What People Are Saying About

Teen Ink™ ...

"No one knows teens better than teens themselves. I was struck by the honesty of the writing in this work. This is a truly valuable book for every teenager. And for every parent."

Todd Strasser
author of *The Wave* and *Help! I'm Trapped* series

"It's hard to describe how good it feels when you realize that someone across the country is dealing with the exact same thing as you. *Teen Ink* does that for me."

Merrell Hambleton, age 14

"*Teen Ink* brings out the best in America's youth—they show a conscientiousness in their words and acute awareness of the obstacles they face from within and without. They speak unapologetic truths from their hearts."

Rev. Jesse Jackson
president of Rainbow PUSH

"Today's young people have so much to say to one another. I applaud *Teen Ink* for providing a forum for their voices."

Lois Lowry
author of *The Giver*

"Reading *Teen Ink* once will surely not be enough. Stories are sure to emerge as favorites that will dwell in the hearts of teens everywhere. Young minds still need to be heard; this is our forum."

Shana Hirst, age 17

"Just when you think we have reason to fear the future, pick up this book and see what the hopes, dreams and courage of you̶ ̶ ̶ ̶ ̶ ̶ ̶ ̶ ̶ ̶) for the soul."

Bill Moyers
broadcast journalist

"I believe it is harder being a teen today than it was when I was a teenager. It is important to communicate effectively with your friends and fellow students . . . and I want you to know how much I value what you are doing."

Hillary Rodham Clinton
First Lady

"*Teen Ink* is a companion. With its diverse selections and uplifting pictures, poems and stories, it has become a shoulder to cry on whenever I feel alone or misunderstood."

Jeanette Wheeler, age 16

"*Teen Ink* provides a great platform for serious teen writers to express their unique perspective."

Matt Diamond
founder and CEO, Alloy

"*Teen Ink* is important because it helps adults to see that all teens are not troublemaking slackers."

Elizabeth Fassl, age 15

"In our society, we spend a great deal of energy talking 'about' and 'at' teenagers. The voice that is often missing is that of the teenagers. This book offers a poignant selection of teen voices speaking for themselves. These eloquent writings offer insight into the challenges, losses and changes of teenagers' lives. *Teen Ink* can help us all gain a better understanding of young people."

Alvin F. Poussaint, M.D.
professor of psychiatry, Harvard Medical School and
Judge Baker Children's Center

"*Teen Ink* is highly entertaining and perfect for the everyday teenager. It has a story for everyone."

Ruchir Thakore, age 13

"Warning—*Teen Ink* will expose you to the thoughts and feelings of real teens who are good and sensitive and intelligent and brave and truthful. It is not for the faint of heart. Be prepared for reality literature from young writers that will make your heart sing."

Cathy Greenwood
English teacher

"*Teen Ink* is a teenager's guide to life filled with compelling stories that really get you in touch with teens."

Allegra Miele, age 13

"I've had the pleasure of working with *Teen Ink* for the past decade, and I can't think of anything that does a better job of confirming the power and promise of teen voices. We are producing some great kids in this country, and if you don't believe me, read *Teen Ink*. Our future is in very good hands."

Michael J. Dukakis
professor, Northeastern University, former governor of Massachusetts and presidential candidate

"The writings in *Teen Ink* are like the magnification of the souls of all teenagers who have raised their pens and spilled themselves onto paper."

Chau Thai, age 17

"*Teen Ink* is a forum for teens that the entire family can enjoy, learn from and use to communicate real emotions among themselves."

Chevy Chase
actor

"*Teen Ink* is like the Louvre museum—it has a collection of wonderful masterpieces."

Eddie Liebmann, age 13

our voices, our visions

Edited by
Stephanie H. Meyer
John Meyer

HCI TEENS

Health Communications, Inc.
Deerfield Beach, Florida

www.hci-online.com
www.TeenInk.com

The following pieces were originally published by The Young Authors Foundation, Inc. (©1989–2000) in *The 21st Century/Teen Ink* magazine. We gratefully acknowledge the many individuals who granted us permission to reprint the cited material.

"Two Boys Jumping." Reprinted by permission of Doug Mahegan. ©1999 Doug Mahegan.

"Losing Tyler." Reprinted by permission of Lisa Gauches. ©1999 Lisa Gauches.

(continued on page 357)

Library of Congress Cataloging-in-Publication Data

Teen ink : our voices, our visions / compiled by Stephanie H. Meyer, John Meyer.

   p.   cm.

   Summary: A collection of stories and poems by teenage writers, arranged under the categories "Friends," "Challenges," "Love," "Loss," "Family," "Heroes," "Fitting In," "Memories," and "Creativity."

   ISBN 1-55874-816-4 (trade paper)

   1. Adolescence—Literary collections. 2. Youths' writings, American. [1. Adolescence—Literary collections. 2. Youths' writings.] I. Meyer, Stephanie H., date. II. Meyer, John, date.

PZ5 .T2948 2000
810.8'0352055—dc21

00-044964

Publisher: Health Communications, Inc.
        3201 S.W. 15th Street
        Deerfield Beach, FL 33442-8190

R-02-01

Cover illustration and design by Larissa Hise Henoch
Inside book design by Lawna Patterson Oldfield

*"What I do not put into words
on a page will be erased by time."*

—Isabel Allende

*Dedicated to the
memory of our parents,*

Paul and Jeanette, Stephen and Frances,

*who always listened to our voices
and will always inspire our visions.*

Contents

3. Love

4. Loss

7. Fitting In

8. Memories

9. Creativity

Foreword

by Beverly Beckham

Most teen books are written in retrospect by those who say, "Hey, I remember what I felt like when I was sixteen—the arguments with parents, flunking math and falling in love. I remember the day my best friend decided he didn't want to be my best friend anymore." It's not unusual for used-to-be teens turned authors to sit down and write their stories. Bookstores are full of these tales.

This book is different. *Teen Ink* isn't a collection of adults reinventing their teen years. It isn't a scrapbook of the past, or a touched-up picture of teen life cut and pasted into something it wasn't.

It is, instead, those restless years close-up, personal and in progress. Written for teenagers by teenagers, it brims with the stuff of everyday teen life, the thoughts and worries and dreams and insecurities and fantasies and hopes, not of someone looking back, but of someone looking forward. *Teen Ink* is a collection of stories, poetry and art that is different because it is written from the trenches of youth.

Within these pages, its voices are like the teens themselves: all over the map. Some are soft and sad; others are loud and strident. They're bright with hope and tinged with fear. They're the voices of kids shouting at a rally, kids answering a question in class and kids whispering in the back of a room.

Unlike some collections, nothing is pat here. It isn't a collection of teenagers standing in a row all wearing the same white shirts and sunny smiles. Here are braces and frowns, dress shirts and t-shirts, earrings and nose rings, thirteen and nineteen standing side by side.

It is *Teen Ink*—teens speaking out about being a teen today.

Beverly Beckham is a columnist for The Boston Herald *and is a frequent contributor to the* Chicken Soup for the Soul *series. She is also the author of* Gift of Time *and* Back Then.

Preface

by Dana Marlowe

I remember my first kiss—it was at camp. I remember my first loss when I was twelve—it was my dad. I remember being a part of the in-group on Monday and the not-so-in-group by Friday. The commonalities of our teenage years run deep. They are not only superficial, like using the same zit cream, but they are the big things. We have experiences ranging from loneliness and betrayal to rapture and satisfaction. These years are exciting and dynamic, and it is important to share these events that shape our lives.

Once, a few years ago, when I was having a severe case of writer's block, my teacher said that even though writing is hard, being a teenager is harder. When I was fourteen, I often sat pondering where I was in my life. My confusion explained why I could not put even a single word on that blank page. We are at a crossroads between being runny-nosed kids and briefcase-toting adults. When we read that others have the same feelings, it can help us glide smoothly through this roller-coaster time.

As a teen, I wasn't a nerd, a jock or a rebel. I wasn't popular or trendy. I was just me, although I struggled to be these other types. Undergoing serious changes—some fun, some dreadful—during our second decade is a feeling we all share. We need a creative outlet in which to pour our emotions. The teens in this heartfelt anthology used their pens to do just that. Some of the prose may make you giggle. Other pieces may cause you to reach for a tissue. Some may make you groan, and a few may have you nodding your head. But there is at least one piece that will leave you with that "been there, done that" feeling.

There is no other book written only by teen authors— teens just like us. Although we share the same ups and downs, our stories have unique twists. We know the excitement of hanging out with friends (our coconspirators in fun), the struggle for independence from parents, the death of a friend or family member, and the excitement of a first date. It is comforting to read this work by peers who have similar, yet unique experiences.

As you journey through these pages of nonfiction articles, fiction and poetry, you will experience your fears and hopes through the words of over one hundred teens. Wander through pieces about friends, families, heroes, challenges, memories and love. These words will be yours. The universality of these emotions and experiences highlight the uniqueness of being a teenager.

It is incredible that we finally have a book for teens by teens. The *Teen Ink* magazine (where these pieces originated) impacted my life deeply. After seeing my words in print, I was inspired to continue writing for newspapers and magazines. An opportunity to get published can alter one's life.

This anthology will reach into your soul and speak to you in a way that says, "I know you; I am you; you are me." This is our soul's vision and voice.

Introduction

We recently overheard a friend tell her daughter, "Oh, what I'd give to be a teenager again. No responsibilities; nothing to worry about." Her daughter immediately responded, "Are you kidding?" We listened as she reeled off the stresses of being a teenager: school deadlines; sports and the pressure to win; cliques and fitting in; coping with love and friendship issues; dealing with personal crises; not to mention her uncertainty about college and career choices.

As editors of *Teen Ink* magazine during the past decade, we have heard from hundreds of thousands of you that these are some of the challenges you face every day. However, you still find time to be creative, have a social life, work, be successful in school and have fun. The teen experience can be both terrifying and exhilarating. We hope this book confirms that you're not alone.

Since *Teen Ink* is written completely by teens, you will find universal experiences represented—from the tragic to the triumphant. In these pages you will share stories of pain and bewilderment, and tales of strength and inspiration. You will need tissues and laughter to read this book. But, before you start, let us tell you how the *Teen Ink* book series evolved.

Eleven years ago we created the nonprofit Young Authors Foundation and began publishing *Teen Ink* (then called *The 21st Century*) as a monthly magazine written entirely by teens. Each month, we select pieces to publish from the thousands sent to us by teens everywhere. We have no reporters or staff writers; we rely completely on teens like you to submit writing, art and photography for the magazine and our online edition, *www.TeenInk.com*. Today, the magazine is read in thousands of classrooms nationwide, and since 1989 we have received more than three hundred thousand submissions and published twenty-five thousand pieces.

This first *Teen Ink* book represents some of the best stories, poems, essays and artwork we've published over the last decade. After we selected our favorite pieces, more than thirty-four hundred teens in schools across the country read sample chapters and told us which they liked best. The result is this compilation selected by teens like you! We hope after reading this book, you will send your work to be considered for our magazine and future *Teen Ink* books. (See pages 325–326 for submission information.)

As parents, editors, magazine publishers and now book compilers, we have been fortunate to have this unique insight into the lives of so many extraordinary teenagers. It is with great joy that we share these works so that everyone can appreciate all that teens have to offer. You deserve our greatest respect and gratitude.

Stephanie H. Meyer
John Meyer

All the royalties from this book are donated to The Young Authors Foundation, Inc.
For a donation/subscription form and to learn more about the foundation, see pages 327–329.

Welcome

This is truly your book. All the words and images were created by teens and gathered from work that appeared in *Teen Ink* magazine.

Join teenagers from across the country by sending us *your* voices and visions to be considered for the monthly *Teen Ink* magazine and for future books in this series.

If you want to participate, see the submission guidelines on pages 325–326. To learn more about the magazine and to request a free sample copy, see our Web site at *www.TeenInk.com.*

Teen Ink
Box 97
Newton, MA 02461

Friends

Photo by Doug Mahegan

Losing Tyler

by Lisa Gauches

To the observer, we appear to be two average high school students. He pores over a college guide, and I write my college application essay. Chewing on the end of my number-two pencil, I'm trying to think of words to live by. That's my topic.

My mind wanders away from the blank page, and so does my gaze. I watch Tyler. His forehead creases slightly, and I know in a few seconds he'll snap his head slightly to the side to get his hair out of his face. Counting down—three, two, one . . . His head tosses back slightly to the left. It's mere habit now, since he cut his hair short months ago.

I also predict in a few seconds he'll swear in Gaelic. He does, and I laugh. It's one of those situations where you know the other person better than you know yourself. And lately, I have found myself observing him more and more.

The expression on his face probably mirrors my own, our eyes filled with stress, frustration and bewilderment. Where did the time go? Days seem to drag, but years pass quickly.

I rest my head in my hands and watch him. Words to live by still haven't come to me. I have known this person for twelve years. He's been my best friend since preschool; when I have a problem, I go right to him.

As I watch him, he coughs, and I worry. I almost ask him if he wants to go outside for some fresh air, but it was his idea to go to the library, so I say nothing. At first glance, he looks fine, perhaps a little tired. But I see the circles under his eyes, and the holes he has punched in his belt because of the weight he's lost. That's the third new hole this month. Without looking up, he says, "Stop staring at me."

Without moving, I reply, "I'm not."

Once, when I was nine, I looked up cystic fibrosis in the dictionary: *a common hereditary disease that appears in early childhood, involving generalized disorder of the exocrine glands, and a deficiency of pancreatic enzymes.* As a nine-year-old, I was very confused. "That's not what Tyler has," I told my mother. "He coughs a lot, and doesn't like to eat. The doctors must be wrong."

She just hugged me.

For almost as long as I can remember, Tyler has been sick. And it has always amazed me how positive he is. In turn, he's made me positive. I used to be convinced that a lung donor would show up, so sure the geneticists would find a miracle cure. But lately, as I watch him grow thinner and thinner, my positive feelings have turned into a facade, and I worry all the time.

I know he grows frustrated, too. Frustrated that he won't have the chance to do everything he wants to, frustrated thinking he shouldn't go to college and waste his parents' money on an education in the middle of which he could die.

Tyler's angry, too. At the world, at God and, some-times, even at me. After all, I'll get to do things he won't. But he would never admit this. In fact, he hides it well. Only I, who have known him so long, know these things.

I'm angry, too, but for selfish reasons. Soon I'll have no one to talk to. No one will ever understand me the same way. I'm losing the best friend anyone could ever have. God is taking back the kindest, gentlest person I'll ever have the privilege of knowing.

And I still have to think of words to live by.

I feel a tear slide down the right side of my face, but make no move to wipe it away. I don't want him to look up and see me crying. I'm usually good at keeping tears in, but he always knows.

He looks up and, with his left thumb, he wipes away the tear and smiles at me. The same smile he smiled at me twelve years ago, when he offered half a peanut but-ter and jelly sandwich to the little girl across the table who had forgotten her lunch.

Tyler looks at the top of my blank page to where I have *Words to Live By* scrawled, and smiles again.

"Always remember, Lise, these words to live by: 'Our sincerest laughter with some pain is fraught.'"* ▣

In memory of Tyler G.

1982–1999

Quote from Percy B. Shelley.

The Girl with the Red-Violet Hair

by April Weber

I often sit and watch the girl with the radiant red-violet hair. She sits there with eyes so shadowed and glassy it's hard to tell their color. I watch her and I wonder what happened to the girl with the pretty blond hair and soft blue eyes that sparkled when she laughed. With a sad heart, I wonder if she remembers those days when we were younger. Does she remember the times we spent together, or has she already burned them away?

As I watch her float through her classes, I wonder where her mind is. Again she makes an excuse for her drifty behavior, and silently I ask her if she enjoys coming down as much as she likes getting high. Does she like that desperate feeling? Does she like feeling afraid and lonely? I watch as she sticks a piece of gum in her mouth. Does she think it will help? Does she think the eye makeup disguises what she has done? Does she really believe bathing in that perfume is going to hide the smell? She smells like an ashtray. There's no hiding it.

I wonder if she even realizes what she is doing. Does she remember what she did last night? What happens when she forgets to be careful? The next time she and her drunk friends pile into the car, will it be the last time? What happens when she takes the wrong pills with too much alcohol? Who will be there to help her? Surely she doesn't expect her stoned friends to save her life.

I wish I could grab this girl by the shoulders and shake some sense into her. If only I had a mirror that could make her see what she's doing to herself. I wish it were possible to make her understand that the sweet, blond-haired girl I once knew has been ruthlessly slain. ▣

Photo by Kristin Cronkhite

Kayla

Fiction by Christopher Scinta

I will refer to her as Kayla because that's what she liked to be called. Her given name was Maggie Kayla Strausser. Everybody called her Maggie—except me. I met her twelve years ago at summer camp when we were barely seven years old. The day we met, I immediately showed her what a charming young man I was by pulling her hair and mocking what I thought was a strange name. She had always hated her name. Needless to say, I was not her favorite campmate. Oddly enough, Kayla and I became friends in spite of our first encounter.

Kayla was very plain with a gawky, insecure nature. She was short with a round face and long, stringy brown hair. She wasn't what you would call attractive, if that term can be applied to a seven-year-old. She was not much of a conversationalist, except when she talked to me. We clicked. She would always complain about how she was homely—ugly even. I couldn't help but wonder who was feeding her these thoughts, but I would just laugh it off and tell her how beautiful her eyes were. She'd try to hide her tiny smile, but I knew that it meant something to her.

We grew up together on the same street in a small town in northern Wisconsin. The summers were warm, and the winters cold, and our playful activities adapted accordingly with snowball fights in winter and tree jumping in summer. In autumn, we'd gather leaves and then wrestle in them; in the spring, we picked flowers.

Wintertime was always the best, though. Sledding trips and fireside secret-telling were a blast. She was the kind of best friend who would tell you everything. Her eyes always showed what mood she was in—and they were beautiful.

Our school was small, with only twenty-two children in our grade. By the time we were in fifth grade, we had been best friends for four years. We still did the ice cream trips, except now we went by ourselves. We still hung around each other's houses, except now we could stay out until 8 P.M. instead of 7:30.

Our "graduations" from each grade were joyous occasions when we would celebrate our departure from some teachers and lament the loss of others. We were too young for real homework, so we spent most of our time after school making exhausting journeys to the drugstore to spend our leftover lunch money on candy. Kayla and I enjoyed our perfect friendship long before the trials and tortures of adolescent boy/girl relationships began to creep into our lives.

By the time we reached high school, Kayla and I were inseparable, not in the romantic sense, but almost as a brother and sister. Of course, high school brought truckloads of the opposite sex. I began looking at girls, and she started noticing boys in an entirely different light.

Kayla never really did grow out of her gawky stage. I felt horrible when she began to realize that many boys are the cruelest and lowest forms of life on the planet if you're not model-thin. I tried my hardest to work through various growing pains with Kayla. I had some of the same problems she did, but she was more concerned about what everybody was looking at. It's hard to tell an insecure fifteen-year-old girl that she is pretty. It's even harder to get her to believe you. I would never forget to remind her of those eyes, but I guess there comes a time when hearing it from your best friend just isn't enough.

The summer before our sophomore year was terrific. For my birthday, Kayla did an absolutely precious thing. She made me a box with a sliding lid and three spaces for pictures. On the left side, she put a baby picture of me. On the right, she put one of her. In the middle she put a picture of the two of us together taken a few weeks before. In the box were a bunch of pictures of us, some things we had made together at camp, and a book of our favorite quotes, jokes and song lyrics. I wanted to cry, but I didn't. I never do. It was probably the most thoughtful and beautiful gift I had ever received. I promised her I would keep it forever and add things to it. She hugged me tight. I told her that she was the best friend a guy could have.

Later that week, we were talking on a pair of two-way radios. I was sitting on my sun deck, and she was sitting on hers. We could see each other and would talk on our radios late at night so as not to get in trouble with our parents. In my backyard, there is a creek that empties into a small lake. That night I asked Kayla if she wanted to steal my parents' canoe and row to the lake. She did, so we started down the river at 2:30 A.M.

The lake was totally quiet, and we just sat there laughing at stupid jokes and poking fun at our teachers. Kayla decided it would be hilariously funny if she pushed me overboard. I immediately retaliated with a quick flip of the canoe. As we rowed back home, dripping wet, she made me promise that someday we would go on a canoeing trip in the Adirondack Mountains.

Toward the end of that summer, Kayla met a boy, Allan, at the town park. She told me about how he was nice and had asked her out for coffee. They went and apparently had a great time. I was happy and relieved to know somebody had begun to take an interest in her. Fortunately for me, she still had enough time to do all the adolescent stuff that had become our routine. She would go out with Allan a few times a week. I was happy that she was finally getting what a sweet person deserved. I had never met him, but he seemed like a pretty good guy. She was content, and that was important.

A few weeks after school started, Kayla called me late at night. She sounded upset and said she needed to talk. It was late, but I was not very tired. If I said no, it would have been the first time in ten years, so I walked to her house. On my way, I thought about her. I figured the problem had to do with a boy. The usual "I'm-not-pretty-enough-for-him" conversations that ended with me trying to convince her of her special qualities were getting to me. I didn't know if I was up to it that night. She was waiting for me, sitting on her deck.

When I saw her face, I knew I was wrong.

She began by telling me she had lied. As I sat there wondering what Kayla could possibly have lied about, she told me that "Allan" was not a real person. All the times she had said she had been out with him, she had really been at the doctors. Earlier that day, Kayla had been diagnosed with leukemia, a form of cancer that is sometimes fatal. I couldn't believe she hadn't told me sooner. A million things raced through my mind. I just stared at her. I slowly drew her into a hug as she sobbed on my shoulder. Although she was insecure, she was one of the toughest girls I had ever known. This was the first time I had seen her cry.

Kayla began treatment almost immediately. We tried not to let her illness get in the way of our routine. We would still go to class, go out to eat and talk late into the night. Only now our conversations contained an occasional mention of a scary hospital room or a new form of therapy. She slowly began to show signs of being a cancer patient. Her hair became thin, and some fell out. She needed more and more sleep. Occasionally, she would not be hungry. She made constant trips to the hospital, sometimes staying overnight. Besides this, our lives remained pretty much the same—until Kayla entered the hospital permanently.

I tried to visit her as much as I could. The hospital was about a thirty-five-minute drive from our town. I took the bus since I couldn't use the car in the evening. I had been in hospitals before, but they had never felt like this. Kayla was on the fifth floor with other cancer patients. She was usually sitting up in bed in a white nightgown. I would stay for a while, and every day I brought her something. Flowers were a favorite because we dried them and hung them all around her room. They were messy, but smelled sweet. We played games with the pigeons and named them according to the noises they made.

We would talk and talk about everything. Our first summer at camp. Our snowmen who got into a fight over whose nose looked more like a carrot during one winter. The ducks we chased from our tree house because we feared they would steal our buried treasure.

How we cherished those visiting hours.

I finally realized what it was like to miss somebody. It was worse than somebody going on vacation or moving away because it was a constant string of postponements and cancellations due to unscheduled tests with uncertain results. The worst was knowing the cause was a sickness affecting somebody who was almost family. I had never had a family member this ill, and it was horrifying to think about what might happen.

Kayla's condition worsened. She became weak and could not walk the hospital corridor or get up anymore. I still visited, but the nurses put restrictions on us. Kayla slept a lot and was often sleeping when I went to see her. She often wrote me letters and left them for me. I read them and wrote back. Eventually Kayla could only receive visitors for ten minutes. In spite of all of this, I knew she was fighting. She always cracked a smile on her pale, now-thin face. In the few minutes every day I talked to her, she would always joke. I remember her commenting that at least she wasn't fat anymore. I laughed and told her jokingly to gain it back, otherwise our weight would be uneven when we finally took our canoe trip.

One evening, I came to her room and she was sleeping. I sat next to her bed and read through the book she had given me long ago. Flooded with memories, I began to hear music that accompanied the written lyrics. As I sat reading, she stirred and I stood over her bed as she looked up at me. I felt her put something in my hand. "Put this in our box," she said with a smile.

I let her fall asleep without looking at what it was. I walked to the bus stop and stood there with my hand clenched tightly to the cold, damp pole. When the bus pulled up, I got on and slowly opened my hand. It was Kayla's hospital bracelet.

Kayla left me four days before my seventeenth birthday.

I closed the box she had given me and carried it outside. As I walked out my front door, I became aware of the drizzle, not unlike when we had pretended those were drops of sugar-water years ago. I stood there looking down the street toward her house, where the handprints in the front sidewalk now seemed so small. I walked to the car that had driven us on high-speed ice-cream truck chases and countless playground romps. I placed the box gently on the passenger seat and turned the key. I drove down our street and turned at the stop sign we had desperately tried to steal for our make-believe parking lot. I drove until I reached town. I passed our old middle school and the drugstore that sold gummy bears by the pound. I pulled into a parking lot, turned off the car and got out. With the box tucked tightly under my arm, I slowly adjusted my tie and walked up to the large brick building. As I entered the funeral home, I walked to the right. At the third door, I came to a sign that said "Maggie Strausser." My heart sank.

As I looked at my Kayla lying there, she appeared to

be sleeping. The makeup with which the funeral home had attempted to hide her ailments suggested otherwise. Her eyes were closed. I had never been unable to see her eyes before, and I burst into tears for the girl with the beautiful eyes. I cried and cried. I cried for her pain. I cried for her insecurity. I cried for the girl who had never seen a tear well up in my eye her entire life. I slowly bent down to kiss her softly on her thin forehead.

I realized, right then and there, that I loved her because she looked so beautiful. ▣

Photo by Michiko Kurisu

Raindrops and Tears

by David Cevoli

Was it a tear or rain droplet that made the wet splatter on his white shirt? I couldn't tell. We stood apart in that dim room full of people. I tried to read his expression. I wanted to know what he was thinking. We hadn't spoken much since the end of summer. The two of us were together almost all the time then.

I think when I'm older and reflect on one summer of my childhood, this is the one I will remember. Sometimes at night we would hang out on my roof, look out at space and talk. We talked about everything up there. I remember once when he got drunk at a party, I stayed up all night and guided his stumbling body to the bathroom every twenty minutes so he could exorcise the demon alcohol. Another time we found a cliff that hung over the stream running through some nature trails near our homes. We walked to the top and jumped off together into the stream. We stayed there all day, jumping off the cliff every so often and then lying in the sun to dry.

The beginning of junior year, things suddenly changed. He was always busy. We stopped hanging out. His girlfriend from upstate came down to visit her father every weekend, and he was with her and just forgot about me. Eventually the friendship ended, and we never spoke. During the fall and winter months, I felt growing resentment toward him.

Sometimes I'd see him at parties with his girlfriend, and we wouldn't even say "hello." We were together in school all the time, but never acknowledged each other. Something stood between us that we couldn't overcome.

I could barely stand to look at him.

Now we stood, separated by a room of people: me standing there like a hypocrite, him shaking hands and hugging people who tried to console him with trite phrases like, "If you need to talk, you know you can call me!"

As if they were as close to him as I had been.

His mother's body lay in the adjacent room. I walked in and shook hands with his father, who seemed to be taking it well. We talked a little, then I walked away and looked outside. The light rain almost drowned the voices of the friends and family at the wake. I stood in the corner watching people. Some were crying, and some were talking among themselves. The dim lights cast crystalline shadows over the room.

I was torn between compassion and anger. I had to say something. I strode across the room and touched his shoulder.

"Can I talk to you outside for a moment?" I asked.

"Yeah, okay," he answered weakly.

He followed me into the rain. As we stood face-to-face in the road illuminated by the light from inside, I watched his shirt being covered by small rain droplets.

"We haven't spoken much lately," I said.

"I know," he replied. There was a pause. "I'm sorry," he said. "It's my fault."

I wanted to say that I could have been there for him, but he knew. As we embraced, I felt my tears dripping onto his shirt. I glanced up at the night sky, past the clouds hovering overhead. The moon glowed large in that dark sky like two moons had molded together to form a unified, indestructible force.

Then we walked inside together. ◙

Mystery Thawing

Fiction by Heather M. Walker

She always smacked her Big Red gum hard
As she waltzed into class,
Her jaws working in vivacious determination
As she chewed with forced effort
Her spiked leather collar
Was dark black
Like the heavy eyeliner
that encircled her icy blue eyes
That were dubbed purple
Behind tinted contacts.
Her spiked stiletto heels
With a metal skull
Super Glued to each toe
Made long black marks
On the imitation marble tile floor,
And made loud clicking noises
That echoed down the hall like hoof beats.
Her hair was dyed ebony black
With thin purple streaks
The color of nothing natural
And everything manmade,
And stood in dark contrast against her
Smooth china pale porcelain face,

Chiseled with china-doll features,
And cheekbones that were high and defined
And garnished with a generous helping
Of purple-red blush,
And her lips that were painted twilight purple
And outlined by thick black eyeliner.
Her fishnets were tight and black
And her tiny leather skirt
That came one inch from being obscene
Was tight, purple and shiny
And squeaked when she walked
And jingled the gold-link chain
She used as a belt
Against the silver zippers and shiny buckles
Of her $875 leather jacket
That was specially imported to her
From a top designer in France
Named Pierre AdVassio
Who no one had ever heard of
But she thought was cool
Because it was French leather
And took her almost 2½ years to save up for.
Everyone looked up as she walked into class,
Up from their books about the Salem witch trials
George Washington's cherry tree,
And other things like
The laws of relativity
That no one ever needs to know,
To stare into her eyes,
Normally hard and icy
And even Hell in its mighty fury couldn't melt,

Though everyone was most sure
It burned in her veins.
She called herself "Mystery" ever since ninth grade,
And tattooed a fire-breathing snake
On the right side of her neck,
That crawled seductively down her shirt
To wrap itself around her left hip bone.
Today, something captivated our attention
As Mystery sat in her chair,
Maybe it was because she didn't cross her legs
Seductively like she did
Every day
In every class
Every time she sat down.
Or because her jaws stopped chewing her gum
And she let it sit wet and hard on her tongue,
Instead of her consistent chewing
That was always as much a part of her
As her dragon-snake tattoo.
Or maybe it was because her eyes
Looked different today,
Behind her purple-tinted contacts,
Like the ice had melted momentarily.
Murmurs hummed in the background,
As books of Washington, Aleister Crowley and Newton
Closed, and all attention focused on Mystery,
Whose eyes were focused obliviously on
The metal skull with a knife in its eye
Super Glued to the tip of her left four-inch heeled shoe.
I remembered the summer of ninth grade,
When her boyfriend and brother were shot to death

In a robbery at a gas station in Boston,
And she was there to see it all.
She blamed herself because she got away
And could do nothing to help them live.
She told me once she thought it should have been her
Losing her life on the cold tile floor.
Her hair had been light blond then,
Her eyes as blue as a pure gas flame,
Her flesh was not marred with tattoos,
And she wore blue jeans and sweaters,
And Nike sneakers, and only wore makeup
On formal occasions.
That summer, and ever since kindergarten,
We had been best friends,
We talked about Corey White
Whom we secretly swore
Would become a plumber
Because he wore his pants like one.
We used to play Barbie,
And dress up like movie stars
In our mothers' formal gowns
And recite lines in old black-and-white movies,
And smoke long pencil "cigarettes"
To make our parents laugh.
I remember in third grade
We saw Bambi
And she cried her eyes out
When his mother got shot.
I remember the red-orange plastic walkie-talkies
We had and used every night
To talk really late, past our bedtimes,

Because it made us feel "cool"
And didn't ring like the phone and wake
Our parents up.
I remember the time she stole a pack of gum
From a Shell station and almost got caught
And swore never to chew that brand again,
But that changed, because she's been
Chewing it for three years now.
She never cried at the funerals,
And no one saw her cry at a sad movie
   anymore.
She never talked to anyone,
Unless it was to criticize
Or curse at someone,
Or maybe just life in general.
Everyone thought she was hard and tough
And never needed anyone.
She even stopped talking to me,
And decided to call herself "Mystery,"
To dye her hair purple and black,
   And be hard.
But today she looked different,
And for the first time in too long
A silver tear fell from her eye
And smeared her eyeliner
Down her pale cheek,
And for a moment I saw the blue in her eyes,
Peek out from behind their purple shields,
And I saw what she fought so hard to hide—
   Fear. Pain.
Someone whispered, "It's been three years!"

Someone else asked what finally made her cry,
And in the back of my head,
A tiny voice said,
"She's thawing. . . ."
I walked to her desk, remembering how she used to be,
And wrapped my arms around her shoulders,
Amazed when she returned the hug
And sobbed like a child losing innocence,
Against my brand-new purple sweater
I'd just bought the other day for $30
But I only smoothed out her hair (too black)
And coaxed her as classmates gawked in astonishment
At her sudden display of emotion.
I never cared that her eyeliner stained my sweater,
Or that people in the hall stopped to look in,
Or the teacher just called our names for the fifth time,
I just bent down to her ear
And whispered tenderly, softly, so only she could hear
"Welcome back, Sarah."

The Trees That Cried

by Jacqueline Savage

Out of the corner of my eye, I watched his chest slowly lift. It gave a silent heave, and he gradually let the air out. He was sighing, a big and painful sigh. It seemed like I was always making people sigh.

I looked out the window of the car, turning my head so I didn't have to see him. I relaxed everything in my body, and tried to make my mind as blank as my face was. My eyes, which felt lifeless, stared onto the wet, gray pavement moving quickly by. I was trying to remove everything from my mind. It wasn't working.

"I wonder," he said, "how much responsibility you take for this relationship?"

I thought about that. He was sure I never thought about anything he said, but I did. Especially about this.

What was happening? We were the best of friends for so long. My childhood was almost entirely focused around him. I never worried about what he thought of me. In the back of my mind, there was a security that was so deliciously safe—that unfailing security of knowing he would always love me.

My mind drifted back to the time of the weeping willow trees. I was really young, not more than five. I'm sure he thinks I've forgotten, but how can I explain I'll never forget it? It was late fall, and really cold out, but I wanted to see the trees that cried. It fascinated me. So we went, all bundled up, and talked for hours under those gigantic trees. I begged for an explanation of their name—why they cried. I knew he didn't really know. So he made up the best, most extravagant story he could think of. We stayed out there in the cold, just us. That is what we were—the best of friends.

The car pulled to an abrupt stop. I looked up at the big school building I now had to face.

"Bye," I muttered.

"Bye." One syllable filled with so much pain.

That was the problem. We got into stupid little fights over everything. And when things were fine, they weren't really fine. They weren't good or relaxed. It was all so tense, and every time we fought, it left a bitter taste in my mouth.

I thought about what he'd asked: How much responsibility was mine? A lot, I'm sure. Probably most is my fault. Sometimes I catch him watching me. I can almost remember what it was like at those moments. But I know I'm a romantic. I make up things all the time. Like with the weeping willows—I don't know how much of that is my memory and how much is my dreamy imagination. Still, at these times, I wonder what he's thinking. Is he proud of me, the person I'm becoming? Does he still love me?

A friend of mine once told me that no one really understands him. I wonder if that's true. At first, I became indignant. I wanted to yell, "I know him! I understand him! Better than anyone!"

But that's not really true. I'd like to think it is, but it's not.

Maybe I should just try to talk to him. I haven't quite figured out yet what went wrong. Maybe it's just our love has changed. It's not bad, just different. I'm growing up, and things are different, but I don't want him out of my life. I still need him, more than ever. Maybe we will never again sit under the weeping willow trees. Maybe that friendship is gone. But a new one can grow. It's possible, isn't it?

Because I still love my dad as much as anything in this world. ▣

Photo by Seth Compton

Can You Stand the Rain?

by Jillian Côté

Can you stand the rain?"

"Stand the what?"

"The rain, Sarah, can you stand it?"

"Yeah, I guess. I don't understand."

"Come on, we know she can. Of all of us, Sarah can stand the rain. Now put your hand on the table."

"Let's do this in one year. Same time, same place."

"Same waiter!"

Between our bursts of laughter, I looked around the table. It was the day I'd never thought would come. In less than forty-eight hours, these three closest to me would all be hours away. It was the last time we would be together like this. We were four crazy teenagers in the middle of the Macaroni Grill, our hands on the table making a pledge we all wondered if we'd keep.

Kate was bouncing in her seat. I could pick her out of a crowd anywhere. I don't know if it was her auburn hair or petite figure, but she was the type of person who was always at the center. She never knew what was going on, though she pretended to. It was her sponta- neous personality I loved. She had no rules, no bound- aries. She laughed, tilting her head to the side—her signature pose—as her eyes scanned the restaurant for our waiter. She squirmed, tapping her hand on the paper tablecloth. Soon she'd be in Vermont, and I didn't know who was going to keep me crazy.

Across from me was Michelle. She smiled one of her "I understand, Jillian" smiles. Michelle had been through more in her life than I ever would. She was strong; stronger than she, or anyone else, knew. I'd seen her come up from being slammed on the ground when it seemed like she could never go on. Michelle had come to me with her fears, secrets and wishes—and had been there for mine. She always managed to make me smile and give me that extra push. She knew I was scared, but she wanted me to be strong. She could read my mind, and I was afraid that soon she wouldn't be able to. Vermont was taking her, too, and I wondered if she'd ever know the difference she'd made in my life.

On my right was Sarah. She was excited, I could tell by her eyes. Sarah knew the world was ahead of her and she wouldn't stop until she had it in her hands. If you didn't accept her, you might as well move out of her way. I could see her in ten years dressed in a navy-blue suit making her closing argument before a jury, the courtroom stilled by her words. If anyone would make it through these next few days, it was Sarah. She was the only one of us who was "sane," and she knew it. She said we were sisters in a past life. She would soon be a freshman in Maine; I didn't know how I'd make it without my sister.

I was a part of all three. I held Kate's insane personality in my hands, Michelle's sensitivity in my heart and Sarah's intelligence in my head. I was two years younger, ready to enter my junior year. Sarah could tell my feelings by my expression, Michelle by my eyes and Kate by the constant tapping of my foot. I was scared of losing these three who had unintentionally guided me through some of the hardest years. I was always running to catch up, and now I was afraid they would lap me without looking back.

How was I going to get through hectic weekdays and depressing weekends with them out of reach? How was I going to laugh things off? Who was going to tell me all I needed to do to succeed? Who was going to give me advice on life, trig homework or petty problems? My mind was spinning. I felt like thunder was crashing down. I could no longer hear the clanging of plates. The hum of voices had dimmed. Time, my biggest enemy, was right at my heels. I could feel myself falling.

Then Kate kicked me. "No tears," she said.

"I love you, honey," Michelle smiled.

"I'll e-mail you all the time, Jilly," Sarah confirmed.

I believed them. Their words pushed me faster, further ahead from what I always thought would let me down.

"So, we have to stand the rain, guys, right?" I questioned, my words shaking. "We have to get through everything, no matter what."

"We can do anything," Kate laughed.

"I can do it!" Michelle exclaimed proudly, putting her hand down.

"Obviously I'm in," Sarah said, placing her long fingers on top of Kate's.

Three pairs of eyes turned to me. "Yes," I said with confidence, finishing the pile. "I can stand the rain." ▣

Sam and His Tomatoes

by Kate Staples

As I walked through the front door of the large brick building, I was met by festive summer decorations, but the beach balls and umbrellas did little to enhance the bleak hallways. Instead of hot sand slipping through my toes, my footsteps echoed on the cold tile floor as I approached the elevator. I pushed the button for the second floor and fidgeted with the wrapping on the cookies I had made that morning. I knew I had reached my destination when the doors opened and I smelled disinfectant and urine, the overwhelming aroma I tried so hard not to notice. I made my way down the corridor to Room 229. As I stepped inside, I saw Samuel staring out of the window at the cars. He was humming and hadn't noticed I'd arrived.

"Good afternoon, Sam," I greeted him, walking over to where he was sitting. His eyes seemed puzzled and excited at the same time. It was the same look he gave me every time I visited.

"I brought you a present," I told him as I placed the shiny bundle in his fragile hands. "They're chocolate-chip."

"Those are my favorite," he said with a smile, revealing his teeth, stained from sixty years of smoking a pipe that now lay in hibernation on the window sill.

I glanced at the pictures of Sam's children and grand-children who only visited on holidays. My eyes rested on the picture of his wife, Rose. He watched, and I could see the loneliness in his eyes as he struggled with the wrapping, his arthritis clearly getting the best of him. I reached over to help, and we both took delight in my morning's labor.

"If you'd like, I'll show you my photo album," he suggested.

"Sure," I replied. I knew the drill. On top of the album were the tomatoes Sam must have just picked from the garden out back. He was a Georgia farmboy who had often taught me the right way to grow tomatoes. He once told me that people came from all over town for his tomatoes. I just smiled; I couldn't imagine going out of my way for a tomato.

We slowly went through the pages of the album, yellow and worn with age. I listened intently to the stories I'd heard a million times, but it never bothered me to hear them again. I couldn't help but smile at the enthusiasm with which he told them. Nothing made him happier than when he spoke about his wife. Rose had been his best friend, and he never let me forget how much he adored her. Her death had had a great impact on him. He hadn't been the same since. I lingered a little longer that day, listening to his tales and sharing my own. I knew how much my visits meant to Sam, not to mention how important they had become to me.

As dinnertime approached, I got up to leave. I could see the disappointment in his eyes. This was the hardest part of my visits. I hated leaving. I often thought how lonely it must be staring out of the window all day, waiting for someone to help pass the time.

"Wait," he almost yelled. "I have something to give you." He reached for the tomatoes on the nightstand and carefully placed them in my hands. "I don't need these. Take them home." I smiled as he held onto my hands a second longer. I watched as he slowly returned to his place by the window.

As I hung up the phone the next evening, I could feel the tears burning my cheeks and a bowling ball forcing its way into my stomach. I sat down at my kitchen table and picked up the once-green tomato. It was now a light shade of red. I held it in my hands and wiped the tears from my eyes, and somehow managed to find a smile. ▣

Matt Keegan
(Sitting Next to Me)

Fiction by Kristen E. Conway

Matt Keegan is sitting next to me. Matt Keegan is sitting next to me on the way back from the annual field trip. Matt Keegan is sitting next to me, and his words are echoing through my head. *You're just scared, Gina. That's all.* I turn around and look at my best friend, Shane, sitting in the back of the bus all by himself. Matt's words leave my mind long enough for another thought to enter. *It's Friday night. How long before Shane's high?* As that thought lingers, Matt's words return. *You're just scared, Gina. That's all. You haven't lost your faith. You're just scared.*

"Gina," Matt speaks from the seat next to me. I turn quickly. I don't want Matt to realize I had been staring at Shane. I turn so I can see Matt's profile. Before today I have probably talked to Matt for a total of three minutes.

I look into those deep brown eyes and stare at the piles of soft brown curls. "I can see why you're so confused," he says. So many girls would die to be where I am sitting now. But I'm not looking at Matt, I'm listening. "I doubted my faith when my grandmother died. She was hit by a car a few years ago. She was in a coma for a week. I just sat there wondering how God, who was supposed to be so loving, could also be so cruel and let her suffer."

I turn so that my back is resting against the bus window and I'm cross-legged. Matt does the same thing, so we sit face-to-face. Our knees press against each other, and my long legs feel cramped. His back is against the arm rest. It must be more uncomfortable for him than for me. I know he won't complain.

"What happened?" I finally ask. I don't want to pry, but I want to hear the whole story.

Matt is still for a second. He takes off his glasses and folds them gently. He closes his eyes and rubs his lids before he picks them up again. He doesn't start talking until the delicate wire rims are perfectly placed on his nose.

"I realized Grandma wasn't suffering and there was nothing I could do to save her." A small tear is gathering in the corner of his eye. I can almost feel his pain. "I realized I was the one who was suffering." He tries to hold in a sniffle.

I try to crane my neck back to look out the window behind me. "It's different watching my friend suffer," I try to tell him. I can't look him in the eye anymore.

"No, it's not," Matt says. He places his hand on my chin and guides my face back so I am looking at him again. "Your friend is dying slowly, and you have to watch. There's nothing you can do." I let out a small, forced chuckle and look back at Matt. "What was that for?" he asks.

I suddenly feel ashamed. It's almost as if Matt has walked in on me while I'm getting ready for a shower.

I'm embarrassed at what he can see, but I'm also ashamed. I'm naked. All my emotions are exposed with nothing covering them.

"You're the only person who's ever told me that," I say. He looks puzzled. I try to explain. "That there was nothing I could do about it. Everyone seems to think that if I were a good enough friend I could convince him to stop. They don't see how I've tried. They make it seem like I don't love him because I don't make him stop."

"I'm not accusing you, Gina." He emphasizes the word "I'm." We sit silently. I place my hand on my knee. I feel Matt's warm hand cover it.

"You're right," he says.

I know he's not talking about whether or not I can make Shane stop. "About what, Matt?"

"Your suffering is different from what I went through with Grandma." My eyes stray briefly to Shane, and then back to the deep, mahogany eyes. I wonder why Matt believes this. I don't even believe it, and I'm the one who said it. Matt takes my hand and grasps it tightly. Yesterday I would have died of sheer joy if this were happening, but now it's only a comfort.

"I never thought there was a way to save her," he explains. Something is trying to hold my eyes to his, but I feel the need to turn my head. "You feel you can save your friend. I knew my grandma was going to die. You have to live not knowing whether this will kill your friend."

I look away, staring blankly at the teachers in the front of the bus. Matt grabs my other hand, interlocks his fingers and places our hands on his knee. I look at him. He wipes the tear from my cheek. "You're scared, Gina," he repeats. He doesn't let go of my hand as he takes my chin. "You're scared, Gina. You haven't lost your faith. Don't ever lose your faith. You're just scared."

This time he lets me look down. A tear falls into my lap. We stay with our hands resting on Matt's lap offering each other silent comfort until the bus pulls into school.

Once I'm home I go straight to my room. I bury my head in the pillows and the tears cascade down my cheeks. I'm crying because Shane is dead. Shane the person is alive and off partying somewhere, but my best friend, Shane, the one I knew, is gone. ▣

2 Challenges

Photo by Jessica Mazonson

It Hurt Not to Cry

by Deanna Harris

He drove a long time, up a winding pass going nowhere in particular, just driving. Then suddenly, he turned onto a dirt road.

"My father and I hunt here," he told me as we continued around the switchbacks and along the edges of cliffs. He told me stories of four-wheeling, campfires and unexpected weather. Then we reached our destination. "It's beautiful up here, isn't it?" he asked as he parked under a cluster of snowy trees.

"Yes," I agreed. Spring was always my favorite season. I looked out the window and saw a flower blooming in the snow.

We talked for an hour about nothing and everything. As he spoke I became entranced. I focused on the way he moved his lips and the sound of his voice.

I did not think things would go that far.

After, he tried to tell me it was not his. "I had an operation and the doctors weren't careful. I can't have children," he explained.

I knew better. I never saw him again.

• • •

I think I knew I was pregnant right away. I ignored it all summer hoping it would go away. It did not.

I went through hell trying to hide it from my parents and friends. After six months though, no matter how hard I tried, people began to notice. When I told my friends, at first they seemed supportive. Later, I lost all but one friend. My brother found out through rumors at school. Then, one Sunday, my mother noticed. She asked me straight out. I burst into tears, and she knew.

"Why didn't you tell us sooner?" she asked. I tried to choke back my tears.

"I was afraid of Dad and what he would do," I finally got the words out.

"We have to tell him," I heard her say. I begged her not to, but I knew that it was no use. She left me in my room, crying and asking God why something like this had to happen to me.

I heard my father yelling, "Why didn't she tell us!" Then the house fell silent. I slowly went up the stairs to face him. The corners of his eyes were wet. He wrapped his arms around me and whispered, "Why are you scared of me? Don't ever be scared of me again." He said nothing about the baby.

During the next week, I saw the doctor, got vitamins, and suddenly had a huge appetite. My mind had been under so much stress it had not been paying attention to what my body and my baby needed. When that was lifted, my body screamed for what it needed.

We talked about options. My parents were understanding, saying it was my decision. My mother brought up the idea of adoption. Although we discussed it, we decided we did not want to wonder how and where the child was. Mom had done some research.

"Open adoption," she explained, "is where you choose the parents, get letters and pictures, can visit, and the child knows who his or her biological parents are when he or she can understand." It took me time to make the final decision.

• • •

We spoke to a social worker, who explained the process of open adoption for us. We talked about feelings in each of us. We were determined to get through this as a family.

At our next visit we were given files of five adoptive couples. Each contained a "Dear Birthmother" letter, pictures and a description of each family's lifestyle. Some had adopted children, and others were waiting for their first.

We decided unanimously to consider a couple who were waiting to adopt their first child. They enjoyed the outdoors, traveling, dancing and other things we enjoyed. They were not afraid to tell us what they were really like.

It was almost Christmas, a perfect time for the present they had been waiting to receive for years. It also happened to be the adoptive father's birthday. While going through their pile of Christmas mail, they ran across my letter.

We met a few weeks later. They came to our house, and we looked at pictures together and basically told our life stories. It was awkward at first, but eventually we had a great time.

• • •

Soon I went to the doctor every other week. I called the adoptive parents after each visit and sent them my ultrasound pictures. I stayed in school even though it was hard having people stare at my stomach. Even my friends talked behind my back. I got so big I did not fit in the desks. I had to sit at tables, away from the class. I spent my "Sweet Sixteen" birthday on the couch with my feet up, eight-and-a-half months pregnant.

Two weeks after my due date, I was sitting in my math class taking a quiz. I got a phone message, "Call your mom immediately." I found out I was going in to be induced the following morning. I could not finish my quiz.

• • •

Bright and early the next morning, my mother drove me to the hospital. I was scared to death. They gave me a hospital robe to wear. I was given an inducing drug intravenously, and then we sat and sat and sat. It got very boring. We played cards. They fed me liquids, and I had to push the IV rack up and down the halls.

At two o'clock the adoptive parents came. They were all smiles. It was wonderful to see two people so happy. We talked until my parents took them out to dinner. My parents (being who they are) proceeded to describe what they would have for dinner, knowing I was starving since all I had to eat was chicken broth.

Later that night, there was still no baby, but I was hurting. The guys became bored and bought a cribbage board. I was very tired from labor and barely noticed. The doctors said the baby was tired, too. They replaced the inducing drug with a sleep aid. I was sleeping in no time.

• • •

The next morning they started the inducing drug again. This time my labor progressed more rapidly. As I got closer, they lost the baby's heartbeat and had to attach a monitor to his skull. A few minutes later, it hit. The pain was excruciating. My father was there the whole time. I remember saying to him, "Daddy, I don't think I can do this." It was then I found the most influential tool in the decision-making process: lack of choice.

The doctors called in the anesthesiologist, who started rattling off his medical jargon. I did not hear a word. All I felt was the pain. "I don't understand you and I don't care. Just give me the anesthesia!" I yelled. Finally, he asked me to sit on the edge of the bed and lean over. I could not hold myself up, so my father was kneeling on the floor holding me up while the doctor gave me the numbing medicine. With every contraction, the pain decreased. I lay there, unable to move even if I tried. The doctors came back into the room.

"We have to do a cesarean section," they said.

I had stopped dilating, and the baby was too big.

Surgery scared me. My heart was pounding. They wheeled me into a room filled with blinding lights. I was so tired. My eyelids felt heavier than they ever had before. Then the nurse came back and said I was going to feel them push on my stomach. I heard the baby cry. A boy! Nine pounds, six ounces! I saw him for a split second and then fell asleep. I could not stay awake any longer.

I woke up in intensive care to nurses ordering Chinese take-out. I looked at the clock and dozed off again. I opened my eyes and found a nurse pinching me. She looked at me and said, "Your father wants to see you." When they wheeled me into my room, it was filled with flowers, balloons and stuffed animals. I talked to my father briefly and fell back asleep.

The next morning was the worst of all the days. They removed all the tubes. I had to walk to get things moving again. It hurt. They practically had to push me off the bed to get me to go. Even when I tried, I was so weak. My whole body felt droopy.

My son, Keegan Allen, and his adoptive parents came to see me often. They fed him, and I watched because I was too weak and uncomfortable to hold him. He was the most beautiful baby I had ever seen.

After a couple days, I was able to walk better. They told me I could go home Sunday.

• • •

The social worker came and we filled out the paperwork for the adoption. By noon, it was final.

We went to the hospital church for the Entrustment ceremony. It was almost like a wedding with tears of joy and sorrow. I placed Keegan into the arms of his adoptive parents as they promised to love and care for him. There was not a dry eye in the room, except for mine. I am not sure why I did not cry. I love my son very much. It hurt not to cry.

• • •

A week later I was back at school, still walking slowly. I will always be known as "the girl who got pregnant."

As for my home life, it got better. I was no longer afraid of my dad. Communication lines in the family opened, and my brother and I became best friends.

Keegan's biological father signed the adoption papers and gave his picture to the social worker so Keegan could see what his father looked like. He never stopped by the hospital to see Keegan, and still denies Keegan is his child to his fiancée and friends. ▣

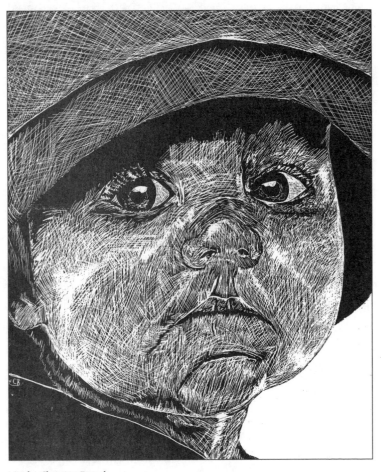

Art by Christine Brasch

Crimson Tears

by Laura Yilmaz

The few remaining pills rattle against the thin plastic bottle I hold in my hand. My head aches with a dull pain. She is upstairs now, taking a shower. She should be all right.

I drag myself into the living room and collapse onto the couch. I am too tired to reach for the television remote, so I lie there, staring at the blank screen. I want to vomit.

Mom called not too long ago. She asked how the night was going and if *she* would be okay. I told her all was well. Now I wish I hadn't. As much as I want my parents to have fun at their gathering, I need someone here with me. I can't handle my sister alone—not tonight.

I realize that I have dozed lightly and quickly shake off the heavy blanket of sleep that creeps over me. Then I notice something unnerving: silence. She is supposed to be taking a shower. . . . Why isn't the water running? I glance at the clock. It's only 8:37. I'd better check that she's okay.

I lift my body from the cushions and go up the stairs. The bathroom door is closed. There is no sound. Nervously I call her name.

No answer.

I call a second time with more authority. Again, I am met with silence. It is deafening.

I push gently on the door, but it will not open more than an inch. She has pulled out the drawer nearest the door, preventing it from yielding to prying eyes. But that small crack is enough to see. Red. Red against her naked flesh, running down her forearm in a graceful arch. It drips to the floor, forming a small pool.

I am afraid.

She sees me, waiting, hoping. She is a child, as innocent as the first blossoms of spring, still untouched by the morning dew. She cries. I plead. Still, she will not open the door. She screams.

I run. I run down the stairs, my eyes flooded with fear . . . but, surprisingly, they remain dry. I snatch a knife from the kitchen and run back upstairs. The drawer bars my way. I am angry. I stab at the rigid wood and force it back. The door gives way.

The knife clatters to the ground. Her body is racked by heaving sobs. I am not crying. I wrap my arms around her frail body. She is shaking. I comfort her—she relaxes a little. She is a baby, crying for her mother. The blood streaks across her face, mixing with her tears. Her wrists are pouring out all the hatred and fear that she has locked inside for so long. They weep more bitterly than she does, two steady streams of crimson tears.

I cannot cry. I wish my parents were home. They are not. It is only 8:39. I am the mother. I am the father.

As I bandage her wrists and speak in soothing tones, I silently pray for 10:00 to come. I want to be a child again. . . . ▣

Just Like a Movie

by Erik Bernstein

One morning four years ago, my mother came into my room to wake me for school. She asked if I had opened a door that was ajar. I was really tired and had no idea what she was talking about. Suddenly I heard my father's voice. It felt like slow motion and seemed like I was in a movie when he said, "We have a home invasion." It didn't register, but then I saw an unfamiliar man holding a gun to my brother's head. I felt sick. The man must have been six feet tall, and looked very strong. He wore a red bandana around his face, and plastic gloves.

Before I knew it, he threw my brother out of the way and pointed the gun at me. He demanded, with anger in his voice, that I come to him. I did what he said. He put his left arm around my neck and pressed the gun against my right temple. I felt the coldness of the metal against my head and, from his trembling, his fear.

Looking into my mother's eyes, I knew she was no longer in control of my life, or hers. He told us if we did not give him money and jewelry he would shoot me. I had three hundred dollars in my wallet from my bar mitzvah. Without hesitation, I gave it to him. Time slowed. I didn't want this to be reality. I waited to wake up. We watched him trash our house looking for more jewelry and money. He took a number of valuable items that had always been in our family.

My mom was begging him not to hurt us. He told her to cooperate and nothing would happen. The next words I heard were about me: "You have a nice boy here. You wouldn't want anything to happen to him, would you?" This frightened them—and me. My brother must have been scared. He speeded up his pace. The man angrily commanded he slow down. Every time he yelled, the gun pushed harder against my forehead. It started to hurt, but I was not worried about the pain. I was worrying he might pull the trigger. *Is this the end of life, here and now?* This thought traveled through my mind and pierced my soul. My main question was, *Why?* I thought I would be hysterical and crying, but for some reason I was the calmest one there. I did not say a word the whole time he had the gun on me. I just did what he said, knowing I was powerless. I prayed to God, begging for our lives.

When my dog started walking around, the man got scared. He pointed the gun at my dog and told my mother to put the dog in a different room, or he would shoot my dog. As my mother obeyed his orders, the man herded us into the garage and opened the trunk of our car, making us get in. It was tremendously cramped with four of us in there. He told us if we got out, he would shoot us. My mother kept asking if I was okay. It felt like forever as we lay there, wondering what would happen next. All of a sudden I heard a car pull up outside. Someone honked the horn, and I realized it was my school car pool. I hoped they would drive away and not have their kid knock on our door. Finally, I heard the car leave. A few minutes later the man came back and told my brother to get out.

The trunk was less cramped. I started to shiver, not from cold, but with fear. I heard the phone ring, but then that, too, stopped. My father and I couldn't take it any longer. We had to escape. My father opened the trunk and told me to run to our neighbor's. I ran as fast as I could, not noticing that my dad's car was missing from the driveway. I banged furiously on the door, yelling for mercy. At last a man opened the door. I couldn't talk straight, but he eventually understood and called 911.

My mother ran to me, and her face told me something was terribly wrong. Tears were running down her face as she yelled and screamed. I will never forget that moment. She grabbed the phone from the neighbor and yelled at the operator, "He took my son. He took my son." My stomach dropped.

Five minutes later three police cars surrounded the house. It felt like a movie, and my mind was trying to find the director, but this was real. The detective took pictures of the mess while the police talked to my parents and dusted the house for fingerprints. My friends were at school smiling and laughing, with no idea what I was going through. Finally my parents checked the answering machine and found a message from my brother. The man had dropped him off downtown. The police picked him up, and our family was reunited.

Returning to my room that night was difficult. The fear came back; my hands shook furiously. This is where it all started. I looked through my possessions to see what he had taken. Suddenly I came across a silver necklace my friend had given me for my bar mitzvah. Hanging from it is an ancient symbol to protect and bring good luck. It came from Israel. At first I didn't know how this mezuzah brought good luck, but I realized it brought me the best luck anyone could ask for. It protected me. It also gave me a memory to help me be more aware of my existence. After this horrible experience, I see how much I have in life. I appreciate everything, especially my family, friends and memories. Life flies by; no one knows when it will end. ▣

Dear A. J.

by Kelly Murphy

To anyone who reads this letter, it is important that you understand its context. Over the summer our high school lost one of its own. Arthur J. McEachern, "A. J.," died early one Monday morning while working at a construction site. Just seventeen, his premature death left behind a shocked family and community.

Since his death, his classmates have been grieving as best they can. This is my best. This letter is to a friend whose life ended too soon.

Dear A. J.,

Your locker now lies empty in the senior corridor. Your friends walk through the hall and remember what it was like to see you smile. Anna embroidered your initials on the guys' hats. She did a fine job. Friday night, your fellow soccer fanatics are dedicating their game to you. The football team wears a shamrock with your initials on their helmets. Maybe it brought them luck in their first game because they won, but I'd like to think that you had something to do with it. I know you were watching. Some of your closest friends got tattoos with your initials. The rest of us are just trying to cope.

I found an old picture of you taken before the sophomore boat trip. Boy—were you cute. In the picture, several of your female classmates are crowded around you. You always knew how to attract attention. It was no wonder—you had such a gorgeous smile.

We are trying to decide how we, as a class, are going to memorialize you. Nothing seems to do your life justice.

We miss you. The senior class just is not the same since you left us. We will never forget you. But after the tears have all been shed, you will always continue to make us smile with the life you led. And even after death, you still have the girls' hearts. I know you took a piece of mine that summer morning.

May God allow you to rest in peace. You will forever live on in our hearts.

Sincerely, your friend,
Kelly Murphy ▣

Safe for the Night

by Amanda Hager

By my calculations, there aren't enough pills in the box." James's voice was low and flat.

I was terrified. How did I respond to that? He sighed, and I knew I had to say something or risk having him grow cold again.

"James . . . ," I struggled. "James, don't say that. I'm here for you, always, you know that. Please don't say that. . . ." I fought to keep my voice even and hide the fact that I was about to burst into tears. "Please . . . as clichéd as this sounds, that's not the answer." Neither of us could say the word "suicide."

"Manders, I know. You're. . ." He paused, and I could picture him sitting on his front steps, bundled in his coat at 2 A.M., baring his soul over the phone. "You're my closest friend, my best friend, and I don't consider many people . . . if anyone . . . my friend. You're special, hon. But right now . . . it really seems like my best option."

I cried silently as I listened to him in so much agony. I could hear him breathing as he thought of what to say next, and when he spoke, I could hear the pain.

"I hate to say this to you, Manders, but you don't know how much I hate my life right now. I told my sister about this, and all she said was, 'That's selfish.' It's not, though.

I used to think people who killed themselves were the weakest, most selfish people, but I was wrong. It takes an incredible amount of strength to go through with it." He sighed again. I pictured him staring up at the cold winter sky, wishing for a way out.

"James, it's a permanent solution to a temporary problem." I could hear the strain in my voice, and I knew he could tell I was crying. "What happens if you do it and fail? Then what? And what if you actually succeed?"

Two hours later I woke up, the phone still cradled against my ear.

"James?" There was a minute of silence before I heard movement on the other end.

"Manders? What time is it? You sound like you just got beaten up."

"Gee, thanks. You don't sound much better. It's four. We fell asleep."

James chuckled softly, his amusement genuine.

"Hey, we slept together, in the loosest sense of the term. I guess we should hang up then, huh. We have school in what . . . four hours?"

I laughed, "Yeah, talk to you tomorrow. Think happy thoughts for me?"

"Silly Manders—I will. Cross my heart. G'night."

"Good night, James."

I sighed as I hung up the phone. I'd kept James safe for another night, but I couldn't make him happy. We'd known each other for five years. At least he trusted me enough to talk to me. At least he trusted me, period. I stayed curled up on the couch, thinking back to when James and I had first met. We'd talked on the phone for three years and knew each other's deepest, darkest secrets. When he was a junior and I was a sophomore, we discovered we both volunteered at the Haunted Graveyard, and decided it was time we met. From that day on, we were inseparable. We talked on the phone every night, and when James got his license, we went to the movies together. Much to my dismay, his work schedule and the distance between our towns made it almost impossible to see each other more than once every few months.

When the school year rolled around again, James made it a point to stop at my school to see me. Without a car, I was forced to take the bus. James waited patiently in the parking lot, and I'd scamper to his car for a hug and a few minutes together. I looked forward to those morning hugs more than anything. At 6′3″, James towered over me. I barely came to his shoulders. In his arms, I felt safe and warm, as if nothing could hurt me. If I was having a bad morning, just seeing him would calm me, and a hug would keep me happy all day. I loved him.

That night, I realized that maturity comes not simply from growing older and wandering through life, but from life's harder lessons. Lessons that come in the form of a tall boy, a bit too thin, who learned to trust, one step at a time; a boy who taught me more about myself, life and pain than anyone before or since. And I knew, at that moment, that James would be okay, that I'd see him in the morning. I'd kept him safe—at least for the night. ▣

Wendy and the Monkey Bringer

by Elizabeth Ames Miller

I will never forget the day my brother was sent to jail. I try to block the year surrounding that incident from my memory. No matter how hard I try, I can still recall it vividly. Maybe it's better that I don't forget.

The whole incident felt like it was from a horror flick. My brother was caught at the pier for possession of cocaine with the intent to sell. I wasn't there, but I can imagine how the scene unfolded. When Sean realized the cops had discovered him, he began to race down the railroad tracks that ran parallel to the river. A vicious police dog chased him, and the police caught, arrested and dragged him to jail. My brother, the one who helped to dress me as a child and played with me in the pool when no one else would, was arrested for attempting to deal drugs.

Every day we hear of slimy drug dealers getting busted in the streets of big cities. No one feels any compassion for them because they are responsible for thousands of drug-related deaths each year. These men deserve to die or be sent to jail for life! But this was not a big city or a drug dealer. This was my town and my brother.

We think that the trash who get arrested every day on the streets have no families, or anyone to care about them. Sean has my mother, my father and me. We all care about him. I love my brother more than myself sometimes.

I remember going to school during those days as if nothing had happened, and then coming home to an empty house and crying for hours out of guilt for leading a normal life. When my parents came home from work, it was my turn to be the strong one. They both showed emotions in their own ways. My father was always the type who got angry instead of upset, while my mother was exactly the opposite. She sat in a chair, crying for hours.

I remember feeling so helpless just watching them. There was nothing I could do. Before the arrest, little family feuds would always be settled with an "I'm sorry," even if I wasn't. This was different. Nothing could change the past. It was all too much to comprehend. We all felt guilty for what had happened to Sean. Even though the psychologist explained that it had nothing to do with us, we couldn't shake that guilt.

School had been an escape for me. Seventh grade was one of the best years ever. I had been elected vice president of my class. I spent all my energy on schoolwork and friends. Everything was fine until one particular social studies class. A fellow student stood up at the end of class, in front of everyone, and asked me, "How does your brother like his jail cell, Liz?"

Every eye in the room focused on me. What could I say? "He says it's better than any hotel room in the Hilton!"

After that class, I couldn't walk. I sat at my desk, paralyzed, and stared out the window. My world had been shattered, twice. School could no longer be my escape. I had lost all respect for myself. I felt an immeasurable amount of guilt every day because I was living in our house, smiling occasionally, even laughing with friends, while Sean was in a miserable jail.

It took time and thought, but I learned to feel better. One should never feel guilty because one's life is happy. I grew to realize that my brother had made his own mistakes. There was little I could do for him—other than to continue assuring him that we all loved him—until he was ready to do something for himself. I love my brother and for the past five years he has made his life one that some may envy. He is loved for himself and what he has made of himself. Sean has turned his life around.

Recently, I went to a concert of his in our town park. He sang a song he wrote called "Wendy and the Monkey Bringer" about a drug dealer named Charlie and a user named Wendy:

> *It's Charlie and he's brought some more.*
> *But she's got to pay*
> *And it's all he can say.*
> *You've got to buy if you want to fly. . . .*

Sean sends his message to anyone who will listen:

> *So Wendy flies, she flies away.*
> *If you're looking for Wendy,*
>   *She's not home today.*
> *Now Wendy's in heaven,*
> *And it's a long-distance call,*
>   *And a long way to fall,*
>   *To go home.* ▣

Leaving Dad

by Kimberly Burton

I used to think my parents were like machines
And programmed themselves with series of if/then
   statements
If the child sneaks out at night, then deliver lecture
   #458
If her friends are bad for her, then it's lecture #342B

And they had concrete problems, not like mine
which required crying over always
Because I am not a machine.
My life would never be perfect.
If the child is afraid, comfort her.

Then one day I learned that Dad picked up all the
   pennies he saw
and threw them onto playgrounds so the little kids could
   find them
and he knew that made them very happy
that's why he did it.
Dad is like that sometimes.
And he and Mom sometimes stared at children running
   around in malls
If the children are happy, then you will be, also

And Dad watched me like that, too
We'd be at a track meet and I would be high-jumping
and when he was truly afraid I would miss that last
*   attempt at 4'10",*
he stopped videotaping and watched
As if I were his life and responsibility
If the child misses, tell her how to clear it
And then I thought about how Dad would feel if I
*   missed*
He would tell me that I tried very hard, even though, he
*   noticed, I didn't lift up my knee enough*
Never, "I wanted to see you at State another year."
Or "I wish you would have made it."
Dad rarely spoke of himself when it was really
*   important.*
Unless of course it was to tell a story I would benefit
*   from*
If the child looks back, then smile.

But in the eyes of my parents, I can see them.
And how everything I do affects them, just a little. . . .
Their computer responses are forced and hard
but beneath I decided lies something more.

Themselves.

And when I leave I will leave Dad behind.
He will help me pack to go away to college and
probably talk with the other parents.

Because that's what Dad does.
And who am I to know how he really feels?
After all these years, he was always my dad.
Talking to me. Watching my fascinating life
If the child must go away, then leave her to go.

It all seems so simple now.
They will let me go because that is their parent-computer
    response.
And I will say good-bye to them
But I am older now and wiser
And want more than anything
for them to realize how much more
I know there is.

Don't Be Afraid to Ask

by Greg Walters

Icould tell from her quivering chapstick-smeared lips I had gone too far. My ability to tell people what I really thought, my sarcastic attitude and what I thought was witty charm had gotten me into trouble before, but this was different. I found myself wishing I could snatch those tainted words and stuff them back in my mouth, no matter how bad they tasted. Unfortunately, the damage had been done, and I was left with nothing to say but "I'm sorry. I'm so sorry." Her reaction—or lack thereof—to my apology deemed it ineffective. My last option was to hold her. The tears I felt through my shirt burned like acid, but seemed incomparable to the scars I had left with my words. So there we stood, both crying. From what seemed like a mile away, someone whispered, "I'm sorry. I love you."

• • •

"Wow," I said, looking wildly at my exhausting pile of homework after only four classes. It was only a few weeks since school had started, and reality had just set in. Teachers were getting impatient with late assignments and all I could think about were my girlfriend, food and sleep—none of which I was getting enough.

Plus, some of my classes were so unbelievably dull I often found my mind wandering. My only refuge was the few teachers who kept me interested. The others were just a bunch of. . .

"Mr. Walters, are you following?"

I almost leaped from my chair. I smirked and said, "I've already finished the article . . . ma'am."

"Then perhaps you would like to summarize it for the rest of the class?" she retorted.

Great, I thought. "I would love to," I said, putting on my most innocent smile. "I just need to know where the class left off."

"Well, since you are too good for our speed of reading, why don't you start where we were—the beginning." Point, set, match. A call rang out from the gods. *Whew, saved by the bell. I must be the luckiest person on the face of the. . .*

"Mr. Walters, we'll be expecting your report tomorrow."

"Fantastic," I mumbled on my way out.

Finally, physics. Physics was always a relief because it was last and we could play with awesome gadgets. And I sat by my girlfriend. This, however, was no play day. The words on the board sent chills down our backs, shakes to our hands and stress to our temples: "Test Today" it announced, laughing at our lack of preparation. We nervously awaited the torture. The teacher passed out the test and said, "Good luck."

Luck? I thought. *I need a miracle, a revelation, some kind of supernatural help.* Prayer seemed like a logical solution, but when I opened my eyes, I found myself anywhere but heaven. Some complained, others whined, some collapsed and some did what I thought was utterly wrong. They approached the teacher looking for answers. Not answers to their questions, but to the questions on the test. It's logical: The teacher made the test, therefore he has the answers. If he planned on telling the class the answers, however, he wouldn't be giving a test. Under normal circumstances, I would speak out, but this time was different. She, the girl of my dreams, had joined their ranks. I could only bite my lip, take the test and keep my mouth shut—for now.

When the physics test was behind me and homework was done, it was a time of great rejoicing. I picked up my girlfriend and we went to the movies. Everything was going great: the movie had been funny and sad; she smelled incredible, like a garden of thousands of flowers right after it rains. It was a huge mistake to bring up the test, but I did.

"So, how do you think you did on the test?" I asked nonchalantly.

"Really well," she answered excitedly. She was slipping into my trap.

"So, do you think you really earned that grade?" She gave no response, just a perplexed look. "Because," I continued, "last time I checked, we are tested on our own knowledge, not our ability to tap our teacher's."

"What's that supposed to mean?" she said, starting to realize where I was going.

"Well, I think trying to get a teacher to give you the answers is wrong. Possibly even cheating."

"Cheating!" The sparkle in her eye was replaced by fire. "Are you calling me a cheater?"

Her words ripped through my ears like razor blades, and I knew it was time to stop. Being the insensitive male I was, however, I proceeded. "You said it, not me." There was at first astonishment, then anger, and finally tears, complete with quivering lip.

The ride home was quiet. I reached for her hand a few times, only to catch the cold metal of the parking brake. Those minutes dragged on longer than classes had that day; it was almost a relief when I pulled into her driveway. I followed her to her door, and with her eyes still wet from tears, she said, "I don't want to talk about this right now. We'll work it out later. Right now I'm angry and tired, and I want to go to bed." I walked back to the car, cursing myself. I guess to keep an opinion bottled up is not a good thing, but to share it and hurt someone's feelings is worse. That's a test question I'm not quite sure about. Hey, maybe I should ask the teacher. 🔲

Cartoon by Jessica Consilvio

Would You?

by Amanda Batz

If I asked you, would you kill someone for me? Would you take a knife and stab someone in the back for no reason? Would you put a gun to someone's head and, if I said so, would you pull the trigger? Ask yourself if you're willing to take a human life.

Every time you get behind the wheel while intoxicated, you agree to these terms. You put a contract out on everyone else on the road. Do you understand the meaning of a contract? This means you become a hit man, hired by the alcohol you consume. You also agree to the terms of the contract, including the consequences. Do you know what the inside of a cage feels like? Do you want to know?

I could spout off all the statistics about drunk driving, but you say you will never become a statistic. I could tell you that driving under the influence is a punishable crime, but you think you won't be caught. I could tell you that even though you think you can still drive like an angel after a few cold ones, your reactions are slowed and your judgment impaired. You would rather believe the angel part because, hey, who am I to tell you about your motor skills.

You think bad stuff only happens to other people. You've read about accidents involving alcohol. You've seen commercials, billboards and after-school programs about the dangers of driving under the influence (D.U.I.). People have warned you what could happen, and you say you've heard it all before. Well, listen again.

When you get in the car, you might notice a woozy feeling. You shake it off. When you turn the key, the engine starts. You push down the gas pedal, and the automobile accelerates. Other cars on the road notice your vehicle is weaving; you, however, do not. When you see headlights coming straight toward you, you don't react quickly enough. Even though you take your foot off the gas and push the brake, you're going too fast.

The front of your car caves in from the force of the impact. You are thrown against the steering wheel as the air bag inflates. When you regain consciousness, someone is pulling you out of the wreck. Later you find out they used the Jaws of Life to pry your car door open. They say you're drunk, but you disagree. Then you take a look at the other car—a good look. The engine appears pushed into the trunk. There is no movement inside, except for the smoke and broken glass falling from the window frames. You realize your car is actually in their lane.

You realize the accident was your fault. You realize the people in the other car will never get a chance to see the damage to their car. You realize they will not be going home to their families. As the ambulance comes and the police cars and fire trucks begin to arrive, you realize you are drunk. You realize the people in the other car are dead, and you killed them. Would you care? 回

Coming Back to Life

by Melanie Race

When I woke up on Friday morning, I didn't quite know where I was. Then, as I looked around the room and realized I was in the psychiatric hospital, it slowly came back.

I remembered that I had refused to get up for school on Thursday. Then I had written a letter to my aunt and uncle—with whom I'd been staying—and left.

I had no destination. I wandered around, stopping at the bank, playing on the swings at the playground, and finally catching a bus into the city. I remembered staring out at the harbor and walking along the river. I felt lost and confused, and I was cold and lonely.

I can't remember exactly when I decided that my life wasn't worth living. I had a bottle of sleeping pills, and I sat on a bench in the train station, swallowing the small white pills a handful at a time. I felt more frightened than I'd ever felt before. There were policemen and an ambulance with flashing lights.

Then there were ants crawling on the ceiling and blinking lights in the sky, but the nurse said they were in my head. I just wanted to sleep. They wouldn't let me, and made me drink charcoal to absorb the pills. Finally, when I was stable, I was transferred to another hospital.

That's where I awoke on Friday morning.

Not again! I thought. I had been in the hospital before, though never for anything quite as serious. I was diagnosed with depression at thirteen. Since then, I had had four major depressive episodes and been hospitalized twice. I knew just what to say to convince the doctors and social workers to discharge me.

The first few days, I refused to talk about the problem. "I just had a bad day," I said. "I'm fine now."

But, of course, it had been more than just a bad day. I definitely wasn't "fine."

In fact, I hadn't been fine for a long time. I couldn't concentrate on schoolwork, and my grades were dropping. I rarely slept more than four hours a night, so I was tired and irritable. I wasn't eating and had no energy to do the things I used to enjoy, like swimming. I tried to convince myself that if I waited long enough, the dark clouds would disappear. But I realized that this time I wasn't fooling anyone with this false optimism and my empty assertions that I was okay. Still, I couldn't reach out for help.

Finally, I began expressing my feelings on paper. Writing about hopelessness and frustration made it easier to talk. I realized that people were willing to listen, and wanted to help. At last I took a very big step — I decided to risk trusting people again. I was amazed how much better I felt. Letting go of that fear opened many doors for me. It's also good to feel able to tell others when I am feeling bad—before it gets to contemplating suicide.

Of course, re-establishing trust in people was only the beginning. There was still a long, hard road ahead. I was forced to face things and people I cared about, which was not always pleasant.

One of my major issues was my mother. It seemed as if she and I were in constant conflict. Before, when this had become too much to deal with, I had left home. Too late, I realized my mistake. I wanted to return home, and my mother wanted me to come back. However, each of us wanted something that the other could not give. Realizing that home might not be a healthy place for me was very difficult. I needed to take care of myself, and that meant being where people accepted me for who I am, depression and all. I have found that place in my aunt and uncle's home, and though it is not my home, for now, it is a good place to be.

Another issue that I was forced to confront was how to cope with my feelings. I tend to keep them bottled up, until eventually, when the pressure becomes too much, I explode. Once I realized that this was a dangerous way to live, I was able to become more open and express feelings more appropriately.

I am not completely well yet. I am making progress. I am sleeping better, and my concentration has improved. I have more energy and have started to enjoy school and work again. Most important, I feel better about myself. I have finally accepted that there are many things I cannot change, so I plan to focus on those I can. I have learned that life may not always be easy, but it is always worth living. ▣

Saving My Brother

by Holly Hester

Oh my gosh, find him!" a voice screamed hysterically. I squinted into the intensely blinding sunlight and frantically scanned the vast blue horizon. Beads of sweat formed on the ridge of my forehead. My heart took on the beat of a drum, painfully pounding harder, faster. My breath came quickly, increasing in speed as my anxiety rose. With every new pump of adrenaline, an overwhelming wave of nausea engulfed me. Foamy waves crashed along the shore, stealthily swirling and swallowing, grabbing like deceiving hands. Sea gulls screeched and dipped toward me, warning, condemning. The rustling sea oats whispered accusations of blame.

Suddenly I heard distant cries, muffled by the wind and crashing waves. The scenery spun wildly around and around as I feverishly searched the landscape in the direction of the small voice. In utter disbelief, I caught sight of a flaxen head bobbing between two gigantic waves. His tiny frail arms splashed madly in desperation fighting the sucking currents of the undertow. I shot across the scorching sand, stumbling over tanned bodies sprawled out across the shoreline, oblivious to sharp shells slicing the bottoms of my bare feet.

As I tore into the water, I realized in horror that the flaxen head had disappeared! My weakening knees caused my body to collapse, and I instinctively began to swim to the spot where I had last seen my drowning brother. Surging waves tossed me to and fro, forcing bitter saltwater down my throat. The intense glow of the noon sun created a reflection of flickering flames across the surface of the ocean, resembling the golden hair of my brother. To my left, I heard a faint gurgling noise, then a splash. I turned to see a tiny pale hand emerge from the water, grasping the air in agony. In one swift movement, I dove toward my brother and grabbed hold of a frail, cold arm. I tugged at his body and led him to the surface of the water. He coughed and sputtered and instinctively began to cry. His warm body clung tightly to me as tears streamed down his sunburned cheeks. I struggled through the turbulent waves and staggered back to the safe sands of the shore. My brother laid his small white head on my shoulder as his shrill cries subsided to soft whimpering.

An overflowing surge of relief drained the energy from my body. I began to shake with the thought of what could have happened. As I stroked the golden strands of my small brother's hair, my eyes grew blurry with tears. As we sat in silence, we watched the warm orange glow of the setting sun, together. ▣

Weight of the Matter

by Christina Courtemarche

I started out at 123½ pounds at 5'6". And that was a good weight. I was happy. I know now that I was thin, even underweight. And I wanted to stay at 123½, 5'6".

So I decided to eat less.

I stopped eating breakfast. And then lunch. I wasn't hungry anyway, right?

My stomach would growl painfully. And it felt good.

Next I was weighed at 110½ pounds. And this was not good, the doctor said. My mother wept and moaned that she had failed. And I wanted to stop it.

Soon it became a sick, twisted game. How little could I get away with eating in a day? How many days could I go without driving my mother to tears? How long before anyone noticed me diminishing to nothing?

Yes, I heard the stories. If you were too thin, your body would live off your muscles, eat away at your heart.

Heart attack.

Without calcium, your bones become weak. Without the right nutrition, you die.

You don't sleep.

No oxygen to your brain. You can't think straight.

You don't have any energy to do anything. There is

only one main thought and action—lose weight.

And you are cold. Even in the dead of winter you were never this cold. Layers of clothing can't keep the freezing out. Icy hands and feet. Numb fingers and toes. Blue nails. Chapped lips. Pale skin. Maps of thin, ugly veins.

In the dark, in your room at night, it's like already being buried in that box. It's dark and cold down here. And lonely.

And there's a screaming in your head. It is fear and no one else can hear it. You don't want to gain weight. You don't want to die. You don't want to make other people unhappy. You don't want to be sad.

But you are afraid to be fat. You're afraid to die. And the screaming continues, piercing your eardrums.

Ninety-two pounds. A nutritionist, a physician, a therapist and a weigh-in are your constant companions.

The all important weigh-in that controls your entire life: 97; 104; 108; 108¾, 118; 114; 116; 119; 119½.

Right now I'm 118, 5′6″ and *fat*.

And there's no one down here to hear me scream. ▣

From the Other Side of a Locked Door

by Caroline Richards

Shades drawn,
chair against door,
she faces the mirror,
and turns ever so slowly,
watching her body's reflection in the glass,
and raises her arms and points her toes—
now a side view:

Thick of stomach
quivers
imperfect.

She'll run more,
six miles tonight,
bike, lunch and dinner,
and no snacking.

A glass of juice,
or an apple,
if she has to. . .

Someone's calling through the keyhole.
There's piano to practice,
homework to do.
She blocks the doorway with her body
and wipes her eyes.

She knows she's falling
and she wants to let them catch her,
and hold her,
and save her—
they would do it for her, too.
But she's played on too long now,
there's no turning back.
Hung head and empty mouth,
it's all about control,
and she knows who's boss.

The Tattoo

by Alissa Deschnow

Tattoos—permanent markings in different shapes, different sizes and all with different meanings. To some they express individuality, to others they're about groups of friends and youth. Tattoos sometimes have names: a person's mother, their lover, their dog. Some have pictures: roses, flowers, skulls, bones, dragons, ladies, you name it. All of them are permanent.

My tattoo is of a different sort—self-inflicted—reminding me of a time when I was alone, and sickness was spreading through my mind. How desperate I was to move on, to shed this mortal world for one of everlasting peace. When I look down, I can almost see the drying blood on my wrist, smell the hospital and feel the charcoal being pumped into my stomach. I was so hurt, so alone, so afraid. But life went on, and I was still in it. The wounds of flesh, spirit and mind healed with time and help. All that is left is the tattoo to remind me, through hard times, that I am a survivor, and tangible proof that there is:

Life after pain. 回

3 Love

Photo by Michael Pagano

Firefly Eyes

by Jennifer Corbett

There is a bluish shine on his face from the light of the television. We're just sitting in silence and watching new videos that we have both seen a zillion times. He seems interested nonetheless. I'm more interested in the patterns created in his eyes by the dancing light. His long eyelashes cast shadows like spiderwebs over his big curious eyes. He turns the volume up. Chords and rhythms and back-up singers fly out at me. The music is loud enough to shatter eardrums, but I don't hear a note. I am too involved in rediscovering his beauty. He raises the remote to the television again, but this time to change the channel. He seems a little frustrated when the picture doesn't change. He sits up and re-angles the remote, trying again. He finds something in black and white, and goes back to relaxing. Not even the chipped tooth on the right of his smile mars his portrait. Sensing my stare, he glances at me, but then after a little smile he quickly turns away, as if I were about to take his picture.

He asks if I want a drink. I tell him some apple juice would be good. I klunk my head back on the sofa with a sigh. He comes back trying not to spill our drinks, looking like he's walking a tightrope. One of the Beverly

Hillbillies makes him laugh. He looks at me to see if I found the humor, and, of course, I'm smiling, but not because of the television. Because my heart feels like singing every time I see that smile make his eyes light up like fireflies. He seems to have an aura of comfortable pleasure following him, like he has rainbows stored in his pocket. His knee is touching my pant leg and it feels like a good dream.

He shifts his position and now I can see what earlier I hoped I had imagined. On the other side, she is also gazing up at him. Their hands are tangled together like a big knot of unity. I brace myself as my heart crumbles to the floor, and only hope that while she looks into his eyes, she is seeing in him what I see. ▣

Love Gone Wrong

by Jennifer Coleman

No, I am not a professional, just a plain old teenager who was dragged into a big mistake. Do you know what it is like to be in love? When you catch yourself staring into space, daydreaming about that special someone? Or maybe it's the giggly feeling in the pit of your stomach when you're with him that you relate to the best. Well, whatever it is, it is an addictive feeling that not even your best friend can talk you out of. Now, here is my story. . . .

It was a week after my sixteenth birthday when my life started changing. It was a slow process, but in the next fourteen months I became a whole new person. I went from being energetic and bubbly to a quiet person who had withdrawn from the world. I was so wrapped up in the thought of having an older, more popular jock for a boyfriend that I didn't see the change.

Now when I look back, I can see how powerful addictive love really is.

I gave up everything for him. He and my best friend were at each other's throats twenty-four hours a day. He didn't like her because she wasn't "cool" enough. She kept telling me that something about him just wasn't right. Of course, I wouldn't listen; I was in love.

He wanted me to give up a friendship for him. She and I had been close for two years, so it didn't seem logical to throw that away overnight. But I was in love, so who do you think I listened to? I gave up a valuable friendship for him. Mistake number one!

It was that first summer that all my goals, values and dreams were crushed. The problem was by this time I didn't need to be my own person. I had someone running my life for me. I didn't need to make decisions for myself. I was told what to wear and where to wear it.

That was the first time I sensed something was wrong, but by then I was so scared that I couldn't stand up to him. He had become abusive, and was getting more and more physical. Not just gritting his teeth, he was now pushing and threatening me with his fist in my face. Although he never hit me, he had his ways. Otherwise, I wouldn't have had a reason to be scared.

He had his list of people with whom I wasn't allowed to talk. If I was caught chatting with anyone on this list, he would punch walls, windows, anything in reach, anything but me. Because I "loved" him, I didn't want to make him hurt himself, so I obeyed his stupid rules. Mistake number two!

The next incident was not my fault, but his. When I finally broke up with him (over a year into the relationship), he decided he didn't like that. He called every night at 2 A.M., and every time he drove by my house he leaned on the horn. This was fine. I understood his anger—but then he started threatening me. He swore that he would hurt me and kill anyone I went out with.

I did go out with another guy. The next day I received

a call letting me know he knew where I had been, who I was with and what I had done. This scared me. I wondered how often he had followed me. I began to worry.

What happened two weeks later was the last straw. I was at a party with a bunch of friends. We were dancing in the backyard when a friend noticed someone in the woods. We laughed at her. When I was leaving I had an eerie feeling in the pit of my stomach, so I asked a friend to walk me to my car. There he was in his truck across the road. I went back inside and called my parents. When my mother came, he was nowhere to be seen.

But as we were saying good-bye, he appeared from the woods in a rage. He screamed he was going to get me, that I had never given him a reason when I broke up with him. He made it clear that he would be sure I would never have another boyfriend. That was it. My mom and I called the cops. I filed a restraining order. I wasn't going to let him control my life anymore. Correction number one!

Now, what I want to ask is: Why? Why did I let some-one do this to me? This is the part that I can't deal with. I feel so strong some days, and other days I feel like crawling into a hole. I understand that this is a problem that hundreds of teens go through every day. I just want you to know that you aren't alone. There are plenty of people who understand and can relate to you. They all can make it through, and so can you!

Now I just have to follow my own advice. ▣

I Rested in Your Arms

by Mary Mattila Cooper

I rested in your arms,
your rough, tickling cheek
   against my throat—
you kissed me,
your mouth warm and wet,
   and I smiled,
more from remembrance
   than passion.
Sunset hovered before us,
violet, orange and rose, and
an icy river the color of your eyes
   curved under it.
I stroked your back pensively,
delighting in the way cloth
slid across your shoulder,
   but my soul no longer buckled.
"This isn't breaking up,"
I told myself,
"I feel nothing breaking."
It was only changing—melting,
not unlike luminescent
sea-ice dissolving in
spring but still

there, after all.
Later, I turned to watch a
rectangular glow pass
over your profile,
lighting your eyes from the side,
caressing each dark curl
    in gold.
You felt my stare and
clutched at the wheel,
veins rising, square hands
    suddenly cold.

We parted after a few
    dry kisses,
my mouth grazing reddish stubble
and yours pressing my cheek.
I turned at the top of the stairs,
wind parting my hair in a
    thousand places,
and watched your white car
    grow smaller,
disintegrating, a little
regretfully, into the past.

The Hole in My Heart

by Olivia King

He looks deep into my eyes, not with a look of love or caring, but of guilt. "Who was she?" I ask, trying to hold back my anger and hurt.

"Some girl . . . you wouldn't know her," he said calmly, as if not knowing her would lessen the blow. I try to look at him, but I find that all I can do is focus on the floor and hope the tears swelling up in my eyes don't start pouring down. I can feel him slowly moving closer, and his hand rests on my shoulder to comfort me. I quickly shrug his hand away, not wanting the reassurance that everything will be okay.

Everything will not be okay. I want to scream at him, and tell him how hurt I am. I want him to feel the pain I'm feeling. I want him to tell me he lied, that he never really cheated, that it was all a sick joke. I could forgive him for a joke, but not for this.

I can no longer hold in my emotions. Tears roll down my face and burn my cheeks. I begin to sob and sniffle and my head begins to hurt. I look up just long enough to see that he is also crying. *Good,* I think, *Cry. Feel pain. Hurt inside, just like me.*

We sit for what seems like eternity—but is only a few minutes—without talking. We both are crying. "I'm sorry," he mumbles over and over, "I'm so sorry. I never meant to hurt you. I'm sorry. I'm sorry."

His apologies make me cry harder. I think of all the times he told me he loved me and how it all meant nothing now. I think of him with another girl, laughing and having fun. He finally leaves me to drown in my emotions. I wonder, *Should I forgive him? Should I leave him? Will I be able to see him with another girl, especially the one causing all this pain? What should I do?*

I know no matter what I do, it will never be the same. There will always be an empty feeling, like a hole in my heart. ▣

Art by Gregory Platt

New Frontier

by Travis Ostrom

Never before in the history of my class had a girl and boy attempted to transcend the boundaries of friendship—until that earth-shattering day in third grade.

Most kids our age had more interesting things to occupy their time than thinking about the opposite sex, but it was different for us. We were interested in girls and they in us.

As interest grew, we asked each other, "Do you like Amy? Colleen? Lindsay?" and, though it was a lie, we always replied with a bashful, but stern, "No." We all wanted to make our move, but feared the fire of peer scrutiny. One bold sacrificial lamb would need to submit himself to the wolves to clear a path. That brave soul would be my best friend, Bailey.

One day, Bailey and a few of us were at a popcorn- and pizza-grease–covered table at the roller-skating rink. We had spent the day skating, playing outdated video games and chasing each other. Although this was what we usually did, that day our normal activities somehow seemed less than entertaining.

It began when Rat—I think his real name was Martin— asked Colleen if she would couple-skate with Bailey.

Whether he was sent or self-motivated is not important—
what matters is Rat skated across that rink, lit by fluorescent flashing lights like a scene from *Saturday Night
Fever,* and asked the groundbreaking question. We
watched, with eagerness and excitement. Bailey pretended not to care about the verdict, but we knew he
was as consumed with interest as any of us. It was almost
unbearable, watching Rat skate toward us, knowing he
had the answer. All we could do was wait for his short
legs to bring the message. I struggled to keep from
screaming, "What did she say?" Finally, he reached us.
"Well, when I asked Colleen if she would couple-skate
with Bailey, she said she might, if he asked himself. But
she said it would be just as friends." A sigh of relief and
disappointment escaped from Bailey. He knew "maybe"
was much closer to "yes" than "no," but he also knew
how hard it would be to enter the wolves' den and make
the request face-to-face. He began his approach and we
circled the skating floor trying to get a better view without being too obvious.

"What do you think she'll say?" Matt asked.

"I bet she's going to say yes. Why else would she make
him ask in person?" I reasoned. A year later I learned an
"ask-in-person" request is not a guaranteed yes, but this
time it was. We watched them step onto the rink hand-
in-hand. All eyes were on the couple as they nervously
skated away from the giggling group of girls. That first
awkward step onto the rink was like Neil Armstrong
heroically setting foot on the moon and opening a new
frontier for all mankind. It was a gun-blast signaling the
beginning of a long and exciting race. When we saw the

two join hands, we burst into a frenzy of excitement and looked for someone to skate with. I searched with a ferocity found only at the most primal level of man until I spotted a likely candidate. I approached purposefully and asked, "Lindsay, will you skate with me?"

She replied with disgust, "No!" I was let down, but not deterred. I was on a mission. Slightly less assured, I skated up to another girl, only to be met again with a condescending, "No." I was still sure I could get a girl to skate with me. I mean, if Bailey could do it, then I certainly could. I was filled with urgency; I was racing against time, or more accurately the end of the song. Any girl would do. The next girl to enter my sight was Pauline, and I hurriedly approached her. A third time I asked, "Will you skate with me?" I felt confident she would agree, but this encounter unfortunately followed the same theme as the previous two. With my heart broken and bleeding, I returned to the refuge of my equally unsuccessful friends. We sat, not saying much.

After a while, I saw Pauline slowly coming my way. I could not imagine what she would say. She sheepishly explained, "I'm sorry I didn't say yes. I was just afraid my brothers would make fun of me. Do you still want to skate?"

"Of course," I replied, and we awkwardly grasped hands and skated off into the shimmering light of the spinning disco ball.

This experience made me wary, but hope remained. After all, there was a grand, new frontier awaiting. ▣

Bringing Home a Stranger

Fiction by Pamela Jourdain Moul

I sat at my office desk, staring down at a pile of papers at least ten inches thick. How was I ever going to get through this mess? Two hours remained, and then I would be free for the weekend. I had nothing scheduled, and, for the first time in a while, neither did he. I planned on staying home, cooking for the two of us and snuggling. Oh, it would be such a wonderful weekend. Just the two of us, sitting in front of the fireplace, watching the first winter snowfall with a blazing fire to warm our feet. We would sip hot chocolate and milk, talk about nothing at all, and just enjoy each other's company.

I closed my eyes and let my mind wander back to when I first saw him. He was walking on the other side of the street as I was hurrying to work. I stopped at the corner and noticed him almost immediately. The way he walked intrigued me. He walked with his head high and shoulders back, though he did not seem snobbish. His body was lean and trim, like an athlete's. Before I could stop myself, I doubled back and chased after him.

Three blocks later, I had gained enough courage to reach out and tap him. He turned, his eyes immediately meeting mine. I held out my hand and introduced myself.

He said nothing as we shook. I asked him if he would like to join me for a cup of coffee. He remained silent.

"Looks like the cat's got your tongue," I remarked as I turned to leave. I had not meant to sound sarcastic, but he must have taken what I said the wrong way. His cute smile turned to a scowl as I started to walk up the street, leaving him behind. As I moved on, I reasoned that stopping him was a foolish thing to do, that I never would have had the guts to follow through with my invitation.

I bit my lip to keep from turning around and saying anything more to him. I kept my eyes in front of me and quickly made my way back to the office. As I gripped the door handle, I noticed a reflection in the glass. I turned around slowly, not sure of what to expect. Silently, he held out his hand. I'm not sure what pushed me to take it, but I did. He led me away from the building and down the street. I lost count of how many blocks we walked, but by the time he stopped, my feet were very, very tired.

I looked up at the building we were in front of. It was my apartment building. I looked at him, my eyes opened wide in disbelief. I had never seen him before, yet he knew where I lived.

He prodded me up the stairs and through the door, straight to my apartment. I put my key in the lock, but before turning it, I studied his expression carefully. His eyes were half open, and his mouth was turned up into a slight smile. His body was tense, as if he knew that by turning my key, I would no longer have my safe little world, protected from all the harsh realities of one-night stands. I would throw myself into the world of givers and takers, of con men and women. I would condone the behavior I despised.

Yet some unseen force had convinced me that there was nothing to fear. My hand turned slowly and the door swung open. I followed at a distance, though I don't remember feeling afraid of him being in my home.

I stood in the living room and watched as he opened the door to my room, as though gaining strength to continue his game. I followed quickly, expecting to be angry at his audacity to invade my privacy. But as I stepped over the threshold and saw him lying on my bed as though he owned it, I reminded myself that I had given him permission to know my secrets. I had given up my privacy when I unlocked the front door.

He looked in my direction, signaling for me to join him. I did so quickly, and that sealed my fate. We have been together for seven years, eleven months and thirty-one days. Today was our eight-year anniversary.

A loud ring brought me out of my daydream. It was my phone. My secretary ran down my agenda for the next week. As she spoke, I glanced at the clock. One hour and forty-five minutes left. I interrupted her and told her I was leaving early, that I had a headache and needed to go home. I tossed my papers into the drawer and grabbed my briefcase. Everything could wait until Monday. Right now all I could think of was him. I needed to be with him.

I hurried down the street, rushing past all the people with whom I would normally stop and chat. He was waiting, as always, in the hall chair where he takes his post an hour before I even leave work.

My tired legs carried me up the stone steps and through

the heavy door. He raised his head to look at me. He looked absolutely wonderful. His eyes sparkled as I slipped off my coat. His mouth turned into a smile as I quickly glanced through the mail. He shifted his weight anxiously as I walked toward him. I opened my arms and he jumped right into them, his head nuzzling my chin.

"Did you miss me today, Charlie? Today is our eighth anniversary, did you remember? I have a present for you." I stoked his fur gently as I carried him to the kitchen. Settling him on the counter, I removed the package from the refrigerator. His nose picked up the scent immediately.

"This is your present, Charlie Cat. Where's mine?"

He jumped off the counter and disappeared. He returned a few minutes later carrying something in his mouth. He dropped it at my feet, hopping back onto the counter. I glanced down and found, much to my disgust, a dead mouse.

I rubbed Charlie's head before I filled his plate with fish morsels.

"You really know how to charm a lady, don't you, Charlie Cat?" I said before removing the dead animal.

He swished his tail wildly in response as he attacked the best piece of fish he had ever had. ▣

First Date

by Lindsay Danner

Lisa Loeb is singing
the perfect song
as we sit sipping Mochas
in the back booth
of Starbucks—
neither of us talking—
both of us staring hard
into each other's eyes—
your foot rubs up against mine
under the table
and you mutter "sorry"
and take a sip of
your coffee
accidentally leaving
a dot of whipped cream
on your upper lip
and I laugh
and you turn a
few shades darker than
a plum
and swipe your
tongue over the
fluffy white stuff

that I so badly
want to reach over
and brush my finger across
because just to touch you
right now
would break the ice
and maybe then you'd say
"thanks" or something
and we could start a real
conversation
and I could actually
go home tonight
and tell my mother
who'll be waiting patiently
in her favorite armchair
just how great
our first date was.

Storybook Love

by Lori Kessler

People often talk about their desire to fall in love like in a storybook—and I silently laugh. When I was little and read fantasy stories or watched movies about Prince Charming, I dreamt about falling in love that way. My family convinced me that it never happened in real life. My parents never wanted me to have hopes too high for something they did not believe could happen. One thing I have learned over time is that parents are not always right.

When I was in seventh grade, I went skiing during winter break with my family. At the hotel, I met a boy named Anthony. We spent only two days together, but we were inseparable. We enjoyed each other's company and had a lot in common. When it came time to go home, I was devastated. I knew we could have something special if we had the chance; there was chemistry between us. But Anthony lived six hours away, and we were too young to drive. We exchanged addresses, promising to keep in touch, although it seemed unlikely we would ever see each other again.

My family and friends called me immature because I said I missed Anthony. When I got excited after receiving a letter from him, they laughed and told me nothing would come of it. Nobody understood how I felt. I knew I was young, but I didn't believe there was an age limit on love. There was a feeling that came into my heart whenever I thought of Anthony. My parents called this silly, an infatuation that would pass, but they were wrong.

I don't believe in the word "impossible." Things can happen if you really want them to. For years, Anthony and I wrote to each other. We called. As we got older, I sometimes thought I would never see him again. The letters arrived farther apart, and the phone calls now came only every few months. I never told Anthony how I felt about him since everyone tried to crush the idea of anything ever coming of it.

Now I am in eleventh grade. It has been four years since I met Anthony. We know almost everything about each other and, although we haven't met in years, I still have the same feelings. The only difference is that I am older and more mature, and can act on my feelings.

I received a letter from Anthony a few weeks ago. On the last page he wrote,

Lori, we've known each other for a very long time. I know I haven't seen you in years, and this may sound absurd, but I am in love with you. Not a day has gone by since we met that I haven't thought about you. You know me better than I know myself, and I need to see you again before I go to college. I can picture spending the rest of my life with you someday. It may sound crazy, but you are the only girl I can see myself raising a family with. I want you to come to my prom, and spend the weekend so you can be there for my graduation. These are two of the most important days of my adolescent life, and I want you to share them with me.

These were the most heartfelt words anyone had ever said to me. So many different feelings rushed through my head. Even when I was a little girl in seventh grade, I sensed that the feeling that Anthony and I belonged together would still exist in me today. Maybe one day Anthony and I will be married. Or maybe we'll only remain pen pals until we grow old. Or we may lose touch over the years and only exist in our memories. All I know is that I have had the honor of experiencing storybook love, and I will never stop believing in destiny. ▣

Photo by Andrew Raymond

Happy Valentine's Day

by Jason Dunlap

"Do you want to go up to the top together?" I asked.

"Sure, let me go with you," she said, smiling. I had seen her waiting alone: a tall, brown-eyed girl with a long, blond ponytail and snow on her jacket.

We got on the chairlift to ride to the top of the mountain. I looked down and saw her skis were longer than mine. It was Valentine's Day and I had spent the morning alone, so even sitting next to this girl made me happy. Then she turned and asked, "So, where are you from?" I looked right into the deepest light-brown eyes I had ever seen. She fluttered her eyelids, as if she thought I was confused, and looked at me with patient questioning.

"Um," I stammered. I shook my head a little and heard the most beautiful laugh in the world: understanding, honest and heartfelt. She giggled and looked at me again. "I mean, well, I'm from a town about an hour south of here, with lots of apple orchards," I managed to say, trying to recuperate.

The ride up the mountain through the light snow had begun as a way to get to what I love, but I ended up loving what I got. Next to me was a girl so beautiful and friendly, I began to wonder if she could really ski. So I asked, "Where are you going to ski now?"

"I don't know yet," she admitted, blinking those heart-beat eyes and shrugging her shoulders, "anywhere."

We talked for awhile, gliding through the fog, looking down on snow-covered tree branches and quiet trails empty of intruding tracks. *This is amazing. This can't be happening,* I thought. Lost in her laughter, hypnotized by her bottomless eyes, I began to seriously consider my ability to ski in my condition. "Can we ski together?" I asked.

In a daze, I heard her say, "That's great with me."

We skied together for what I hoped might be an eternity. Every time she made it to the bottom first and waited for me. After telling her how incredibly fast and talented she was, I was rewarded with the everlasting memory of her smile, laughter, ponytail and brown eyes all at once. It felt like my day, my life, had just begun. Admitting I had to leave with my parents at 3:00 P.M. was a guaranteed promise of near-future regret.

On our last run, I still only knew her first name: Carey. We made excuses to stop and spend time together. By now it was clear to both of us that we had connected in a special way. She laughed at everything I said. We glanced, smiled and stared at each other even when we weren't talking. Then I went with her down to the spot I could take my skis off and go inside the lodge.

The next ten minutes and what they would bring weighed heavy on my heart and made me catch my breath at the same time. I didn't want it to end, or to say good-bye. Too much had happened in that short period of time, cutting it off too soon seemed inconceivable. We both quietly took off our skis. She bit her lip and faced me with her eyes melting my heart, bringing a thousand feelings but no words.

"I have to go fix my hair and go inside, too," she stuttered, looking down. We walked in, and as she went down one hallway and turned to see me step toward another, we both stopped. "Um, see you later," we both said, barely hearing the words.

Each step away was harder, and the urge to run back and find her grew unbearable. Through the window, I saw her walk out and put her skis back on. I ran outside, hoping to find her. I looked around, with the desperate hope of expressing the huge feeling in my heart, but she was gone. All I could do was whisper, hoping she could somehow hear me inside her heart, "Happy Valentine's Day." ▣

Daydreams of a Cashier

Fiction by Alison Lemon

Here's your receipt, ma'am. You saved $9.44. Have a good day," I said for what felt like the hundredth time that day. My voice began to sound strange: cold, distant, robot-like. I wondered if others noticed.

My next customer unloaded her groceries onto the belt. As I waited, I looked at the clock and sighed. *Only 4:30. An hour and a half to go,* I thought.

It was May and the late afternoon sunshine streamed in through the front windows. Outside, a mother tried to put groceries in her car while her three small children ran in circles shouting to each other. Two older ladies sat on the bench, probably discussing chicken recipes.

A girl I sometimes saw in school, whose name I couldn't remember, walked by holding her boyfriend's hand. They were both smiling and laughing really hard about something. It made me smile too, but at the same time I felt a twinge of sadness in my stomach. I thought of my own boyfriend and how far away he was.

When I snapped out of my reverie, the woman was holding coupons in her outstretched hand. I must have looked startled because she chuckled softly.

"Do you have to work much longer?" she asked.

"About another hour and a half," I answered.

"Oh, that's not bad," she smiled.

Easy for you to say, I thought. *You'll be out in the sunshine in less than five minutes.*

"No, not too bad," I replied.

"Where are you hiding the peanut butter this week? Every time I come, you've got the whole store switched around. Besides, I'm an old lady. My eyesight's not what it used to be and. . . ."

My mind suddenly conjured up little elves sneaking around the store, late at night, hiding peanut butter from unsuspecting customers. A giggle escaped my throat. "Aisle five," I said, still smiling.

"Thank you. You've been very helpful. Hope the rest of your shift goes fast."

So do I, I thought.

"Hi, how are you?" I asked my next customer.

"You have some nerve charging $1.29 for a head of lettuce," he shouted in response.

"Well, um, that's the price." I never knew what to say in situations like that. All my customers seem to share one common belief: that I, personally, set all the prices for the store.

"You can get lettuce for half that at Victory," he raged on.

Somehow I doubted you could get lettuce anywhere for sixty-five cents, but I wasn't inclined to share this. Instead I smiled and said, "Did you see some of our other prices, though? We have a great sale on cereal this week."

"Well, you can't make a salad with corn flakes!" he said, taking his lettuce and storming out.

"Hi," I said to my next customer, without looking up, wondering if I'd make it through the rest of this day.

I started to look for a price on the flowers I had just been handed, when I noticed what they were—a dozen perfect white roses, my favorite.

"That will be $14.99, please," I said. "They're very beautiful. White roses are my favorite," I said as I took the money. I was taken aback when I saw the white-gloved hand that held the twenty-dollar bill. There were few people who wore gloves like that, gloves that had never seen a speck of dirt. I somehow doubted Mickey Mouse was vacationing in New England.

"I know. That's why I bought them for you."

My knees grew weak when I heard that voice. I put a hand on the register to steady myself. I was almost afraid to look up, but at the same time was compelled to do so. As my eyes rose, they traveled up the impeccable blue of a Marine's uniform. Each gold button was polished to perfection and glistened in the afternoon light. My eyes passed the smile that always melted my heart, and rested on the eyes that held the warmth of the May sunshine and sparkled like the finely polished buttons.

"I don't believe this. What are you doing home?" was all I could manage to say.

"I had to come home; I was lonely. I miss you so much. Sometimes I just miss . . ."

"Miss . . . Miss! I gave you a twenty-dollar bill. I'd like my change."

That's when I realized I had been staring at the back wall, a twenty-dollar bill clutched in my hand. I turned to the man buying the flowers. He was middle-aged and balding. He had no white gloves, no gold buttons. The only blue he wore was his torn T-shirt.

"I'm sorry, sir," I said, beginning to count out his change.

"My mother-in-law will be out of the hospital by the time I get these flowers to her," he commented to the woman behind him.

I sighed and looked at the clock. An hour and fifteen minutes left. ◙

"See You Later"

by Rosa Rockmore Baier

She had seen him every day for a year, sat beside him at lunch and driven in the air-conditioned coolness of her car with him at her side. She listened to his worries and loaned him her ear to mend his troubles. She watched the swing of his walk and the expression of his eyes. She had loved him.

But now, the year was over. They no longer had classes together, no longer ambled through the school corridors in conversation. She could no longer imagine his eyes beneath her lids at night, and the sound of his voice became stranger in the halls when they passed.

Sometimes now—but this was rare—he appears at her art class, surprising her, laughing at her speechless wonder. He sits and watches her draw or cut collages, and he talks a little. But the silences, she feels, are conspicuous. She cannot sort through thoughts fast enough to find the magic topic to keep him talking so she can remain silent. So she turns to her project, and pretends to be absorbed in it.

But even while leaning forward, eyes close to the page, she is aware of him next to her. His very form, his presence, wraps around her mind, and she dreads the moment he will stand, take his book bag and vanish into the schedule that has taken away their time together. Soon the moment comes, some ten, fifteen, maybe twenty minutes later, and he rises to leave.

"See you later," she says, though she knows she will not. She is happy, but the happiness brings tears because it is elusive, and it will not last. It is happiness that glosses over the darkest of despairs and can turn, instantaneously, to grief. She has lost him; she knows it.

But worst is her awareness of his other life. She passes his girlfriend in the halls, looks her over piece by piece, one day the arms, the next the legs. There is nothing wrong separately, but together the slim building blocks make up someone she finds awful. "Awful" doesn't describe the feeling, but rather it is a feeling that defies description. There is nothing physically wrong with her—in fact, she is beautiful. Is it jealousy? Perhaps, or maybe just the primitive eyeing of a rival animal from a distance, across a clearing, or this crowded hall.

She tries, however painfully, to imagine those arms and legs intertwined with his. Her hands on his chest, or his on hers. The pictures are there in her mind when she chooses to see them, and sometimes when she does not. Hot breath and wet lips, closed eyes, soft skin.

She wishes—what does she wish? There are no definitive ideas, only an empty longing. Does she want that girl gone from his life? Yes, but then there is the fear that someone else would enter, some other girl. No, it is safer it remains this way.

She played it safe last year and kept her head under her turtle shell, staying in the "just friends" safety. If she hadn't, maybe it would be her hands in his . . . but there is no room for *maybes* now. She wants to forget him, but she also tries to hold their hours together fresh in her mind. The memory slips, though, and she cannot grasp its slimy sides.

She passes him in the schoolyard and smiles, pulling up the corners of her mouth. There is the moment right before passing him to savor, then he's beside her—"Hi," he says—then past. It's over. It's all over. ▣

4 LOSS

Photo by Charlie Semine

Granted

by Andrew Hammer

I wish she was dead," I said quietly to my cousin as we stood in his living room watching our mothers talk one late fall day freshman year. My mom and Aunt Sharon spoke of nothing in particular, simply enjoying each other's company. My mother often embarrassed me, and that day was no exception. I was embarrassed by how she dressed, with her dorky Christmas socks and shirt tucked in all the time. Then there was the way she acted: always so joyful, not realizing what it was like being seen with her. The things she said (and firmly believed) also bothered me, such as "Parents don't expect enough of their children," and "The day I say boys will be boys, you may as well just shoot me."

This was not the first time I felt a strong dislike toward my mother, but it was one of the last. That evening I went home unaware of how much influence my mother had in my life. Nearly a week later, I found out. My parents were disappointed with me and my older brother, Peter. They felt we were making typical teen mistakes and didn't like our choice of hangouts, our clothing that didn't fit and, sometimes, our friends. Most of all they hated our music with its loud banging and screaming.

One night, I became so frustrated with my mother when she threw out my favorite CD that I punched a hole in my wall. I quickly rearranged the furniture so no one would notice. Pulling up to school the next morning, I went through the usual routine. I tried to sit low in the seat of our old beat-up station wagon so no one would recognize me as my mother dropped me off.

I tried to get out as quickly as possible. As I gathered my things my mother said, "Good-bye." I managed to utter, "Bye," as I slipped out of the car.

Not much stands out about that day in school. Just before it was over, however, I do remember glancing out the window at an ambulance speeding down Main Street. It reminded me of my first-grade teacher, a scary, old woman who always made us say a Hail Mary for the person the ambulance was rescuing.

Arriving home with my brother, Peter, I found my little brother, Greg, watching TV.

"Where's Meta?" I asked, noticing my sister's absence. "Out with all the rest of the big eighth-graders?"

"She and Mom went shopping," Greg replied.

I made myself a float and sat down to watch TV.

An hour later we heard the distinct crackle of stones in the driveway. Although I knew it would be my mother, my instinct led me to look outside.

"Andy, who is it?" Peter asked.

"It's a cop. He's just turning around."

Then I realized the cop wasn't backing up.

"He's getting out!"

At first, I worried I was in trouble. Peter and I went to the door to meet the officer. I remained as still as possible and hoped politeness would keep away trouble.

Seeing how slowly he approached, I relaxed a bit. As he reached the door, he took off his hat.

"Is your father home?" he asked.

"No, he's still at work."

His questions came fast, and our responses were delayed as our minds worked hard to determine the reason for his presence.

We turned to each other to answer each simple question. We were too busy trying to put things together to be sure our answers were correct.

"Last name, Hammer?" his voice softened.

"Yes."

"I'm afraid I have some bad news for you. Your mother and sister were involved in a serious car accident. Your sister was taken to Children's Hospital. Your mother didn't make it. I'm sorry."

No one said anything for a second that seemed like hours. Even if words existed for all the emotions I felt, there would be too many to write.

Realizing it was my time for questions, I asked when it had happened.

"At about 3:20."

I paused and asked where.

"On Main Street near Connection Drive."

A few more questions followed. We then went to the phone to call my aunt.

"Aunt Sharon, I have somebody here who wants to talk to you," I said, realizing I couldn't tell her and handed the officer the phone.

Her shrill cry of "No, not Laura!" was heard by all, and still resounds in my head.

The officer left. I often wonder why he left us, three kids, after telling us this news. We were alone. Greg was still watching TV in the living room. Peter took the job of informing him. I remember glancing in to see Peter kneeling in front of Greg's chair, Greg's face in his chest. Both were crying.

I never did cry that day, although I should have. As people flocked to the house, I was continuously told I must not cry. I needed to be strong. A man I barely knew drove to my father's workplace to tell him. No one in the family appreciated this.

The following days were bad: three wakes, the funeral, the burial. Each wore away at me. I was angry at the people who surrounded me during these events. They weren't thinking. They said and did what came to their minds, which left me to decipher many mixed messages and unbelievable theories. The worst included a woman who claimed she knew of my mother's death months before it happened; a Catholic priest who told me my mother was in heaven, as if he had forgotten Catholics believe in purgatory; and a conversation about how seriously injured my mother had been.

I was supposed to deal with all this and remain strong in the process. Mom's death was the worst experience of my life. It caused more family problems than any fight Mom and I ever could have had. It caused more pain than any embarrassing thing Mom ever could have done. It caused more frustration than any teenage mistake I could ever make. And, if I had known this ahead of time, I never would have wished for it. ▣

The Tear

by Lauren Vose

I held my breath. I watched a tear roll down his cheek. More followed. He began to gasp for air and rub his forehead. My knees seemed to give way and I realized I was on the ground. Tears streamed down my cheeks.

His gasps grew to full sobs. They were clearly audible beneath the sniffles and sobs of my girlfriends. Surrounded by more than twenty friends, he stood, shaking in sadness and frustration. Nothing was held back. He wept with everything in his body. I couldn't take my eyes off him, as he suffered in sudden pain and shock. The captain of the football team, sobbing without inhibition. I sat alone, watching, disbelieving what I saw. The tears continued to fall onto his crisp blue shirt.

Had it suddenly hit him that his friend was dead? I had sobbed for two days and felt like I had nothing left. I felt hollow. I felt empty. But his pain appeared raw. Maybe it hadn't sunk in until he saw his friend's body. I, too, had dismissed it as a bad dream until I saw his body laying on white satin.

Tears came, one after another. I sat alone, wanting to rationalize, to somehow get to the source that was causing him so much pain. I watched face after face walk out of the funeral-home door with the emptiness I felt spread across their pale faces.

I looked at him, standing there in agony: the class clown, the "tough guy" who daily made me laugh in class. But something inside didn't allow me to accept it as him. Something unfamiliar had seized his emotions. His usual coolness had succumbed to the powerful reality of fear and pain. I did not recognize him. Every tear that poured from his heart onto his shirt sent a painful feeling down my spine. I wanted so badly to embrace his large shoulders and tell him that it was going to be okay. But as I sat weeping, watching, I couldn't accept it myself.

The flood of tears escaping from his heart was all I needed to see the reality of our shared situation. I had learned to justify my tears, but it took more to accept his. I felt that if something could cause him to break down, if something could put him through so much pain, there must be a lesson here. There was something too painfully scary and incomprehensible about a child's death. No seventeen-year-olds can justify their peer's disappearance when they have earned the right to grow up.

As he continued to weep, I began to realize he wept for lack of understanding. He wept in fear of living without his friend. He also wept in fear of his own vulnerability. He saw a seventeen-year-old boy, athletic, funny and well-loved by his classmates, now surrounded by flowers and sympathy cards. He saw himself in that coffin, which clouded him with a fear he'd never felt so vividly.

Now he began to sniffle, trying to somehow quiet the burning sense of incomprehension ripping at his soul.

He tried to erase the tears from his reddened cheeks. He turned his back to me and took a step away. But this could never be erased in my memory: My friend, the big, tough jock who never takes anything seriously, wept like a child that night.

And another tear rolled off my cheek. ◙

Papa Preferred Roses

Fiction by Gina Nicole Statuto

Green. That's right, green. And it wasn't even a pretty green, it was a sickly shade. You know, the shade of green that you find on ancient Kleenex boxes, or the lining of silverware drawers in old ladies' kitchens. Not to mention how itchy the darn fabric was. Papa would never have made me wear this dress.

And the flowers. Who in their right mind would have chintzy marigolds at a funeral? Papa didn't even like marigolds. He always preferred roses. "But they have thorns," I would say when he would go on and on about how he loved roses. He would gently shift the pipe between his clenched teeth and say, "Yes, they have thorns. But even the most perfect things in life cause pain. That doesn't mean that we love these perfect things any less."

I glanced at the clock. This was taking forever. To pass the time, I started to count the number of men who were bald in the church. One, two, three . . . Should I really count Mr. Laurie? After all, he did have a bit of hair that he oiled and whipped over the side of his head that made it look like he still had a ways to go before he was officially bald. Well, I'd better count him so it came out even. I have always hated odd numbers. Don't ask me why. I guess they just bother me because if you had to split something up with an odd number, it wouldn't be fair.

I was getting a rash on my behind from this dumb dress. I scratched, then my mother poked me in the shoulder and whispered, "Stop that. You look like you have fleas." I stuck out my tongue at her, and waited until she turned around in her seat before I gave myself another good scratch. I wish I did have fleas. Or perhaps some exotic illness that would have kept me home, so I wouldn't have had to be here.

The choir started singing "Amazing Grace." Papa loved that song. He used to sing it when he was bringing the horses in at night. I used to love when he sang it in the wintertime, because his strong voice cut through the cold air and made it seem warmer. I hastily wiped away a tear. I wasn't going to cry. Crying is stupid. I tried desperately to think of something else.

Standing in the corner, I noticed London Willis. I grew up with him. He's my age, which is sixteen, in case you didn't know. He's all right, I guess. The only thing about him that irked me was his nose. I swear, if you didn't know him, you'd think he was a living replica of Cyrano de Bergerac. Actually, even if you did know him you'd think he was a dead ringer for old Cyrano. Today he looked especially bad. He was wearing a sport coat that hung too far over his waist. The sleeves came down over his hands. His mother had probably tried to do his hair, but the effect was anything but attractive. It was slicked back and shone as though he had put shoe pol- ish on it. He looked like a used-car salesman. You know, the kind who yells and screams on TV about how their lot is having a big clean-out sale. They're always having big clean-out sales. Commercials like that make me sick.

Now the priest was reading a poem about loving people as much as you can and all that stuff. Personally, my motto is, "Love as few people as you can because you never know when they're going to die on you."

My sister was sitting with her new beau. She was crying on his shoulder. It was nauseating. Papa would never have let her lean on him in church. I wanted to scratch out her eyes because she was being so disrespectful of my papa. He was patting her hand and kissing her forehead. I could almost picture what he was saying: "Don't worry, my love. I'll take care of you now." Or, "He was a good man." What did he know about good men? He certainly wasn't in that category. I scratched my behind.

"And if the family members would come up now and pay their last respects to Don." The priest's voice broke. My mother was pulling me from my seat. She had her hand over her mouth, and there was a deep worry line in her brow. I waited in line to see my papa. I hated having to remember him like this. I made a vow not to touch him because he would be cold. My father was never cold. He could work all day outside without gloves in the winter, and he would still be roasting like a chestnut. I guess sometimes you just don't realize how warm something is until it's cold.

It was almost my turn. I closed my eyes and waited until the person in front of me had said their last words to my father. He was a rather short man, with odd, circular spectacles that sat at the end of his nose. He wore a double-breasted black suit with white gloves. Yes, I'm serious, white gloves. And I thought London had absolutely no style. His head was bent low over my father, and his lips were moving mechanically. Suddenly, I panicked. I had forgotten that you were supposed to say something when you were at the casket. The gloved man left. There I was with nothing to say. Then I realized that I had already told my father everything he needed to know. He knew what I was thinking already. I could tell that he was all around me. He was telling me that I didn't need to say anything. So I didn't. I never said a word. I stood by his casket for only a moment before I left him a final gift. Delicately and lovingly, I placed a rose on his chest. A rose with all the thorns picked off. ◙

Photo by Kendra Levin

Shadow

by Jessika Teegarden

I remember you running
on a flight of laughter
wind in your uncut hair
eyes crisp with wit.
I ran, gasping, after you
branches snapping back at me
biting at my sunburnt skin
bare feet sparking the grass.
You were the first to kiss me
the first to make me giddy
with insincere love, undeveloped.
I remember it all—
your craziness, how you made
me laugh.
At night I would dream
as I lay awake
about you, a tiny boy
with a world of imagination.
Together we sat by the water
staring at the ripples
we made with our toes.
But I would not jump
from that old brick bridge

though you pleaded with me so.
I would not sneak out at night
to whisper with you into the darkness.
You begged me to run far away
to risk, to experiment, to live. . . .
If, now, I could do it all again,
I would give in to your pleas.
You would find me beside you
running with you instead of
behind you.
I would do anything now
if I could look into your eyes
once alive with spirit, with light.
I would do anything now
to hear your voice, your breath
to jump from the bridge with you
into the shock of cold water.
There, you are still alive.
There, in that place
where we played together,
You were so real, so vivid
and I was the shadow without life.
Now it is so hard to realize
that you are the one without life,
buried in a shadow of memories.

I Love You, Mom

by Jennifer Clarke

"I love you, Mom. See you tomorrow." I said these words every day as I kissed my mom good-bye. Most girls I know don't tell their mothers they love them when they say good-bye. But I wasn't like girls I knew.

As a baby, I was adopted by two loving people who were willing to take me into their home. They became not only my parents, but also my best friends. As I was growing up, I learned that my birth mother was very young when she had me and wasn't able to care for me. I understood and was thankful. After all, I ended up with two people who loved each other very much, and also loved me. Three years later, they adopted another baby, Lori.

Until I was nine, I didn't understood why my parents didn't have any children of their own. Then my father explained that they tried many times, but they were unsuccessful. Part of the reason was that my mom had diabetes. Since I was young, I didn't really understand what that meant. As I was growing up, I would see my mom give herself shots and wonder why she was the only one who had to do that. All I saw every day was a strong, beautiful, healthy woman, who spent her life helping people.

When I was thirteen, everything changed.

It started with a tiny blister on my mom's toe. This may seem like no big deal, but she ended up losing her toe. Soon she suffered a stroke, and just as she began to recover from that, her leg had to be amputated.

This all took place over three years. The toll this took on my family was unbelievable. My mom was in and out of five hospitals, each doing their best to help her. Sometimes she was home for a few months, but something always seemed to go wrong. When the holidays came, my father, my sister and I spent the day in her hospital room. One Thanksgiving we ate turkey there, and another Christmas we brought all our presents to the hospital so she could see us open them.

I tried my hardest to make her feel better, but nothing helped. At home, taking care of my little sister became my job, along with cleaning the house, doing the laundry and cooking the meals. I thought it was unfair, and took it out on my father. I hated the fact that all my friends went out on Friday nights, while I had to stay home and play "Mommy."

It was even harder for me to go to school while my mom was lying in the hospital. By now, I was sixteen. Luckily she was there for my birthday party, and I'll never forget hugging her as tears fell down both our faces. I'm still thankful for that moment with my mother because it was the happiest I had seen her in four years.

But, once again, the happy days became sad. On June 15, I stayed home from school to take care of her. Once again she was admitted to the hospital. At first, no one could figure out what was wrong. She remained in intensive care for a week. She began to do better. Then on July 10 she became very sick, and on the eleventh she almost died.

It was getting harder and harder to deal with. Every time she got really sick, she would always come back and do even better.

When the doctors finally realized why she was so sick, they put her on dialysis, a treatment for her kidneys. It seemed to work. On August 17, we visited her and she was doing extremely well. When I left, I kissed her and said, "I love you, Mom. See you tomorrow."

At 6:30 the next morning we received a call telling us she had passed away during the night.

Today, a little over a year since my mom left, I am closer to my father and sister. And along with accepting my family responsibilities, I have gained respect for my mom. I still don't understand how she managed to accomplish all she did.

As for being adopted, I have no desire to find my real parents. The ones I have had are the only ones I'll ever need. They taught me to be strong and follow my heart. Watching my mom smile through all her pain taught me that I can accomplish anything. I know she's with me through this important time in my life, and she'll guide me in the right direction.

"Thank you, Mom! I love you and I'll see you tomorrow." 回

If Only I Could Cry

by Benjamin Rhatigan

So I was sitting outside the funeral home last December trying to open a Snickers bar with my chapped hands. It was one of those chafingly cold days when the sun is high and I was just aching for it to come down and warm me, but the wind opposed it.

I was sobbing slightly as I watched the leaves breeze away from me in tiny swirls. Actually, a more accurate description would be that I was choking on my sobs and saw the leaves through a thin haze of tears, which, of course, I hastily wiped away. Because I was a boy. And boys don't cry. We just don't.

But gimme a break. It was my grandfather's funeral. I was alone outside seeking solace from my Snickers. Nobody would know. Yet I still couldn't do it. And inside the funeral home? Forget it. Couldn't happen. I was worried people would think I didn't even like the guy since I was shedding about as many tears as he was. But, oh man, I wanted to. I wanted to pour out all my sadness and anger. Just let go. Just let it wash away. It hurt so much.

He had Parkinson's, and I watched while he weakened and shrank until he wasn't even a whisper of the man he once was. I remember walking through the woods to my grandparents' house, bracing myself for the inevitable pain of the visit. My grandfather would enthusiastically say, in his feeble, coarse voice, "Hey, look who's here!" I'd approach his wheelchair, push out a smile, swallow the lump in my throat, and forcefully blink back my tears. Then I would shout, in an equally forced voice, "Hey, Pop, how's it goin'?" And it was such a shame. This rock of a man, this rock of a husband, father and grandfather reduced to such a pitiful state. And there I stood, like some actor from a bad school play, a goofy grin plastered on my face. All I really wanted to do was burst into tears and beat the life out of something.

If only I could cry. I want to cry the way breath is exhaled. Pushed out in one big, flushing gust. I feel unreal when I don't cry in a sad situation. What kind of a monster doesn't cry at his grandfather's funeral? At his sister's wedding? Me. But I'm not a monster, right? I'm just a boy. Ha.

Crying should be as natural as laughing or smiling. Is it a normal expression of strong emotions? That is what upsets me the most. I consider myself to be a loving, open and expressive person. It scares and upsets me when I just can't get my body to do something that I feel is so vital to the process of clearing my soul. I'll keep trying. ▣

Why Me?

by Marcy Griffin

I woke up and it seemed like an ordinary day. When I went to school, it seemed like another boring day.

Then my principal came to my class to get me: the sound of her heels, the silence inside the room, the sound of thunder in my ears. I felt uneasy tension slip through me.

I remember her walking in the room, the long shadow cast behind her. She asked me very nicely to come with her. I could feel the tension in the pit of my stomach, the fear washing through me, my face burning red.

My mind raced through all the things I'd done recently. Was it the time I skipped class or maybe when I pushed Katie down in the snow? I walked down the hall on this bright sunny day thinking, *I must be in deep this time.*

Then I saw my brother standing in front of the door, staring into space. His face was set in a grimace. My heart skipped a beat.

My brother, my other half, the one person I looked up to, was standing in front of me, telling my principal something I couldn't understand. At that moment, I saw pain, concern, fear and tension build in his eyes. I realized it wasn't something I had done, but something worse. I wanted to know why my brother was there and not my mom. I wanted to know what was so awful that everyone had gone through all this trouble instead of just waiting until I got home. Yet I was terrified of the answer.

I couldn't ask because the lump was getting bigger in my throat. My tongue was tied, my mouth dry.

Everything began spinning.

Then my brother told me, "We're leaving."

As we walked out to the car, I realized that my brother had ridden with my mom's best friends. I began to panic and slipped into hysteria. We got into the back seat and my brother put his arm around me and told me our mother had been in a car accident. I didn't understand.

Was she at the hospital, was she in critical condition, a coma or . . . ?

I tried to ask, but the words would not emerge. My brother pulled me closer. As reality hit me, I asked, "Is she okay?" In a voice full of sorrow, heartache and grief, he told me she wasn't all right. All my anger and emotions welled up inside. Then he lifted my head and spoke very quietly, "She was hit by a truck; her car was crushed."

I did not know how to react. I sat in silence, staring out the window. When we pulled into my driveway, it hit me.

I would never see my mother again. One day everything is there, and the next brings an incident of unbelievable tragedy—a person's life changes in the death of a heartbeat. ▣

I Couldn't Let Go of the Memory

by Brian Harrison

ay 16, 1:25 P.M. History Class.

M I'm supposed to be some sort of writer, so why can't I say anything now? We all know that life isn't fair. We all know about death and that we must deal with it. Somehow I know he took his own life. If he had said something, anything at all, I would have been his best friend. But all I ever gave him were brief conversations, in homeroom or the hall, or a "Hi" while he was passing. I liked him. I'm not saying that because he's gone; I did. He was smart and laughed at my jokes. We had things in common. But no one could find enough time to keep him here. I wonder if there was enough time in the world to do that. Maybe this will change the way people act and feel; it takes a tragedy like this to ameliorate what is wrong. Nobody could tell he was depressed; he hid it too well. Nonetheless, somewhere else, at any given time, someone will be made fun of. Geek, loser, idiot; it's hilarious now. For some reason there are people in this world so insecure they look to others to vent their frustration on them. I'm not perfect. I've done it before, even though I've been the victim of plenty of criticism. You need a thick skin. He didn't have one and now we all feel empty. The saddest part is that he had friends, family and teachers who were there for him, but he refused to believe it. Matt was not a major part of most of our lives, but he's affected mine forever. My own problems keep piling up, but when something like this happens the problems all seem meaningless. I could say I feel very lucky, but the tears never lie.

May 19, 3:45 P.M. The Wake.

I've never liked wakes. I know it's not something to look forward to, but they hurt. It still didn't hit me, even when I saw him lying there. It made no sense. Luckily, I was there with friends who felt the same way. He was brilliant. When Matt applied himself, he was amazing. As I sat there, I remembered too many things he did and though minor, they brought me to tears. He could break into the FBI computer if he had the time; he was a hacker extraordinaire. He told me that he used authors of books he had in his room as aliases. He had a sick sense of humor. There is no reason this had to happen. I still can't believe he's gone.

May 20, 10:00 P.M. The Funeral.

This was the icing on the cake of despair. The pain of crying with all your friends is too much to bear. The entire service, I kept praying, asking why. I asked myself. I asked others. Why God? Why Matt? Why now? Why? I prayed for an answer. He's at peace, but he's the only one. None of us can come to grips with this bitter taste of reality. I couldn't let go of a hug. I couldn't let go of the tears. I couldn't let go of the memory. Too many tears, too much pain.

Saturday Morning, 8:30 A.M.
I write this article. I've turned to Elton John's "Funeral for a Friend/Love Lies Bleeding" and "Skyline Pigeon" for help. For me, this is mourning. The crying is enough for some. Elton's saying, "Fly away . . . toward the things you left so very far behind."

I have to say something. Suicide is the cry for help that can be heard by all, but never made better but in vain. Tragedies are not sugar-coated tastes of life; they are unsympathetic lessons that hit hard and leave their mark. This one hit too many of us, but we will pick up the pieces. Even the family, who is going through hell, will eventually pick up the pieces. No matter how utterly useless, like there's no reason to go on, you can always pick up the pieces.

Matt, you never showed that sorrow, that pain, that uselessness, though it was there. There's always a way out. There's a way out of every problem life throws at us. One must remain strong and find that answer, find that reason to keep going.

There are so many wonderful things in life, but they aren't handed to you on a silver platter. A talent, a passion: everywhere we look there is reason to persevere. My passions, music and writing, may never amount to anything, but they are two of my reasons. I had to look for them and when they came, it was a spiritual rebirth. For everything there is reason, justice and worth. Live, and you will learn, learn and you will grow. Through that growth you will love, and then you will know.

The song repeated the line, "Love lies bleeding in my hand." Let's pick up the pieces, let's stop the bleeding. Let's try to make sure this never happens again. Maybe we make that a reality, but there is too much to live for not to try.

For those despondent souls out there who feel there is no reason to go on living, think again. To find that reason may take days or a lifetime. But the greatest tragedy is to end that search, that journey. Even if that reason cannot be found, know that the search is as great as the discovery. Life is a roller coaster and to give up and scream for the attendant to stop the ride so you can get off is a crime. Stay positive, hold on tight and you'll leave with a smile on your face.

I'll miss you, man. I'm sure that heaven has some system that you can crack into.

There must be some reruns of *Star Trek* up there, too. We'll always be here for you. ▣

A Life Still to Lead

by Sasha Dwyer

The can opener whirls the can around. Over the sound, I can hear my parents talking in the background. Click. The can finishes rotating and I lift it off the magnetic circle. In the background, I hear the phone ringing. My parents' talking ceases as they answer it. Taking the top off the can, I pour the soup into a bowl. I hear my mom say, "What? Ginny? Calm down."

I place the bowl down and turn my attention to the phone conversation. I see tears start to well up in my mom's eyes, and my heart starts to pump. My mind plays the guessing game of what could have happened. She finishes the conversation with "I'll be right there."

My dad and I are now staring intently as she covers her face with her hands. My dad puts a comforting arm around her. I am now standing on the outside, with my bowl of forgotten soup.

"It's Jaime. She's dead. She was in a car accident. She and her friends were driving drunk, lost control of the car, and all of them died." She starts to cry as my dad holds her.

My mind is rammed with thoughts. My cousin? No, it can't be. She's only eighteen, the same age as my brother. How could she be dead? Tears well up in my eyes, and I run up the stairs. Background noises again. I hear my mom tell my dad to check on me. Finally, I hear the heavy thud of winter boots as my dad climbs the stairs. I want to be left alone to think about what happened and to grieve. My dad knocks on the door, and I wipe my eyes and tell him to come in.

"Are you okay?" he asks.

I nod, unable to say anything. He gives me a hug and kisses my forehead. "I am going to bring Mom to Grandma's. Want to come?" I shake my head, glad for the time to be alone. One more kiss and he leaves. I hear softer, quieter steps come up the stairs and stop at my door. My mom knocks and enters. Her eyes are red and her face is tear-stained.

"Hi, honey. Here is your soup."

She hands me a steaming bowl of soup. Why did she think of making that for me now? I don't want it, but take it anyway and thank her.

"I'm flying to Illinois for the funeral tomorrow. Everyone is meeting there. Only a few tickets can be bought so late, so you'll stay here with Dad for New Year's. I'll be back soon." I nod and she continues. "Grandma is in pretty bad shape, so I'm going there to be with her. I'll be back later."

I nod again and she leaves. Finally I am alone with my thoughts. I feel hot tears burn in my eyes and course down my face. I wasn't close to Jaime. I used to think you had to be really close to someone to mourn their death. This is not true. I only saw her once a year. She was older. Though at that second, all I could think about was how young she was—too young to die. A life still to lead. All I could think about was how, when she visited, she had always tried to include me, even though I was younger. Now, I would never see her again. It's hard to imagine never being able to see someone again. I also kept thinking what a waste of a life it was.

That New Year's was a mournful one. Sometimes, when someone dies, you tend to forget things about the person: his voice, how she acted or things that she might have said. But Jaime taught me one important lesson. I will never drink and drive, or get into a car with someone who has. Even though it was a hard lesson to learn, it is one I will never forget. ▣

Art by Jennifer Perry

Saying Good-Bye to Brandy

by Andrea Josenhans

Whenever I walk into my parents' bedroom, I still expect to see her lying on my parents' bed, sleeping. I'd seen her on that bed almost every day. It's hard to accept that I'll never see her there again. I feel as if I've lost a close relative. Actually, I suppose I did. Even if she was just a dog, Brandy had been around even before I was born and I loved her like family. After all, she was part of our family. We brought her on vacations and, when she was younger, she would jump on one of the kitchen chairs while we ate dinner, expecting to eat what we did. We wondered if she knew she was a dog, since she hated all other dogs.

I still remember when I walked into the kennel area of our veterinarian after our three-day vacation. The dogs jumped around and barked like crazy in their cages, all wanting attention. Usually, I would have been happy to give them the attention, but that day I was nervous and sick. Things got worse when I saw Brandy, lying in her cage without moving. She tried to get up to walk to us, but couldn't. There was a white cloth wrapped around her neck to keep in the intravenous tube, and next to her was a dish of untouched food. She hadn't eaten for three days. She would only drink water, and even for that she needed help. I've never felt so bad in my life.

For years I'd been expecting that she might not live much longer. Her sight wasn't very good and she was practically deaf, but she still wasn't in bad shape for a seventeen-year-old dog. I knew that it might happen soon. Unfortunately, you are never prepared. I kept remembering everything Brandy used to do: run around the lawn so fast she'd kick up grass, play catch with a tennis ball, and run up and down the steps, wagging her tail, when we used to ask her if she wanted to go in the car. She let me sit on her when I was two, and chased a Doberman pinscher twice her size when it bothered me. Once when we snuck her into a motel and went out to eat, we came back to find Brandy sticking her head out from between the curtains for everyone to see.

I didn't want it to end like this for her. Only four months ago the veterinarian had told us that Brandy had four more years. I wonder what he thought of his estimation now.

During the next few days, we realized, little by little, the severity of her condition. By the third day, they'd told us that if she weren't better by the next day, we should probably put her to sleep. I prayed that she would be okay . . . but she was worse. The clinic said they could try other things, but they didn't think they would work. My parents decided it was best to put her down. I didn't agree, but I didn't have a say. I suppose that it was better I didn't, because I would have tried anything to keep that poor animal alive, and she probably wasn't happy anymore.

My mother and I went to see Brandy one last time. It was as if Brandy knew that it was the end. As I was saying good-bye and trying to stop crying, she licked my arm and put her head on my hand. That only made me feel even worse. I started begging my mother to give Brandy another day, but her condition had gotten worse and she wasn't even able to stand. We knew it was no way for a dog to live.

I feel bad that I let her die with strangers. I wanted to be with her to the end, but my mother was on the verge of passing out, so, with a sigh, I stood up and stared at Brandy as I closed the cage door, knowing that it was the last time that I'd ever see my beloved dog. I'll never forget that first of August—the day I said good-bye to one of my best friends. ▣

A Strong Man

by Jessica Seifried

My memories are of a strong man, rough around the edges, but truly caring and loving inside. I can remember how smooth his dark brown hair was and how it smelled when he hugged me. I remember him teaching me the right way to swing a bat or kick a ball, how he was the loudest parent in the stands when I hit a home run or scored the winning goal. I recall those family trips and how my mother, brother and I were kept awake, laughing, because he snored so loud.

I can remember how he looked on August 18—peaceful as though he were sleeping, but he was no longer snoring. His beautiful brown hair was in disarray, and its once-comforting, familiar smell was overpowered by that pungent hospital smell. The sheets were pulled high and the lights were dimmed. My mother cried and clutched his hand. My brother clenched his fists, rubbed his eyes and hung his head in confusion. I was surrounded by family, but I felt so completely alone. I felt all eyes were upon me, waiting for a reaction. I ran from the room as my world crashed down on me.

A million thoughts raced through my head. I kept waiting for someone to wake me up from this nightmare. But nobody came. My father was laid to rest four days later.

He had died of a heart attack. Sometimes I think I see his face, or hear his voice in a crowd. . . . My heart skips a beat and I begin to head toward him. But it is never him. He was a strong man, my father, a bit rough around the edges, but loving inside. ▣

Photo by Charles Key

The Rain

by Allison Poole

I remember the rain.
Not much else.
Sitting on the porch crying
Because everybody else was,
And watching my tears
Blend with the rain
To form puddles
Which dripped into the street
And were splashed up by the cars
As they turned into the driveway
Ruining my new dress shoes
But I didn't care
Because they gave me blisters.
I couldn't help but wonder
If the rain could wash my tears
All the way to the ocean
(Which was only around the block)
And eventually to Japan.
We had tried to send a bottle there once
But found it the next day
Washed up on the shore
So I didn't think my tears
Would make it either.

I threw a rock into the drainpipe
That used to be my favorite hiding spot
And it made a hollow sound
Which was how I felt inside
When everybody told me
How sorry they were
And patted my sopping hair.
I just sat out in the rain
Until they all left
Which wasn't long
Because no one wanted to stay.
I didn't wave good-bye,
I just stared into the rain,
The only thing in life
That seemed consistent
And that always has been.
As long as I remember her,
I will remember the rain.

Good Night and Good-Bye

by Robert McKee

"There you go, girl," my mom said as she let my dog loose to run around. Daisy was an outside dog, but she was usually tied up. In the summer when we were out at night, we usually let her run around the yard.

We live in a secluded area with few houses, a dirt road and fields that stretch for miles. It was a beautiful July evening with a "red at night, sailor's delight" sun setting over the dusky atmosphere.

My younger brother Jamie was jumping off the picnic table onto his wrestling buddy in hopes of being the next Stone Cold. My mom was lighting a citronella candle. Summer smells wafted through the air overtaking the exhaust of a passing car. I was watching Daisy run around. I could tell she was excited to be free.

"What a goofy dog," I muttered. I hopped off the wraparound porch and landed in the ankle-high grass. Reminding my mom that it needed to be cut, I ran off to play with the dog. Now Daisy was an all-time great dog, a mutt, but a real winner. She never bit or barked unless there was danger. She had a whitish coat with a few black blotches here and there lightened with age, giant brown eyes that engulfed you with one look, and a wet nose. Her coat was a bit scraggly, since she loved to roll in the dirt and grass. When I jumped in front of her, she shied back until she noticed the friendly face, then she was soon lapping me with her sandpaper-like tongue. I pushed her off and began to wrestle her.

Meanwhile the troublesome cat, Tigger, was lurking inside. He walked with slyness and style as he purred his way onto the windowsill, leaning against the screen with his orange fur sneaking through the tiny holes. Daisy spotted him. Not that she had any intention of hurting him. She usually just wanted to play, but the dog didn't do her usual bark and runs. She noticed the cat and paid no attention. *That is strange,* I thought. *That's nothing like Daisy.*

"I tell you, we could never count on her for protection," my mom commented.

I went inside our warm house. My mom started to read a book, and my little brother was so attached to his wrestling buddy that he blocked out the rest of the world. Daisy wandered off once she lost our attention, down the road, slower than usual.

Later, I came back out to talk to my mom. The evening was quiet once more. The sun was setting, and the night chill was starting.

"Daisy," I yelled. *Where is she?* I thought.

"That dumb dog must have run off again," my mom said. "Go down the road and see if you can see her, Bob, and don't forget a couple of treats."

I came back empty-handed—no dog, no treats.

"Where are the treats?" my mom asked.

"Oh, they got mushy, so I tossed them," I replied.

"Daisy! Daisy!" all three of us called at the top of our lungs.

"Bob, let's get in the car and look for her," my mom suggested. "Stay here, Jamie, in case she comes back." My mom and I started out. We knew she couldn't have gone far.

"Daisy, Daisy," we could hear Jamie calling faintly. I began to yell louder out the window.

The neighbors have a dog, I thought. So I jumped out of the car and ran to their yard. I heard a whimper, but saw no Daisy. My brother came running down the hill to the neighbors, and we searched around the weeds and barn. We didn't see her. Then my brother yelled, "I found her. I got her." I slipped on mud and ran to the dog. I was about to yell at her, but couldn't. She was whimpering and stumbling. Her paws were brown from the mud, and I could tell she was sick. I remembered a few weeks earlier when my mom said that Daisy wasn't eating. She said she tried every kind of food: hard, soft, wet, dry and chunky. So we led her up to the car fifteen yards away. That short distance took Daisy ten minutes. I scooped her up into the car and drove her to the house. As I lifted her out, I held her gently, so as to not break any of her fragile ribs. My mom said, "You know what this means, don't you, boys?"

We both replied in our most solemn voices ever, "Yes." My brother got teary-eyed, and all I could think of were the good times, the sweet memories. Like the first time we got her home when she was just a pup and I was six. I spent that night with her in the basement on the cold floor with my baby blanket to help us stay warm.

I felt so sad that one of the best things in my life was dying right in front of my eyes. I hugged her as gently as I could.

She only had one night to live. That evening, I sat outside with her. I muttered to her and myself, and soon fell asleep beside her. I woke up forty minutes later, looked at her for a few minutes and softly patted her good night and good-bye. That was the last time I saw Daisy. ◙

The Things We Take for Granted . . .

by Cassandra Stuart

Apple picking. Singing in the rain. Sand between my toes at the beach. Snowball fights in winter. Running through the woods. The scent of my mother when she hugs me good night. The warmth of the sun on my face. The twinkle of stars in a summer sky. The taste of ice cream. The conversations, laughter, tears and time shared by friends. The joy of seeing a baby smile. The feel of a cool gust of wind on my face. The satisfaction of winning a track meet. Wearing the symbolic red sweater of our school's senior class.

Colleen and Erin will never do, see, feel, touch or know any of these things again. One rainy morning, one puddle on the road and one tragic car crash later, their lives, and ours, will never be the same. Our friends are gone and so are others' daughters, sisters, nieces, granddaughters, inspirations, loved ones, baby-sitters, teachers, volunteers, students and athletes. They were extraordinary girls with their whole lives ahead of them, running to after-school activities or discussing plans for college. Like us, the most important things on their minds were homework, what was happening that weekend and what was for dinner.

But that Tuesday, September 22, they never returned home, and never would again. They left family and friends in shock, sadness, anger, frustration, confusion and mourning over the loss. Priorities shifted, faith was questioned and our community was truly tested.

To many of us, everything important became insignificant—we all lost track of the latest homework assignments, the dates of the athletic events and just about everything else. We suddenly realized that the only way we could get through such a loss was together. The moment we discovered the deaths of our friends and classmates, we pulled together and clung to one another for dear life. Superficial facades faded away, strangers hugged, parted friends reconciled, parents held their nearly grown children as protectively as fragile infants, students leaned on teachers and teachers leaned on students. Compassion, understanding and love replaced competition, exclusion and animosity. The responses and outpourings of support were utterly amazing.

I am thankful that our class and community have bonded so tightly in these trying weeks, but I beg you not to wait for such a disaster to appreciate all you have. Savor every chocolate-chip cookie, hug your family and friends often, smell the next rose you walk by, talk to the girl at the back of the class, stroll the beach barefoot, smile at strangers, hug those who look sad, apologize to those you hurt and never forget to say "I love you." This could have been anyone—your friend, sister, brother, cousin, classmate, teacher, parent—absolutely anyone. Treasure every day you are given and be thankful. ▣

Passing the Guardrail

by Elizabeth Pile

I had so much happening that July weekend. I planned to spend time at our community camp for special needs people. I had a college interview. The grass desperately needed mowing. Then there was also my sports physical, a picnic and work. At some point I also had to find time to pack for my trip to New Orleans with my church youth group.

As I dragged out my suitcase, the phone rang. That call suddenly made my needs totally insignificant. When I heard Jared's voice, I thought nothing of it, but his next faint words came in a rush and caused my knees to buckle onto the carpet. "A car accident," Jared said. "Dave's gone," his voice dwindled to a whisper. "He's gone."

My vision blurred with overflowing tears, and I choked on my breath. Dave was Jared's older brother. He was only nineteen. I had laughed with him the day before.

For once, I had no words to say to Jared. There were no words that could bring Davy back. That afternoon was only the beginning. The memories have yet to fade.

. . . Driving to Jared's grandparents' house. Passing the shattered glass on the road. Tire marks. Seeing Jared's pale, tear-stained face. His brave attempt to smile. It pierced my heart to see him that way. His outpouring of

thoughts as we walked in the rain: quoting his last conversation with Dave, describing the horror and disbelief
he felt when he saw Dave's body, knowing that his big
brother could not hear him say, "I love you." This six-
foot, seventeen-year-old boy leaning on me for support.
Warm teardrops falling on my head.

. . . The never-ending line of a rural community
expressing its grief at the viewing. Half of the visitors—
teenagers—facing the truth that they are not indestructible. Many did not know Dave at all, but were touched
by his death. A father's sob. A mother's look of numb-
ness. Dave's senior photo on the coffin.

. . . The funeral. A beautiful day. A small church
packed full. Parents easily imagining themselves in the
place of Dave's parents. Jared asking that I remain by his
side. Crumbling to pieces as I, and others, shared memories. Dave's senior class singing "You'll Always Be a Part
of Me," the song they had sung the night of their graduation. Hands reaching out to be held. A final good-bye.

I know too well that the sadness of this experience will
never disappear from my heart and mind. Those left
behind are a constant reminder of the pain, the tears and
the harsh realization of life's brevity that I encountered
that summer weekend. Of course, life goes on.

. . . A family's unsuccessful attempt at normalcy.
Beginning to set my own goals after graduation. Pictures
of yesterday. Crying to a song about a life that ended too
soon. Passing the bent guardrail. A silence too long to
bear . . .

We've said good-bye . . . but we'll always remember. ▣

Sheldon the Fisherman

by Andrea Trask

Death is a vague one. You think that he can't possibly touch you or anybody you know. You go through life skipping the obituary section in the newspaper and holding your breath when you pass a graveyard. Then, with no warning, he appears like a rude houseguest. But when he leaves, he takes someone with him.

I spent most of my childhood at the small bait and tackle shop that my father owns and runs. Daily, I'd play games in the parking lot in front of the building—catch with my brother in the grassy field out back, or (on rainy days) Clue in the small upstairs area my dad called an office. I grew up with the most frequent customers as friends, people like Teddy Abbadessa and Fisherman Jack. And Sheldon Sladen.

Sheldon could probably be best described as . . . I don't know. A man who spent his life fishing and lobstering; a man who was short but made up for it with a personality that could knock you over. A man who was dark, rough and weather-beaten from years spent at sea, yet gentle enough to befriend a toddling girl like me with ease.

He seemed eternal, a man who would always be around. I always thought that when I graduated from high school and helped at the shop during college breaks, he'd come into the shop with a hello and a grin. I thought I would be hearing his little jokes and tidbits of fishing news for years to come. But last spring, my mother gave me heart-shattering news—Sheldon had died.

He had been fishing in his boat outside the harbor and apparently had a heart attack or stroke, became entangled in his line, fell overboard and drowned. I suppose it is a comfort that he died while doing what he loved best, but nevertheless, I was unable to force my dinner past the growing lump in my throat and spent most of the evening crying into my pillow.

True to form, his will stated that rather than be buried he wished to be cremated and have his ashes scattered into the sea. That day hundreds of people gathered on the shore to pay their respects to a wonderful man, and the overcast sky made it seem like even nature was mourning his passing. As the priest scattered the ashes, however, the clouds parted, the sun broke through, and a rainbow arced across the sky—a pathway of God, laid out for the angels to travel and bring a great man home for his eternal rest.

Good-bye, Sheldon—wherever you are, you will never be forgotten. ◙

5 Family

Photo by Anamaria Lugo

Reliving the Nightmare

by Alison Reemer

t was a dark rainy day in November. Washington, D.C. felt gloomy, and the topic was not helping. The building looked like a ghetto from Warsaw. You could see smokestacks and chainlink fences along the insides. Just looking at this building sent chills down my spine. I never thought I could feel this way. It was as if an outside force beyond my control was about to take over my feelings.

I walked into the U.S. Holocaust Memorial Museum with my grandmother clutching my hand for dear life. I knew this was going to be one of the hardest things she would ever do, but if it meant educating me about a horrific event that she had the misfortune of taking part in, she was willing to endure the pain. My family accompanied my grandparents during this traumatic experience. My grandparents relive the nightmare of the Holocaust every night when they sleep, constantly having nightmares of the screams and gunshots that rang out during those nights long ago.

As we entered the first room, I was confronted with four mannequins lined up in blue pin-striped uniforms, typical of the concentration camps. There were pictures of people's arms with their number tattoos, and articles of children's clothing with stuffed animals and books. The Museum revealed the many methods of torture the Nazis used during the Holocaust. There were Aryan eye charts, hair samples, calipers for measuring the Jews' heads. Nothing was left out; there was a complete set of disgusting tools of torture. It was absolutely revolting, and made me feel sick. By this time, my grandfather was shaking and close to hysterics. I could not even imagine what this was like for him, but it was something he needed to do—to educate me about the horrors of the Holocaust that many people deny ever happened.

I spent most of the walk through the Museum with my grandmother, hand-in-hand. She told me stories of when she was a child in her hometown, what it had been like to have the Gestapo walking through the streets, and how one day she was playing with her friend and the next day her friend had been taken away by the Nazis.

After seeing a display of the cities the Nazis attacked, I rounded a corner to see something I never imagined would be included. It was an actual train car used to transport the Jews to the concentration camps. My grandmother took my hand and led me inside. We walked to the window in the corner, and, in the darkness of the car, she began to tell me the story of when she was taken away. "I was just a small girl. They came into my town and shoved us all onto the train. There were hundreds of us packed together very tightly. You couldn't even breathe. There was only one window, and most of the time it was closed. My father was separated from us. He was in one corner, while my mother and I, with my brothers and sisters, were in another. Then one day the

doors opened, and my father ran out. I followed screaming, but I never found him." She stood there staring into
the darkness of the train car. My grandfather began to
relive what it was like standing in line every day just
waiting to get tattooed, but fortunately they never got to
him. He has told me so many traumatizing stories over
the years that I feel they are the two bravest people I
know. As I left the train car, I was bombarded with the
sight of piles of suitcases, possessions of those who had
ridden these trains to the concentration camps.

Yes, these things were traumatizing to look at, but
what I encountered during the rest of my tour was even
more horrifying. My next stop was at the crematories.
They showed every detail of these death chambers, with
mannequins in actual Nazi uniforms carrying piles of
bones from the crematory on stretchers. I started to feel
sick. I wanted to run, but I stayed with my grandparents.

Next, as we passed through the glass hallway engraved
with all the names of the towns in Europe, we stopped
to find my grandparents' towns. The look of happiness
on their faces when they saw the names truly warmed
my heart.

Shoes. Millions of shoes. Piled in a large room from
wall to wall. Just shoes. Whose shoes? I kept wondering
if any of my grandparents' shoes were in that pile. There
were shoes of all styles and sizes. High-heeled shoes,
boots and tiny baby shoes. They never had a chance to
see the world.

As my family and I entered the last area, my grandfather began to lose control. It was a single room with a
flame burning in the middle. He began to cry and shake,

and I didn't know what to do. We let him walk across the room to the window that looked over the city. There was a look of fear in his eyes, as if he thought it was all happening again. That day was the most horrible experience for my grandparents since the Holocaust. They were forced to relive their fears. I learned a lot about who my grandparents were, where they came from, and most of all, what they had had to endure. I learned about my history, and me. I came to realize that I am special because I am the granddaughter of a Holocaust survivor. It is my job to make sure that no one forgets it happened. ▣

Holding On

by Kaidi Stroud

We loaded the car to visit every summer—
four animated girls were enough to leave you out of
*   breath.*
You won me with a Mickey Mouse ice-cream pop.
I won you with a mug made of Carolina red clay.
We cut out construction paper hearts,
and sent them to you with our love.
You cherished them all
because you knew that things would change.
Things would grow older.

When I got older we drove down for a brief visit.
I noticed your hands shaking as you cut your meat,
your voice trembling as you quietly spoke.
You still had pink construction paper piled in your
*   drawers.*
But I didn't have time for paper hearts anymore.
You bought me a Mickey Mouse ice-cream pop.
But I didn't eat ice cream anymore.
But now, Granddaddy, if you could only buy me one
*   more pop,*
I'd eat it just for you,
to pretend that things hadn't changed

the way you knew they would,
and to love you as I did then, and as I do now—
both at once.

Because now I realize that you were just holding on
to the hand of a little girl who was too young to hold on
*   with you.*
And now that I understand,
that little girl has long since run off out of sight.
And now that I understand,
it is suddenly my turn to do the holding.
So here's my hand, Granddaddy,

Hold on.

Skating Paradise Lost

by Joseph DiPasquale

Normally, after my third hour of freestyle, lethargy would start to creep into my legs, and I would work on spins or choreography instead of jumps or stroking. But, since this was my last time to skate on home ice, today was special: I was joyously anticipating my move to Cape Cod to train for the year. There was nothing I would not sacrifice for figure skating. I had decided that my skating would benefit if I left home to train with Eve Scotvold, the legendary coach of Nancy Kerrigan and Paul Wylie. The stars of skating excellence in my eyes blinded me from my initial fear of leaving my family.

My parents came with me for that first week in Cape Cod while I settled in with my host family. I started immediately with a grueling skating schedule: four hours of freestyle, two hours of figures, two hours of ballet and one hour of weight training—just the type of rigorous training that I had hoped for. The whole experience was sublime. Not only was I in skating paradise, but my parents were there with me.

The last day my parents were there, my father dropped me off at the rink at 6:45 A.M. I was so eager to get on the ice that I neglected to kiss him good-bye. Instead, I grabbed my lunch and ran inside to the rink.

In the middle of the 11:00 A.M. freestyle, I suddenly locked eyes with my brother. He was standing off the ice by the snack bar. Bemused, I rushed to the boards to find out why he was there. When I noticed my mother and ten-year-old brother close behind him, I began to worry that something was wrong. I couldn't help but shudder at the sight of my mother's watery eyes as she put her hand on my shoulder and said, "Joe, I have something to tell you. . . . Daddy's dead."

The next few days are a blur. I felt as if I were experiencing a nightmare from which I was powerless to escape. The world continued on its ruthless path before my glazed stare. I left Cape Cod with my family, weeping during the three-hour trip home. My heart was torn by my father's sudden death and the abrupt end it brought to my stay in skating paradise. Like a child, I tried to ignore the situation in the hope that it would go away. His death was extremely hard to accept: I left the wake early and was the only member of my family not to speak at the funeral.

Over the weekend, I needed to decide whether I would stay at home or return to Cape Cod. I knew that my father would have supported any decision I felt was right. My skating aspirations, however, left me little choice. Dad died on Thursday; I was back in Cape Cod by the following Tuesday.

When I returned, I was apprehensive about my new living situation, school system and skating coach. I had courage. I was sure of my father's blessing as I entered this brave new world. I will think of him as I gather the incredible strength needed to deal with his death away from home. ▣

IN MEMORY OF NED MARIO DIPASQUALE
(1942–1994)

Photo by Whitney Wiggin

Bargaining with God

by Kelly Donald

When I think of my family, I consider it "normal" —two working parents, a daughter, a son, and even a white picket fence. Our family life was stable and dependable—until one January day.

It was a Sunday morning and I was getting ready to baby-sit. My door was shut. Suddenly I could hear my mom running up the stairs, screaming my name. I thought Dad must be playfully chasing her, as he often does. I opened the door to watch the fun. It might have been the tears in her eyes or her terrified look, but I knew something was really wrong. Soon I was downstairs with my family, each with our own tears and terrified looks. My father was in the basement seated in a chair, his limp body being supported by my brother. He could hardly talk; only murmurs came from his mouth. His eyes were squinted and he was breathing heavily.

My mom sent me outside to "wait for the ambulance." I wasn't in any state to argue. In the two or three minutes it took for the medics to get there, my whole life changed. What was happening? What would I do without my father? Why him? Why me? Why hadn't I told him that I loved him?

I could hear the sirens in the distance. They sounded light years away.

When help finally arrived, I begged them to hurry. The medics went to my father and, after a quick exam, put him in the ambulance and rushed him to the hospital.

At the hospital, the hours dragged like years. Finally the doctor came and told us what had happened. His medical jargon meant nothing to me, but I did catch the word "stroke" here and there. My father, *my* father, had a stroke? How could this be happening?

My dad stayed at the hospital for two days. Both nights I bargained with God. I knew that if there was ever a time I needed his help, this was it. I swore that if he spared my father, I would never ask for anything again. I vowed never to take my father for granted again. I promised away everything I had to have my father back. I wanted my crumbling world to be normal again.

I just hoped God was listening.

On the third day, the doctor met us as we were coming in. He said he had to talk to us. *This is it,* I thought.

He sat us down and started to talk. I did all I could do to concentrate on his words. Finally I heard "fully recover." I burst into tears—at last—happy tears. My prayers had been answered. I had a father.

Since then, I realize that nothing is *ever* certain. Now, when my parents say something, I listen. When the family sits down to dinner, we enjoy each other's company. Dinner time isn't just time to fill our stomachs. It's a time to fill our heads and hearts with memories to last forever. I have come to believe firmly that you don't realize what you have until it is almost taken away. ▣

Christmas Cookies

by Helen Comber

"Are we there yet?" asked a sleepy voice from the back of the dark car. It was the tenth time my little sister had asked. Sadly, I had been counting. Long and bumpy car rides from New York to Ohio aren't exactly exciting. The only thought that kept us all from mutiny was knowing we were going to a place we dearly loved.

We have gone to Grandpa and Grandma's for Christmas for as long as I can remember. Christmas at home barely feels like Christmas. My mom spent her childhood there, remaining there until the day she said "I do" to my dad. Theirs was a small town, our second home, and we loved its sleepy atmosphere.

As we pulled into the driveway, I could already feel the warm glow that enveloped the house at Christmas time. In the front yard was Grandpa's annual light display, with the large wooden nativity scene painted in bright colors. There was no snow, which disappointed us, but what the house held was most important to us.

Grandpa came out first, as always. "How are my grandkids?" he asked loudly and happily.

"I can't move my legs!" groaned my youngest sister.

Grandpa ceremoniously hugged us all, youngest to

oldest, as he did every year. The air was filled with cries of "We're so glad to be here," and "My, my, how much you've grown!"

Tiredness faded. It was official. It was finally Christmas.

"No one goes in empty-handed!" yelled Dad. We grabbed our bags and pillows from the car and went inside to the family room, always warm and inviting. Colored lights were strung, and, in the middle of the room, the Christmas tree glowed; every shadow was deepened, every detail softened. An old, fuzzy-sounding Christmas record played on the stereo, perhaps Bing Crosby. This room was magical.

In the dining room, another smell emerged. Grandma had been baking again! But that was no surprise. We always found her there, always with something ready— maybe her Spanish chicken and rice. If we were really lucky, it would be spaghetti with meatballs.

Mom always got the first hug from Grandma. They had a special mother-daughter moment we never intruded on. Then it was our turn, and we all got a loving hug. We talked about school and the trip. Then Mom joined her for their cooking session. We knew all too well where Mom's cooking genes came from, although the prestigious position of "best family cook" came with age and experience.

Grandma was of medium height, thin, with deep chocolate-brown eyes. Her hair was short and curly; my mom called it "salt and pepper." She wore grandmotherly clothes, pastel sweatshirts with flowers and matching pants. Grandma had a sweet voice and was always ready when you needed to have a good talk. She got up early every day to go to church with Grandpa, and could often be seen saying the rosary.

I always thought Grandma was quiet. She wasn't shy, but rather waited until it was her turn, always thinking before she spoke. I rarely remember her raising her voice, but boy, if she did, you knew you had really done it. Grandma, at rare and special moments, could be funny. Her jokes were few and far between, but whenever she told one, we laughed.

Grandma spent most of her time in the kitchen. She would stay home and cook while we went downtown to skate or see the elaborate holiday train display. It was hard to believe such heavenly food came from that humble kitchen. Grandma was a miracle worker.

Of all the food produced from that ancient oven, the best was Grandma's Christmas cookies. After dinner, we could choose two from her vast selection. These decisions were among the hardest of my life. There were the green, buttery wreaths and Christmas trees that were oh-so-crumbly and melted in your mouth. And her large and chewy sugar cookies with the extra large Hershey's kiss in the middle that I always saved for last. There were butterscotch ones and perfect peanut-butter cookies with the traditional crisscross. And, of course, my personal favorite, the chewy candy canes with the minty icing and cute pink stripes. Grandma, always caring, would make plates of cookies we would deliver to her neighbors.

Christmas wasn't Christmas without being there, or having Grandma's Christmas cookies. But I knew—everyone in my family knew—that Grandma had cancer. I tried not to believe. It was easy at Christmas to deny anything was wrong. As all my aunts, uncles and cousins opened presents that year, it was blissful. When Grandma received a warm robe from Grandpa, she held it up for the family to admire, her smile shining brightly.

I dreamed of Christmases past—and Christmases to come.

That was her last Christmas. Grandma died two months later. It was so sudden; I thought she had more time, and so did she. She left many things unfinished, many cookies unbaked.

It was a shock when I visited her just before she died. She had been so different at Christmas from the half-delirious woman suffering in bed. Near the end, I knew she was ready. I'm sure she went straight to heaven. I bet she bakes cookies for the angels now.

Last Christmas was our first without her. During the long car drive, I wondered if Christmas would ever be Christmas again. As we entered the family room, everything seemed the same. Grandpa gave us warm, comforting hugs, just like always, youngest to oldest.

When we went into the dining room, however, it was clear something was missing. No one greeted us as we entered the old kitchen. There were no smells of Christmas cookies.

Grandpa pulled out a tin and offered us a cookie, but they were not the same. Grandpa had made slice-and-bake cookies—the kind with green trees and red snowmen in the middle. It was so sweet of him. He meant well. It made me want to cry.

"Boy," Grandpa joked between mouthfuls, "I'm sure glad I stayed home all day to make these."

And we all laughed. But I couldn't help thinking—Grandma would have done that. She would have labored over that ancient oven again this year. I knew Grandpa felt it, too. He loved her so much. And now, he missed her so much. If eating these cookies would give my grandpa comfort, I would eat a whole bathtub full. At least my mom baked some of our old favorites. At a too-young age, she assumed the title of "best family cook."

In the dining room was a new display: a photograph of Grandma as a beautiful navy nurse with white candles burning bright next to some flowers. I gazed at it and thought of her and prayed for her and remembered . . . and the light aroma of freshly baked Christmas cookies gently surrounded me. Christmas had finally arrived. 回

No Visitors at This Time
by Andy Redden

*Long hallways filled with artificial light burn my tired
   eyes*
The smell of high-grade Formica fills the hospital
Long uncomfortable hours, waiting, hoping, but knowing
Bad news, but the machines said he was getting better
Watching them work on his lifeless body
Keeping him alive for the next few minutes
*Everyone destroyed, barely able to cope with themselves
   for the moment*
Tears on leather
Alone
*"No Visitors At This Time," give me the sign, memory on
   my door*
Too many faces, too many people, too much emotion
Escape through The Doors playing in the background
Nice choice of music, my choice
The preacher rambles on, fumbling up the words, lets go
Into the ground you go, bro, "See you on the other side"
I'll pick the stone, your new front for eternity
*The lake and your bike, but I chose the cattails, so
   symbolic*
*I go and wash the stone every day, water the grass,
   think of you*

You taught me everything, brother
How to live, have fun, take care and survive
You taught me to do good, and be true
How to cope with living, to get along with parents and
*   siblings*
You taught me all about life, dear brother
And in your final lesson, you taught me all about death

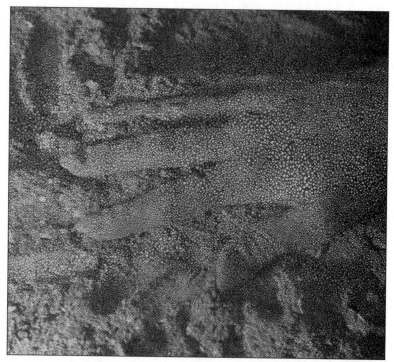

Photo by Abigail Cook

Perfection

by Alexa Lin

The audience's applause died away as Odette left the stage. It was time, and I was ready. My heart pounded from the excitement as the other baby swans and I wished each other luck before positioning ourselves in the wings of the curtain. They were nervous, but I knew how perfect everything was going to be. Tchaikovsky's music began to break through the air as we waited for our cue.

Ever since I could walk, I've been dancing. My mother wanted me to get over my clumsiness and learn to walk gracefully, so she enrolled me in a dance school. From the beginning, ballet was my true love. I dreamed of being Clara, happy in a world of enchantment in *The Nutcracker,* or rising from the grave in *Giselle.* Ballerinas always looked so graceful dancing on their toes and flying through the air. Everything about ballet was magical, and I wanted desperately to be a part of that magic.

When I was ten, I started dancing on my toes because my teacher and foot doctor thought I was technically advanced and strong enough. Classes met six days a week, and I anxiously attended each knowing that only practice could make perfect, and that perfection was the key to happiness.

I was rewarded for my hard work when I was cast as one of the four swans in my school's production of *Swan Lake*. I don't ever remember being prouder. It was my first year on pointe and I was going to dance alongside the older girls, who were thirteen. I told my mother, who placidly promised to attend my June performance.

During the next few months, I worked diligently, ruining endless pairs of blood-stained satin shoes. My toes hated me for torturing them. I gave them no say in the matter, forcing them to work harder, forming blister over blister. I was often discouraged by what I saw in the mirror, but by June I knew I was ready.

On performance day, my father informed me that the lawn needed to be mowed, and that he wouldn't be going. Despite my disappointment, I gathered my costume and headed over to the auditorium. Everything was ready. I knew each square foot of the stage and each curtain wing individually. An hour remained until the performance.

I entered the bathroom to get dressed. My hair was parted in the middle and slicked back over my ears into a bun at the nape of my neck in the true ballerina style. I pinned large feathers to each side of my head as I began my transformation into a swan. I meticulously applied my stage makeup with false eyelashes. To a stranger I would have looked like a prostitute with a funny hairdo, but to me I looked like a true dancer. My feet seemed eager to be squeezed into pointe shoes, and I sewed ribbons for security. Nothing was going to go wrong because I was prepared.

So far the performance had been wonderful, and now it was my turn to add to the perfection. The four of us coupéd onto the stage, hands joined together as our heads looked this way and that. I executed each step with precision as though my life depended on it. I knew my mother was watching, and I wanted her to be proud. Dancing made me feel wonderful and nothing could stop me from this sense of freedom. My feet felt light as they jumped; my legs cut through the air. Everything was so well rehearsed that my mind enjoyed the performance as my body danced. I wanted to dance forever, but the music came to an end as we piqued to our knees. The high stayed with me as the audience roared in awe. We curtsied and left; the ballet continued.

I sat backstage feeling overjoyed that my work had paid off and relieved that it was over. My teacher greeted me with a congratulatory hug, and I looked forward to receiving another from my mother. I had never danced so well, and already I was looking forward to next year's production of *Les Patineurs*.

The rest of the performance was a success. Dancers exited the stage after the final bow to be accosted by proud friends and family. I looked for my mother as my friends were presented roses and carnations. She was standing by the exit with her back to the excitement. I approached her with a sparkle in my eyes and in my heart. She turned around, and I saw that there were no flowers in her arms and no sparkle in her eyes. I asked, "Mommy, what'd you think?"

She replied flatly, "You were the fattest one on the stage."

I didn't want to dance anymore. ◙

My Worst Day

by Margaret Wetherell

I had always perceived my family as being perfectly normal. We always seemed boring. I had one brother, and my parents were still married. We often went out together shopping and for dinner. Over the years, we had typical family arguments, but nothing serious.

Then something happened. It was a Saturday, two days after Thanksgiving, and my parents and brother had gone to visit relatives for the day. They left early in the morning and came home in the early afternoon. My mother was in a pretty bad mood, which I realized the minute she walked in the door. A police officer had given her a speeding ticket.

My mother was tired from the day, so she took a nap. I noticed she went downstairs to the bathroom, and then went back to bed again. A half hour later, I went into the bathroom. What I found shocked me.

On the tissue box behind the toilet was a piece of paper, held firmly down by three empty medicine vials. Curiosity drew me closer. I discovered a suicide note.

The only thing I could think was, *Oh my God, my mother is dead.* I was frozen and didn't know what to do. I began screaming for my brother, who came in wondering what could be wrong. He looked at the note, and together we ran up the stairs yelling as loudly as we could. My father and I screamed at her and shook her to wake her up while my brother called 911.

The paramedics got there in no time and eventually got her out of the house and to the hospital. There she had her stomach pumped and the doctors estimated that she had taken sixty to seventy pills. My mother was in a coma that night, but slowly recovered. She stayed in the hospital for two weeks.

After her release, my family went to a psychologist. During sessions, we were able to express our hurt and talk about our feelings. Since then, we have become much closer and do not argue nearly as much. I want to think that this is a happy ending to my mother's depression, but I can't. I don't know if she'll ever go to this extreme again, but I can only hope she doesn't. I will always be grateful to the paramedics for saving her life. I don't know what I would have done if we had lost her.

I did learn one thing, though: Suicide is not the answer to anything—there is always a better way out. ▣

Constant Fear

by Heather Quinn

When I was little, I would sit on the brown leather couch and clutch my ragged panda bear to my chest—waiting. At six o'clock, I would hear it—the sound of my father's work boots echoing in the hallway. The instant the first thud was heard, everything changed.

My mom would jump up from the couch to make sure dinner was ready and there was plenty of cold beer in the fridge. My older sister and I would stop whatever we were doing. In an instant, we were transformed into "little mice," as my mom called it.

It always seemed like Dad took hours to climb those stairs. But soon enough his foreboding presence would take over the den. He would walk in, take off his smock and sit on the couch, saying nothing. Only after he sampled his dinner, drank his first two beers and changed *Sesame Street* to his favorite program would he speak. He would stare at my mother, watching her every move, ready to fight. Then he would ask how her day was. We all dreaded her answer. If she said it went well, she was a dirty liar. If it went badly, she was a no-good, incompetent mother and a bitch. She was always a bitch. And we were spoiled brats—always.

He would only stay home for a short while. He would be off to the nearest bar within an hour. We never knew whether he would come home drunk or spend the night with another woman. My mom used to try to lie for him. "He's sleeping at a friend's house," she would say in her sweet, soft voice. But we always knew: See, Dad, you always forgot your toothbrush.

In the morning, I would go downstairs and eat my breakfast quickly, trying to slip out without bumping into him. I would gulp down my cereal, drink my juice and sit frightened as my mom quickly made my lunch. Grabbing my Cookie Monster lunch box, I would lift my backpack off the floor and slip out the back door. I would walk slowly, looking into neighbors' windows, wondering if it was like my home in everyone's house. The constant fear and unbreakable silence were perfectly normal.

Walking home from second grade one day, I had a funny feeling. I arrived home to find my family in the den. "Divorce," they said. The best for all of us. I couldn't understand anything except that Daddy was leaving. All I asked was that Daddy take that Budweiser lamp with him when he left.

In the beginning, he would visit three times a week— then two, then one. Holidays, always drunk. Christmas eve, he arrived at 1:30 drunk and on drugs. He begged to stay; Mom let him. For three days we lived in fear, just like before. Constantly drunk, he left food and beer cans everywhere. Finally he left. Visits became weekly again; he brought gifts. I was happy with new toys, but they never made up for the pain. I still feel the pain, every day. I lost my childhood, lost to a beer bottle.

For a while, he took us out for dinner once a week and gave us money for clothes and tapes. But I still hated him.

Then one day, angry, hurt and violated, I walked the streets for hours. The headline flashing over and over in my head. Arrested for drug dealing, Daddy was going to jail. I've yet to face my father since that day. All the pain, all the anger climaxed that day as I slowly read the words in the local paper. He'd been betraying us for years, living a lie. I was devastated; how could he do this to us? I haven't gotten my answer yet. I'm still sorting through all the anger and pain. ▣

Feast Fit for a King

by Emma Hill

My grandfather cooked us breakfast
Every year on Christmas morning
We would all awaken to the sounds
Slipping through the kitchen doorway—
The sizzling of the pan, the whipping of the eggs, the
*   buzz of the timer*
And the gentle hum of a Frank Sinatra tune
Coming from his deep strong throat
As we'd watch him in all his glory
Stride across the linoleum like a king
In his "Kiss-the-Cook" apron and green and red
Checkered towel flung carelessly over his shoulder
Until his regal masterpiece was complete
And the glow of victory on his face
Would lure us through the doorway,
Still in our pajamas and slippers,
Our eyes daring the ornament-covered tree to burn
*   brighter*
Our hearts thumping with great anticipation
Of the day to come
The smell of his aftershave, sweet and familiar,
Passed by our noses as we kissed his cheek
In thanks

The Christmas morning rituals were expected
Like the moon and the stars and the sun
Always there before
Always will be there

My grandfather lay sprawled out on
The snow-white sheets with perfect
Corners, the red emergency button
Next to him on the wall
The gentle hum of the life machine
Replaced the songs in his own throat
With sullen eyes but a proud heart
He refused to give in to the nurse's pleas
To eat his breakfast
Because the cook always preferred
His own eggs Benedict
To strawberry Jell-O.

"What Did You Say?"

by Mark Phelan

Her reaction surprised me. I really didn't mean to say "Leave me the hell alone," but the words tumbled out in a moment of pure emotion. Her face contorted in disbelief and anger, and I knew immediately I was in for it. She managed to get herself under control and slowly—very, very slowly—she opened her mouth to speak.

"What did you say to me?" she asked accusingly.

"Ah, well, um, leave me the hell alone?" I repeated meekly, staring down at our tiled floor, wishing I was anywhere, anyplace but there. Without another word, she simply pointed in the general direction of my room and I knew I was *really* in for it. I trudged up the stairs and waited for the inevitable arrival of my father, who, upon hearing what I had said, would lecture me on the evils of insulting one's mother and the consequences of such an action.

This wasn't the first time my mother and I had had a little "disagreement." I was only twelve years old, yet my life seemed filled with skirmishes, sometimes all-out wars. I hadn't liked her going to my baseball games, still she showed up, shouting and cheering in a way that would make any kid cringe.

I was in sixth grade, and it seemed as if she were a part-time teacher; she constantly volunteered to monitor field trips, much to my embarrassment. When I informed her one day that she was the only parent who offered to go on class trips, she looked shocked, then launched into a tirade about how lucky I was to have a mother who cared enough to bother.

Time and time again, my mother shocked, scandalized or just thoroughly embarrassed me, yet she never seemed to notice. I certainly couldn't accuse her of ignoring me, or not loving me or maliciously trying to hurt me. Rather, it was just that she didn't really understand me, or maybe I didn't understand her. I didn't know what it was like to raise a kid. It might have been one of those parent reactions that made her flip out. She didn't deserve what I said to her. She was just trying to be nice, but she had gone overboard as usual, and tempers had flared.

The sound of a car turning into the driveway jerked me awake. I heard a car door slam shut and fearfully peeked out my window to see my father—the judge, jury and executioner—slowly walk to the house and enter. I knew what was coming. There was a brief pause as my mother related the events to my tired, unsympathetic father, and then a shout calling me from my sanctuary. I took a deep breath.

He stood in the doorway, a figure of doom, waiting to hand out my punishment. Without warning, the storm was upon me as my father, in graphic and gory detail, described to me what would happen to me if I ever even came close to acting the way I had today. Just behind my father lurked my mother, pretending to wash the dishes, but I knew she was listening and probably gloating. The remorse I had felt disappeared in a flash, replaced by pictures of overbearing parents yelling at their poor, defenseless child. As my father's hellfire and brimstone sermon came to an end, I put on my worst scowl, glared at my mother, turned on my heels and stomped up the stairway. Maybe she did deserve it after all. ▣

Art by Chad Fleming

Father Figure

by Pamela Gorlin

Who is this stranger
who knocks hesitantly
upon the screen door
outside my house.
He glances at his watch
anxiously
it is precisely six o'clock
As it is every week

Who is this man
who sits across the table
At a local family diner
He glances at his watch again
he says we must hurry
As he does every week

Who is this image
before my eyes
who looks so much like me
I am careful of what I say
not really sure why
His opinion should not matter
but it does
As it does every week

Who is this seemingly
uncaring soul
who stumbles over his words
uncomfortably
Then attacks mine
in the next breath
And thinks that
he has the right
to do so
As he does every week

Who is this child in the mirror
A teenager whose eyes
usually shine
with the confidence of
innocence
But now glance about
unsure of anything
especially
her father's love
A child of divorce
and contemplating why
after he drops her off
as she silently cries
As she does every week

The Greatest Gift

by Jinny Case

The day he came into our house was gray and melancholy. Snow had yet to grace the earth with its solemn beauty. The wind, screeching through the naked treetops, was fierce and bitterly cold. The ground was frozen, with clumps of dirt as hard as stones. The fallen leaves and tiny, decaying blades of grass were laced with ice. Jack Frost had frolicked on the windows the night before, weaving intricate patterns on his icy loom.

This was the monotonous tone of many winter days, but somehow the sky was even more overcast and the wind seemed to howl a mournful warning. Our lives were about to change forever.

The baby was so beautiful: his skin, a pale blushing color; his eyes, changing from green to brown according to mood; his hair, a soft, warm auburn color. I fell in love with him almost immediately. No more than five weeks old, he regarded our foreign features with the curiosity and speculation of a small infant, and whimpered loudly for the familiar, if not beloved, face of his mother. She was nowhere to be found.

He was so innocent, so unaware of how precarious life could be, how everything could change forever in an instant. The natural bond between child and mother was nonexistent; in its place was treachery and abuse.

My mother took this child into her home and agreed to care for him until his dangerous situation could be resolved. Days turned into weeks, and weeks became months as the legal process of separating him from his birth mother dragged on. My family soon came to adore this baby as one of our own. The bond between mother and son developed within my own mother and the infant as she cradled him to sleep on winter nights.

Since the problem was unresolved, the courts awarded the birth mother temporary visitation twice a month. A guardian for the baby, appointed by the state, was to be present with the birth mother during these visits, since she had threatened the baby's life. The guardian was also to evaluate the mother, Clare, and her understanding of child care.

Many times this incompetent guardian would confuse the dates, and my mother would end up overseeing the visits. Clare would emotionally exhaust her, pleading for the baby we felt she didn't deserve. To the tiny infant, Clare was just another face. He did not know her.

My mother grew bitter toward the birth mother and the department of human services. What kind of justice system would consider returning a helpless baby to an unfit mother?

A summer came and went, blowing its warm breezes and gentle rains. In its place was the moaning wind and dead leaves crackling beneath our feet; the pungent odor of fire burning in the wood stove; the bitter air, prickling our noses.

The baby was a year old now, a precious part of our family. Worry for him chafed at my heart. In the depths of sleep, I dreamt he was taken away and abused by his birth mother until the tiny body lay beneath the frigid, heartless earth. . . .

The baby's father would not give child support, so, as a result, the department could never prove who he was. How could two human beings be so callous to their own son, a perfect little boy? When so many loving people had nothing, I abhorred them for what they had done to their flesh and blood.

That was two years ago. Now my little brother is three years old. It is winter once again. Tomorrow, my parents will confront Clare one more time in court. I pray that this time will be the last. ▣

6 Heroes

Art by Amy Spota

My Friend, Beth

by Melissa Kleinman

When people think of heroes, different ideas come to mind. Young children might envision Superman or Batman, while adults often picture a doctor or police officer. For me, one person comes to mind—my friend, Beth.

Beth was born with a respiratory problem that makes it difficult for her to breathe. She grew up in and out of hospitals, attached to devices to help control her illness. When Beth was four, the doctors told her parents she would not live to the age of ten. But she was determined, and when her eleventh birthday rolled around, Beth was there to blow out her candles. She proved the doctors wrong, but she still wasn't out of the woods.

Beth went through several more years of doctors poking her like a pincushion, but she never complained. Instead, she would just smile, give a little laugh and continue to fight. With all she had to deal with, you would think she would be too busy to listen to her friends' trivial dilemmas—but she always found time.

I remember asking her once if she ever wondered, "Why me?" She looked at me, replying, "At the risk of sounding corny, I believe God has a purpose for everything. He must have given me this illness for a reason." I asked how she always kept her spirits up, since she was constantly so cheerful it was nauseating. She laughed and said, "If I give up, I might as well die right now. Life isn't worth anything if you don't put effort into it. You must put emotion into it. I fight because of my desire to conquer. What doesn't kill me will only make me stronger." In that moment she showed me what it means to live life to its fullest without regrets.

I'll tell you now that my friend's real name isn't Beth. If I included her name, she'd probably kill me. She doesn't want anyone to know about her health problems because then they'd give her special treatment, which is the last thing she wants. She wants to be an average teenager, understanding that she has to accept love as well as loss. She's the kind of person you wouldn't be content meeting only once because she improves the quality of life by improving the quality of love. She's so passionate that she makes acceptance that much easier and, in my book, that makes her a true hero. 回

Danny Lee

by Tiffani Morehead

I will never forget that day—September 8—my dad arrived at my mom and stepdad Danny's house unexpectedly. When my sister Tina and I saw the shocked, sad look on our dad's face, we knew something was really wrong. He asked me to wake my other sister, Tracy, because he had something important to tell us. I had a million ideas running through my head, but never once did it cross my mind something so terrible had happened.

My dad told us that my mom and stepdad had been in a really bad car accident. My mom was in critical condition. Tracy and I were crying hysterically when Tina asked, "What about Danny?"

My dad replied, "Honey, Danny is dead." That was the most painful feeling I have ever experienced in my life; my heart felt like it had shattered.

It had all happened the night before. My mom and Danny had been at a firemen's concert. She was driving home, and Danny was in the passenger seat. Danny must have seen the car flying over the median divider. His first reaction was to protect my mom. Not thinking about himself, he jumped over her before the car landed on them. Danny died instantly but, thanks to him, my mom lived. She was in critical condition for two weeks. When she got out of the hospital, she lived with my grandparents until she was able to be on her own and take care of the four of us. She wasn't expected to walk again, but with months of physical therapy, she is doing well. When we saw a picture of the car, my mom's side was all bashed in while Danny's wasn't touched. The woman who killed Danny was drunk and didn't suffer a scratch.

Danny saved my mom's life and gave up his own. I am thankful for him being a true friend to his wife, my mother. For that he is, and always will be, my greatest hero. ▣

Exit: My Hero

by Amanda O'Loughlin

You could never tell from the outside of the building that there was an apartment inside, but of course Jay was always different. The smell of leather penetrated your nostrils as soon as you entered the door. Everything was out of the ordinary and extremely expensive, but that was him. He was not just my uncle, he was my friend, he was my hero, he was Jay.

A rush of memories have recently flooded my mind. I remember when I was five years old and a flower girl in his wedding, and I later wondered why he got a divorce. I remember looking out his bedroom window and watching the traffic below, hearing the cheering of the crowd at the baseball game and eating at the Chinese restaurant near his apartment.

I remember when he took my sister and me on trips through the city to the top of the tallest buildings and the grand opening of Tower Records to shop. Jay was the most outrageous shopper. Every time we visited, he would say, "Did you see what I bought?" It was always something extravagant and very cool, but that was Jay. Now I know where I got my expensive taste.

As we got older, though, the trips and sleepovers stopped. We would go for short visits, and a few times my grandmother and I would go and help him work in his garden.

Then things got worse. The garden became too much for him. In fact, the city got to be too much. Jay needed someone with him all the time, and it was easier for him to move back home. So he completely redid the upstairs of my grandmother's house. It was amazing! It looked exactly like his old apartment, only smaller. It even smelled of leather, and he still had something new every time I saw him.

Things were different now. My visits were reduced to sitting on his leather couch and watching TV so Jay would have someone there with him while he dozed. It began to get very difficult, but I wanted to do anything possible. I knew he had limited time left, and I wanted to spend as many hours with him as I could.

I have clear memories of playing cards, happily making him something to eat or taking him for short walks in his wheelchair. Still later, I would sit in a dark bedroom staring out the window while I monitored his intravenous tubes, thinking he didn't have much time left. I tried to prepare myself, but that didn't work.

On January 9, I had been looking forward to sleeping in. I was surprised to be woken up at 8:30 A.M. by my dad.

"Amanda, Jay died this morning, hon." I was in shock. AIDS had taken my hero away.

Jay lived longer than most AIDS patients, but that was not the only difference.

Jay had decided early that he would not let AIDS lick him. He went to schools to teach kids the dangers of this disease, spoke at conferences, worked with the AIDS Action Committee and, most of all, worked with our family.

Although it has been hard since he died, I have thought a lot about how Jay affected my life. He taught me about love, strength and courage. If it weren't for him, I would not have been strong enough to make it through. He was and always will be my hero. No one in the world had more courage. I remember wondering how I could tell him, so I wrote Jay a poem thanking him for all he had done. It was his Christmas gift.

On Christmas Eve, my family went to my grand-mother's house as usual. When Jay was alone, I went upstairs to see him. I gave him the poem wrapped in a box and watched him open it with difficulty because his fingers were swollen.

I watched him read the poem. When he was done he looked up through his tears and said, "This is the best present I've ever gotten!" and hugged me. Afterward, he told me it was very adult of me to tell him that it was okay to die. He had fought long and hard, and it was okay to let go. That hug was so vivid. It was the last time I saw him. I should be thankful I got to say good-bye and, most of all, tell him how I felt.

Some people feel that bad things happen to people because they deserve it, but no one deserves AIDS, especially not Jay. Of course he was not perfect; sometimes he was obnoxious and arrogant, but that was Jay and he was special. He touched the hearts of everyone he met and made a little space there. When he died, his soul broke into a million pieces and went to all those little spaces. Yes, a light went out that Sunday morning, but it is still shining brightly in my heart. ◉

Editors' Note: Here is an excerpt from Amanda's poem that was read at Jay's funeral:

You are always there
You give me strength
And for all of this
I must give you thanks

It should be
The other way around
I should be helping you
When you are down

So when the pain is too much to bear
and I cannot be there
Take this poem and read it through
And know that I will always love you!

Hockey Dad

by Brendan Murphy

While the rest of the world is sleeping, my dad is dragging my warm covers off me so we won't be late for my 6 A.M. hockey game. What started as a hobby is now my passion, and none of it would be possible without my dad.

"Let's go, Brendan. You can do it!" Encouragement like that does not go unnoticed. Every game, no matter what the outcome, my dad always says "Good game," and "You looked great out there." I'm confident, knowing that if I make a mistake or play poorly, my dad will still be there for me. Support is one of the greatest things anyone can have. My dad is my support, without forcing me to become something I'm not. It was my dream to play hockey, he just guided me.

As I get older, the competition becomes fiercer. Each season brings a new schedule with more than thirty games, which my dad eagerly attends. He gets as nervous as I do, but somehow rocks in his seat and keeps quiet. He wants to yell and scream like most hockey parents, but he is different. After each game, we sit down to eat and go over things to work on. Usually he only tells me how proud he is of me.

Remembering all those early-morning games and

late-afternoon pond skates with Dad, I realize how lucky I am to have him. It's not easy getting up and driving to rinks at all hours. My dad not only does that, but also helps me fulfill my dreams. I make sure that every game he attends I play my best, just to show him those 6 A.M. games did me some good. ◙

The Stranger

by Cassandra Summerill

Y ou appeared homeless: dirty, with long, knotted greasy hair. But inside was a very special man, a man who saved a little girl from being seriously injured—or worse. Think back now, over ten years ago. It was the week before Christmas, and Santa was everywhere. Carols played in the background as everyone rushed around the mall finishing their shopping and getting grumpy.

I was two years old and shopping with my mother and baby sister. My mother was getting stressed with a bad headache. She was carrying the stroller down the steps when I fell and started sliding down the escalator. My mom tried to grab me, but was too late. You jumped over her and my sister, and pulled me into the safety of your arms just as my fingers slid past the last step. You handed me to my tearful mother. My mom squeezed me so hard I thought she'd never let go. We turned to thank you, but you were gone. We searched for you, but you were nowhere to be found. My mom took me to the doctor who said I was lucky to have only minor scrapes. He said I could have lost a finger—or worse. Whoever you are, wherever you are, I thank you with all my heart. Without you, a caring stranger, I would not be able to do the things I love to do today. ▣

Our Escape

by Kathleen Waters

I was five years old, sitting on the old brown couch with my blankie and old dog, Bruzer, by my side. The room was dark because we'd lost power again. I had no idea my life was about to change.

I had a weak immune system and was always sick. That night was no exception. I sat with my knees pressed against my chest, rocking back and forth, battling a high fever. The strong smell of alcohol filled the house. The beast that called himself my father was drunk again, and he and my mom were fighting about something. Her voice was shaky and frightened. Hearing my name, I knew they were fighting about me.

My older sister came to comfort me, while our brother, who was like a father to me, tried to get the beast away from my mother. My father was screaming at my sister to stay away from me; when I was sick, he wouldn't let anyone go near me. That frightened my mother.

I lost consciousness, and when I came to, I saw my mother, brother and sister packing everything they could get a hold of. I walked around trying to figure out what had happened. The beast had passed out on the kitchen floor. My mother told me we only had a few minutes;

Joe, her friend, would be there soon to pick us up. I still didn't know what was going on.

I heard a soft knock on the door. My brother held my hand as we walked to the car and climbed in with our few belongings. I looked outside and saw everything familiar disappear into the night. My mother thanked Joe the whole ride. I wanted to know what was going on, but I was too scared to ask. Everything was going by in slow motion. I wanted to cry, but I couldn't. Finally, I heard Joe say, "Well, here it is. Good luck with your new life." My mother said thank you over and over. We got out of the car; my brother and sister held my hands. I heard my mother ask, "Is this the shelter for battered women and children?" It was. A tall lady brought us to our room. It was small and dull with a bunk bed, one big bed and two small dressers.

We left most of our possessions and all the bad times behind that night. I learned it is never too late to start anew. My mother struggled for many years, but she emerged a hero. She is in a health management position now, and my brother is in college. He still acts like a father to me. My sister is starting her own family, and, as for me, I'm trying to do my best in high school. ▣

A Guardian Angel with the Same Name

by T. K. Broderic

They say that there is one person in everyone's life from whom you draw inspiration. I am no exception. When I find myself getting lost in situations I'm afraid I can't handle, or if I don't know how to go from one step to the next, I go directly to my father. I never hesitate to ask him to tell me where to go next. I think I "talk" to him more than anyone else. My father works in ways that are different from most fathers. He never tells me exactly what I should do. He only gives me suggestions. He won't look me in the eye when I do something wrong, or tell me never to do it again. You see, my father isn't here anymore. He hasn't been here for a long time—way too long, if you ask me. My father died two and a half weeks before I turned ten years old. Today, I am seventeen, but it seems like I am thirty.

I don't really remember much about him. You would think I'd have pretty clear memories by age nine, but I don't. It is difficult to think of things we did together, even though there were many. Nothing in particular he said sticks in my head, except his exclamatory "Super!"

and, of course, his big hugs and wet kisses. They seemed unimportant then, but nothing is more difficult to think about now. You don't pay attention to what you have when you are nine; you just know it is there. When it does go away, you don't know how to do without it. Today, it is getting easier and, at the same time, harder. I realize now what I am missing. From his absence, I must draw strength.

Not a day goes by that I don't talk to him, saying "Hello" out loud and winking at his photo on the wall. He still is here in one way or another. Every once in a while, I hear him laugh at me or feel him smiling at me. I know sometimes he thinks I did well and sometimes he's mad. The hard part is figuring out which direction he wants me to go.

It is really hard trying to figure out all these signs, Dad! My greatest dream would be for you to come back so I could see you one last time. A lot has changed since you left. Everything around here is different. I sure could use help keeping the lawn looking nice. I don't know how you used to do it.

If one good thing has come from this, it would be that I see things in a different light now. I can understand the pain others feel more than I would have. I am a more sensitive person; not a lot fazes me.

Plus, I have a guardian angel with the same last name. I realize what a good person he was. I need to live up to his high standard, which, believe me, is plenty high. Thank God, I have two good parents to lead me: one to keep me grounded and one who keeps my mind in the clouds. ◙

A Pint-Sized Mentor

by Jaime Koniak

T his summer I was a mentor. I had the enormous responsibility of leading a group of puzzled six-year-old girls around a strange and awesome environment—day camp. I promised myself I would be a fearless leader, stick it out and show these little women the best summer ever.

There is always one child in a group who stands out and serves as entertaining dinner conversation. Because of her crooked smile, her earnest hands that would caress my face to gain my attention, and the way those crystal blue eyes became flying saucers and her voice dropped to just above a whisper when she let me in on her big secrets, Claire became that child.

It was usual for Claire to scamper across the shoddy field when I arrived, like a caged animal set free to inform me of the latest group news (a.k.a. the other girls' problems) or her own epiphanies. One Monday morning, Claire was not the normal galloping gossiper. When we were in the musty, cramped wooden rectangle known as the freshman girls bunk, I engaged in the procedure that had become as routine as brushing my teeth: the art of covering every bit of Claire's stark white skin with SPF 35. Suddenly the blue saucers of her eyes glared up at my half-closed ones. Expecting a cheery piece of news, I listened to little Claire as she solemnly declared, "Jaime, my poppy died." Having skimmed through the counselor manual and using my common sense, I knew that little girls' statements are often imagined, exaggerations of the truth or retold tales of the past. As I slowly questioned Claire about how she felt about the tragedy, I saw that my favorite, quirky camper was indeed speaking the truth and letting me in on her most important news.

Caught off-guard, I quickly searched for the words to comfort a grief-stricken child. I asked Claire if she and her daddy (whose father had passed away) were sad, and if she had given him a big "Claire hug." Remembering how those small, earnest hands wrapped around my shoulders felt, I knew, at that moment, that a "Claire hug" would be the best remedy for even the world's worst afflictions, and asked if she'd given him a hug.

I did what I thought was a decent job comforting my camper, and shared the news with my cocounselor. Having thought that the incident was basically under control, the "Toothless Fairies" (my motley group) and I trekked down the hill for the morning's fun-filled activities. Dreaming about my plans for later, I was jerked back to my present role as adult when I felt Claire's eyes focus on the equivalent of six-year-old height: my waist. I slowly turned to the skinny girl whose hand I was clutching. Claire quietly cooed, "But he's still in my heart." What I felt at that moment cannot possibly be recreated: a befuddling mixture of sorrow, amazement and respect for Claire. Not knowing what else to do, I stopped trotting to first-period music, squatted down and enveloped the pale, serious little person before me not only for her comfort, but for my own.

On that particular sunny Monday morning, I, the mentor, was no longer the teacher or the fearless leader. Claire had introduced me to innocence in its sweetest form. Although she had no idea, she possessed valuable knowledge and honesty that enabled her to teach a lesson to someone who had lost her sixish simplicity. As I marveled at Claire's latest epiphany, I took in every aspect of her unselfish nature. This fragile girl, while inexperienced and new to the world, had more understanding of death than I did. So, in a sense, I was a student that summer. While in shape and form I may have been the fearless leader and counselor, Claire was the true mentor. ◙

Trapped Inside

by Melissa Bizub

The twisted wreckage of an eighteen-wheeler lay smashed into the side of a ravine with the driver hopelessly trapped inside. One man saved the life of that truck driver three years ago. That hero's name is Mike Bizub—and he is my dad.

It snowed that morning and the roads became icy; my dad had decided to stay home until conditions improved. My mom went to visit my grandma at the end of our road, which is an access road for the turnpike. As my mom came around the bend of my grandma's driveway, she heard a loud noise and our van shook. She didn't realize what had happened until she got out and saw the truck's trailer sticking out of the ravine. She ran to my grandma's house to call the police—and my dad.

When my dad got there, a state trooper told him not to go near the truck; he didn't think the driver was alive. My dad went down anyway, and found the driver, José, alert. My dad talked and prayed with him to keep him calm. The cab of the truck caught fire and my dad put it out with the extinguisher from his truck. When the ambulance came, the paramedics didn't want to go near the truck. They asked my dad to take José's blood pressure and do other procedures. My dad took his blood pressure, but José's legs were crushed between his seat and the dashboard. They had to cut the cab apart to get him out.

Today, José is doing fine; he is walking and has gone back to school. The day of the crash was his birthday. My dad was honored by our town, and recognized by our governor for his heroism. My dad says life is precious; he would have done it for anyone. He doesn't consider himself a hero. I do, every day. ▣

Photo by Stephen Siperstein

Donna Reed, Eat Your Heart Out

by Miranda Noonan

Lying on her back on my bedroom floor with all fours up in the air, she'll impersonate a dead cow just to get me to smile. She refuses to dust, explaining it adds character to the house. Her cure for a broken heart is a bag of M&Ms and a pint of Ben and Jerry's. She considers Donna Reed definite dartboard material. That's Ma for you.

I grew up in a circle of three. Day-to-day living with Ma and my sister Jess taught me the fundamentals of life. Even then, Jess and I were close—a special bond connected us. Ma played the struggling single parent while Dad was off finding himself.

Money was always tight and times were tough. Although Ma had graduated from Columbia University, she worked second-rate secretarial jobs. Those things didn't matter. What mattered to her was enough scrimping and saving to give us the basics of life. Food was basic. Books were basic. Simple Christmas presents were basic. I easily developed a fetish for peanut butter and ramen noodles in exchange for these few pleasures.

There were no stifling ballet lessons or tedious piano

practices, but I learned to dance in the rain and play in the snow. Therapy sessions were in the form of whipped-cream fights. Ice cream was always a possibility, and Sunday afternoons were spent baking anatomically correct bread people.

Ma raised us without raising a hand. Nonviolence was a way of life. She taught us to be tolerant of others; all have a right to existence. We learned not to be prejudiced. To hate is unintelligible to me—especially on the basis of race, religion, beliefs or opinions.

Ma isn't like other mothers. She has never tried to be, nor have I ever wanted her to be. I know she falls into a class of her own, and I am glad. Standing out has always been one of Ma's best points. There are times, however, when I wish she blended in a bit more. Then I realize she should do anything but. Ma is Ma for who she is. I'm not embarrassed by her, and I wouldn't ever want her to change.

With Jess going to college this year, Ma's had more time to write. She's a newspaper woman. She belongs to an almost extinct but elite class of reporters who write with heart in their headlines and soul in their stories. Ma has never ceased to be the most amazing woman I know.

It is because of Ma that I am ready to take on the world. Ma will be right behind me, I know. She'll be riding that Harley she's always wanted, wearing one of her big, floppy hats, and letting her long, red hair fly out behind her. If ever I should lose my way, she'll simply throw all fours in the air and point me in the right direction—second star to the right and straight on until morning. ▣

7 Fitting In

Photo by Sarah Bay

Nappy-Headed with "Limited" Potential?

by Tiffany Burton

I am not the valedictorian, or the salutatorian, and personally I'm glad. When people notice you are academically successful, they expect you to maintain that success. I don't like proving myself worthy in others' eyes. When one needs to prove herself over and over, that only creates two things—ulcers and gray hairs. I share one thought: Live up to your own standards, not the Joneses'.

In elementary school, I felt compelled to read the really thick books without pictures before everyone else. By high school, my peers were concerned with grade points and entering the top ten. I watched others slowly become immersed in the pressures of *magna cum laude*. To me, they were missing what high school was supposedly all about—football games, first loves, movies and the carefree attitude that gets on parents' nerves. I came to the point in my junior year when I just wanted to have fun. If I didn't make the top ten, that was okay, I still planned to be successful and happy.

Long ago, at the age of two, my family had already decided I was a goofy-looking thing with nappy hair and limited potential. My aunts (who are teachers and registered nurses) never thought I would excel at anything. But I started reading at three and my grandmother taught me arithmetic with flashcards. At four, I could read well. My grandmother made me memorize the order of the books of the Bible and the spelling of their names until I saw them in my sleep. No one in my family ever read bedtime stories to me because I read to myself.

In my childhood, certain incidents crept into my memory and affected me, both positively and negatively. The positive effects made me want to try harder and prove everyone wrong. My aunts always talk as if my parents not having college degrees and living in a run-down neighborhood are handicaps. They call where I live the "reservation." I'm the wild Indian, and my family, savages. I never thought of myself as savage, just average.

One day during sophomore year, I went to a football game at the university my cousin attends. My aunt asked me where I planned to attend college. I listed my top three choices, all of which happened to be prestigious private institutions.

"Your parents don't make enough money to get you through one year, let alone four," she smirked. The only thing I thought was, *I'll show you*.

Everything I ever did was to prove something to my family—until now. I joined the National Honor Society and National Art Honor Society. I worked at versatility so I could do, or know, everything about anything. I joined the workforce so I could be called independent, and jumped into community efforts so I wouldn't be labeled lazy and selfish.

Now, I've stopped proving things to my family and started working on being fulfilled. I realized I couldn't keep putting what I wanted to do on hold because my family criticized it. Ever since I was little, I wanted to own a beauty salon and "do some good hair." Whenever I told someone this, they would just look at me, noticing I was halfway intelligent, and ask, "Why?" I usually could see in their eyes, "What a waste of potential."

I was confused. To my aunts I have limited potential, to strangers and instructors I have ample. To me, just knowing I have enough potential to succeed is enough. When I came to terms with this, obstacles in day-to-day life became easier to climb over. Life itself became livable, and I knew I would be okay as long as I was happy.

These are my aspirations for college and life: to succeed for my family, those who thought I had unlimited potential, those who thought I had limited potential and nappy hair, and those who think living in the ghetto is a handicap. ▣

Into the Mold

by Lisa Schottenfeld

Does it irk you that I read Shakespeare for fun?
You laugh when I describe my passion for Hamlet.
Does it bother you that I worry about auditions
while you lift weights for varsity soccer?
You smirk at each other when
you see me tug my tap shoes out of my locker
and I hear your giggles down the hall
as you toss your
pompous track bag over your shoulder.
Does it amuse you when I say I studied for a test
instead of watching that trashy show on TV last night?
You'll have to excuse me if I'm not
up-to-date on the latest soap opera gossip.
Does it annoy you that I don't wear lipstick to school
while you slip into the bathroom between classes
to reapply your favorite Ruby Red?
Are you frightened by the fact that maybe
just maybe
I don't want to fit
into the mold that comes free with your
Teen *and* YM *magazines?*

I Sat with Nikki

by Micaela Golding

Over the years, one thought has haunted me: *Why did others think I was a sellout?* A few years ago, I was a new student at another high school. I made it my duty to observe my surroundings and the people to see where I could fit into this ecosystem. Immediately, I noticed something peculiar. I realized how segregated it was. During lunch, the tables were either predominantly white or black. Nothing like this occurred at my previous school. Everyone mingled. But when I sat with a white student during lunch, the defamation of my character began. My choice of whom I sat with affected the black population. They called me a "sellout." The more I thought about the black students' reaction, the more it bothered me. All because I sat with Nikki.

Nikki and I were both new. We were in the same grade, we had a class together. She was very nice, and we immediately became good friends. I realized we shared the same values. The only problem was that Nikki was white and I was black. This was a taboo with the black population. They taunted me. No black person talked to me. People would stare and tell me that I did not know where I came from. When they heard the argot-type lingo absent from my speech, they ignored me—all because I sat with Nikki.

I experienced animosity from the black students many times that year. Once there was a group of students standing outside school. The area found a way to segregate itself, once again. The whites were on one side, and the blacks on the other. Nikki was sitting on the "white side" where she always sat because that was the ledge she found comfortable. She waited for her stepfather to take us home. As I approached the double doors, there was a group of black students. I summoned my courage to go over to my white friend and kept on saying to myself, *I do not care. I am going to do what I want to do.* It relieved me not to hear gasps or see stares. Instead, I heard clapping hands as they continued playing their game. However, I realized later, the situation had yet to reach its climax. The conversation turned to chocolate. They talked about white chocolate, and how white chocolate was still black. Another incident happened when I entered the lunch room. Three guys said, "There goes an oreo—black on the outside but white on the inside." I mustered up all my courage not to cry. All this happened because I sat with Nikki.

I tried to socialize with the black students, but only resistance greeted me. First I tried talking to them in my classes where there was a maximum of two black kids in a class of twenty-five. They did not address me. However, one day I did happen to talk to one black girl because the teacher paired us together. She invited me to sit with her and her friends during lunch. She said she hated seeing me sit with "them." They all looked at me as if I was from another planet. Their facial expressions said, "So, and who asked you?" When my new friend sat down, one of the others derided me by saying, "Angie, this is Micaela," in the same tone that I introduced myself. Her friends giggled. They said nothing to me during the entire lunch period while I tried to engage them in conversation. However, from their response it was obvious that my input did not interest them. This all happened because I sat with a white girl named Nikki.

I do not understand. A person would never believe that I experienced this today, not in 1963. The media inundates us with materials urging us to take steps toward equality and to promote racial harmony. Am I the only one who listens? Did the train pass every black person at this school? Why are we going backwards? Did Martin Luther King and Malcolm X die for things to go back to the way it used to be, or worse? This is not 1963 when the prejudice occurs from the opposite side of the spectrum, but, today, the prejudice comes from my own people. They did not even know me! I do not understand. They made me an outsider—all because I sat with Nikki. ▣

The Beauty of Diversity

by Anna Tudor

I look at her
I do not see her skin.
It crosses my mind that she is different,
but only for a moment.
I am not concerned with the differences;
I worry only about her tears that fall
and her heart that weeps.

The darkness of her skin
does not affect the diverse beauty of her face
or the beauty of her soul.
I hold her close,
comforting,
wishing I could remove the pain
but I cannot understand the sorrow she knows.
The heartless gestures of a bigoted man . . .

Though we try to ignore our ethnicity,
neither can ignore the hate that surrounds us.
The words of one man,
so harsh,
have opened her eyes.
She suddenly sees me
as "one of them."

She pulls away from me,
still sobbing.
I wish that we could be the same.
But we are not.
And the beauty of diversity
has lost me a friend.

Photo by Yoo Jean Han

Ghetto Girl

by Lisandra Lamboy

I was born and raised in an inner-city borough commonly connected with violence, drugs and crime. Here, minorities are the majority. This grand town made me the person I am today.

My childhood was pleasant. The bright autumn leaves with tinges of orange and gold symbolized the beginning of a new school year, when I met friends and learned exciting new things. Summer began with the scanty deep-green of bushes and trees, bringing fun and play. Every day I wandered outside reveling in the sun's warm rays, and met friends for games of hide-and-seek and tag. In each person and place, I saw potential. I trusted every-one and feared no one. I didn't live in a ghetto, as so many call it. This was my home, my neighborhood—the only place I had ever lived. I saw nothing out of the ordinary—well, maybe a crack vile or two—or heard anything abnormal—well, perhaps a gunshot or two. To me, all of America was the same.

Time passed, and I was no longer a little girl, but a teenager with wonder, curiosity and an interest in life. My voracious appetite for knowledge propelled me to seek ideas and new perspectives from books, teachers and peers. I began to ask questions about others, my surroundings and myself. I opened my eyes, and for the first time truly saw and absorbed what formed my community.

I was fifteen years old. It was a normal day and I was walking home from church. Although the streets and buildings were the same, something was different. I was different. I saw filth and garbage on the street, I saw the buildings "tagged up" with graffiti for what they really were—the projects. A group of teenage boys, with bandanas representing their gang, were hanging out and smoking pot on the stoop, suspicious of cops on the prowl. Teenage mothers seemed tired of having to be adults too soon. Reality struck me. What was once a normal, safe and loving environment became a foreign land. I was suddenly a trespasser in an unknown territory. I lived in the ghetto.

I realized we were living a life full of harsh circumstances. There was poverty, hopelessness, violence and abuse of all types. I saw my friends get pregnant, join gangs to feel accepted or become addicted to drugs to escape reality. Why? Why do talented youth with so much potential do this? Do they think they have no alternative? I constantly wonder how much of life is chosen and how much is forced upon us by circumstance. I truly believe we control our destiny.

I have not lost hope for those who have yet to realize there is more to life than the streets. Although there are many teenagers who do fit the stereotype of my city, there are many who do not. Teens like me want to make a difference, work hard and persevere through life's shortcomings. We are bright individuals, filled with hopes and dreams. We have resolved never to become involved in any activity detrimental to our future.

Reflecting on my experiences, I have wondered who or what has made me strong and goal-oriented. My answer is simply that I have learned from the mistakes and accomplishments of those I have encountered. As a result, I know what I must do to continue up the ladder of success. College has always been a top priority. It is not just an institution that will train me for a career, but a place where I will learn more about myself, others and life. By making myself an even better person, I will be able to discover my vocation in life and what I can do to be of service to those around me, especially my community.

My experiences as a "ghetto girl" have made me the person I am today: dedicated, hard-working, determined and, most important, a leader. ▣

I'm Not Prejudiced, Am I?

by Aaron Shield

'm not prejudiced. I can't be. I was raised in a suburban, white, upper-middle-class household in a little town of thirteen thousand. My parents had always reinforced the idea that all people, regardless of skin color, were equal. I had grown up on the *Sesame Street* scenes where Muppets of all colors played and lived together. Being a minority myself, I had always been sensitive to comments about race or religion, and tried to get my friends to refrain from telling racist jokes, at least in front of me. I even remember teaching my younger sister, when only three years old, not to judge people by their looks. ("It doesn't matter if you play with someone with green or purple or brown skin, as long as they're fun.") So it was pretty safe to conclude I'm not prejudiced.

Or so I thought.

One summer I attended a program at Brown University where I met a variety of people: black, Asian, Haitian, Hispanic. It was a great experience, since at my high school, there was little racial diversity. (Out of the 550 students there were only ten blacks and an equal number of Asians and Jews; the remainder of the population was white and Christian.) I took a literature course, where one section focused on the relationship between people and fear. We confronted issues of race, sexual preference and religion that make people different from each other and, thus, create fear. It was there that I first experienced conflicting feelings about race and my own thoughts.

An African-American girl, Lia, explained the experiences that she had because of her color. Suddenly a vicious thought came into my mind: *Am I perfectly innocent? Do I hold prejudices that I refuse to confront?* I had always tried to be the understanding liberal, the tolerant one who (supposedly) understands and sympathizes with all people. At that moment, I remembered a conversation that I had had with my Hebrew tutor when asked the question: "If you were walking down a city street at night, and saw a man walking toward you, would you be more frightened if the man were black instead of white?" At the time, I thought I was totally unbiased, and after grappling with the question, came to the conclusion that it wouldn't make a difference. I truly believed this, but my teacher remained incredulous. "We have a fear of the unknown," he said. "It's natural. We can't help it—it is human nature to fear that which is not like you. I suspect that deep down, where you can't or won't look, you know who you would fear more." I didn't agree—I'm not prejudiced, remember?

But that fall as my mother drove me through a nearby city, I spotted three young black men. They seemed a bit "suspicious" to me, looking around as if to see if anyone was watching them. As we drove by, one reached into his sock and pulled out something small. "That was a drug deal we just saw!" I remarked, confidently. My mother turned and looked, "He gave the man a piece of gum. Juicy Fruit."

I was stunned. There I was—the unbiased, unprejudiced liberal—a racist. I had assumed that because they were young black men standing on the street corner, they had been exchanging drugs. I had made the assumption quickly, naturally, without a doubt in my mind. Suddenly I was forced to face my own racism.

What I'm trying to say is that all of us, no matter how hard we try not to be, are only human. I realize now that I, like everyone, do fear that which is not like me. However, my realization does not make me cynical. Rather, it does the opposite. I now know that I am prejudiced, but, by recognizing this, I can at least hope to overcome it. I know who I am, and who I can become. ▣

Good Enough for Me

by Alexa Lin

Hey, Chink!"

I'm late, I'm late. I was supposed to meet John at City Hall thirty minutes ago. Why didn't I plan for such a crowd on New Year's Eve?

"Hey you, Chink! "

Up the stairs. Don't step on my feet, please. Only one more subway ride to get there. I hope John's still waiting.

"Chink! I'm talking to you, you Chink!"

. . . just about to step into the subway . . .

"Bitch."

Made it. Good.

It wasn't until a week later, walking to math class with John, that I realized I was the "Chink" the people in the subway were talking to. I told John, but his puzzled face just looked at me as though my story made no sense. I'm Chinese. It wasn't the first time the thought had entered my mind. Every day I look in the mirror and notice that I am still Chinese, just like yesterday, and just like every day before, but sometimes it becomes more than just a glance in the mirror, like it did that New Year's Eve.

I've grown up a lot since my blissful childhood that protected me from racism. In middle school, being Chinese was all I thought about. *I'm Chinese. I'm Chinese.*

Hey! I am Chinese. What did this mean to me? At one time, it meant I was embarrassed. Now I value my culture, and I accept growing up in America with parents who aren't American.

I was the first in my family to be born here. I remember reflecting on my birthplace with my mother at the age of nine. She said, "Being the first to be born in this country means nothing. Why not be the first to attend an Ivy League college? That is important."

My family lived in a city for my first three years. I went to a Montessori school where the class was taught to read, to fold toilet paper over twice to get maximum usage with minimum waste, and to say, "No, thank you anyway" if we didn't want a celery stalk that Molly brought to share. Nikki was my best friend. I had a crush on Mark. Being a "Chink" in America was not with me then.

When we moved to the suburbs and I entered public school, things began to change. I missed Black Nikki. White Kevin replaced White Mark as the boy of my dreams. And I noticed I was the only Chinese person in my class.

My best friend was Sarah. I remember finding her older sister's cigarettes and unwrapping them to make a collage of the tobacco leaves. I remember dressing up as Cinderella's ugly stepsister for Halloween. I remember having a funeral—coffin, flowers and all—for our pet bee, Buzzy, whom we had captured a week before. I remember sharing Sarah's pain when her parents divorced. But it is Sarah's grandmother from Ohio whom I remember most clearly. She often sent Sarah these delicious, flawless, fat lemon cookies Sarah always shared with me. One time her grandmother came to visit.

"My grandmother doesn't like you," Sarah said casually.

"What do you mean?" I didn't understand. I had never met her grandmother. Why wouldn't she like me?

"I mean, she told me Chinese people are filthy, selfish and rude, and she says that she would never let you into her house. But don't worry, Mom and Dad still love you."

"Oh," I replied, glad that Sarah's parents loved me.

In middle school, being Chinese became even more apparent and damaging. Still the only Chinese person in my grade, I allowed my race to isolate me.

At this age, I loved getting my picture taken with friends in the mall, and putting them together in a photo album.

Oh, look at Sarah's eyes—they're so big and round. And Amy's blonde hair. I wish my skin was pale like Kelly's. Cathy's green eyes are so pretty, I would think.

I wanted to be like them. I wanted to be white. I spent middle school wishing I was like everyone around me. I never went out with friends because I was afraid to ask my parents for permission. "You don't understand. It's a Chinese thing," I would always say. I made being Chinese my life, my everlasting problem. I cried myself to sleep every night. My teachers showed concern. "You don't understand. It's a Chinese thing." My friends stopped asking me out. "You don't understand. It's a Chinese thing." I hid from my "Chinese thing," and I hid from my life.

Everything began slipping away, and all I could do was cry. I felt even more alone in such a large school.

My mother gave me Amy Tan's *The Joy Luck Club*. At first I cast it aside. A year later, out of boredom, I read it. Then I read it again. And again. It didn't fill me with overwhelming relief, but it helped. Thanks, Amy. Thanks, Mom. I couldn't believe the similarities between my life and those in the novel. It wasn't just *my* mother who placed a mirror facing out my window to reflect away "bad things" when I had the flu. It wasn't just *my* mother who called me a ghoul when my hair looked wild. I finally understood that being Chinese is part of who I am. My best friend is overweight; Oscar Wilde was gay; and I am Chinese. I am a person, I am a human being, just like everyone around me.

Last October, my boyfriend, who happens to be white, told me about his mother's conversation with a neighbor.

"My son is seeing a Chinese girl right now."

"Oh, really? That's nice. They're usually a nice group."

But it's no longer only my problem. Racism, unfortunately, is everyone's problem, no matter which end or side you're on, and I know that it still exists. Racism hurt me growing up, but it won't hurt me anymore. Through regular comments of, "Are you two sisters? You look alike," and, "You know you did well on the math test. All Chinese people are good at math," I've gone from accepting to correcting. I do not resent people for their ignorance—I pity them for having such funny minds. I am not sorry for being Chinese, but for being so easily influenced. I had a hard time setting my race aside to find myself. But now I have seen a part of my true self, and being Chinese is a part of that part. I am ready and willing to move ahead in search of the other parts. Where do I fit in? I fit in here, in my own warm spot, in this big world with everyone else, and that's good enough for me.   ▣

It Doesn't Come Naturally

by Danielle Compere

I have a dream that my four little children will one day live in a nation where they will not be judged by the color of their skin, but by the content of their character.

—MARTIN LUTHER KING JR.

Martin Luther King Jr. hoped this idea would have a great impact on us. I had this dream, too, but one day it was dampened by the insulting words of a young boy.

The April breeze swept across my face on this cool, sunny day as I stood on the baseball field waiting for my brother. I stood there as the wind blew tiny dirt particles in my eyes, with the smell of freshly cut grass carried by the whistling wind. It was his eleventh birthday, and my family was picking him up from practice to take him out to eat. They sat in the car, while I went to get him on the field. Most of the team had gone; there were only two kids left. I returned up the hill to the parking lot to tell my parents he was coming. A couple of minutes later we saw his tall, dark frame coming up the hill. He was covered in dirt with his cleats stained with mud.

My mother asked, "How was practice?" as she handed him his ice-cold water bottle.

He looked at his feet and then back at the family, and said, "It was alright, but I got in a fight."

As with all mothers, panic flushed over her face and a twinge of fear ran in my heart.

"What happened?" my parents asked in unison.

"Oh, I got in a fight with some kid who was talking junk to me," he said as he rolled his eyes trying to keep the tears from coming. "He always bothers everyone."

I could tell he was not telling us something. The coach came to the car, and shook our hands with his chubby, pink fingers. He said a kid named Matt had called my brother a racial slur, and my brother had knocked him to the ground. The coach told us not to be too upset, he would handle it. When he left, all eyes stared at my brother.

He was upset. We asked what Matt had said.

"He called me a n———."

Our faces dropped and I felt like I had been stabbed in the heart. He kept speaking, but as soon as he said that word it was as if I were removed from my body and I couldn't hear what others were saying. The word kept appearing in my mind, *you n———* . . . *you n———*. I couldn't think; I was mad, upset and scared all at once. I kept asking myself why, but could not find an answer.

Everyone was upset. This was a day my brother was supposed to be happy. It was his birthday; this shouldn't have happened. We moved here to get a good education; we didn't think we had to go through this in the process.

A few long April days passed, but my anger remained.

One day, we went to his game. It was a beautiful, cool starry evening, but the thought of Matt ruined my peaceful thoughts. I got a good look at him that night. He was very small, about 4′3″. He had crystal blue eyes, and his hair was the color of brown autumn leaves. He walked very slowly with his short, lean legs. He looked harmless, but looks can be deceiving. I kept thinking of him as I walked toward the concession stand where I smelled freshly baked pizza. The fourth inning was over, and I could hear the baseballs hitting against the metal bats while the team practiced for the next inning. I was in line waiting for my pretzel when I saw Matt nearby. He looked at me with fear in his eyes, while I glared with mine lit like fire. We stared at each other as if everyone else had disappeared. I wondered if I should keep walking. I did not want to lose my temper, so I walked right past him with my head held high as I felt a breeze and heard the conversation of the birds behind me. This ignorant child is not going to make me lose my dignity. I did not turn back. I had become a new person. I would forget him; he was not worth my time. He cannot be blamed for his ignorance. His racism is taught.

It doesn't come naturally. 回

8 Memories

Photo by Beth Ezell

My Grandpa

by Kathleen McMillan

I can almost see him sitting there: pink-faced, freckled and partially bald, with that peach fuzz of red hair circling his head like the first tufts of hair on an infant. Surrounding him are pages of the Sunday papers and his favorite coffee mug with the brown lettering spelling BOSS, leaving a faint ring on the dull dining table. Placed in front of him is a plate, usually polished clean, but occasionally smudged with egg yolk from when he pushed his English muffin across the plate in a habit my father has also picked up.

I remember his navy blue pants that always seemed too big, his V-neck alligator sweaters, and his variety of scaly caps with the signature "McMillan" with its green shamrock and gold Claddagh pin. I always looked forward to Sunday visits to Grandma and Grandpa's.

Memories flood my brain. I was only eleven years old when he died. I was just a kid, but I thought I was so cool. I wasn't. That day I took refuge at Blue Jay's Sub Shop with my mother's cream-colored bike. I sat at a table in the corner ripping a napkin and swirling the red and white straw in my cherry cola. My friends, Jen and Todd, were like inanimate objects to me. They listened as I rambled on as if I were a senile old bat talking to her cats. "My grandpa had a heart attack," I said. For two seconds I felt different. As though I was finally the center of attention and someone was finally listening to my heartache. Then I remembered and I felt lousy again. I wasn't crying, though. My mother said, "Honey, he'll be okay. Probably." Probably was the key word. I went to Blue Jay's to get away.

At eleven, time meant nothing to me except that if it was dark out, I should be home. I dialed my number. "Mom, how is Grandpa?" I asked.

"Kathleen, come home," she said, her voice cracking a bit.

"No, he is alright, isn't he?" It could not be that. . . .

"He died. I'm sorry." I slammed the phone down, ignored my friends and took a running start onto my bike.

I can never describe how hard it was to get up the steep hill to my house. My legs were like spaghetti, and my knuckles were white because I was holding the handlebars so tightly. I never thought I would make it. But, of course, I did. It was like a bad dream where you're trying to run, but your feet won't move. I didn't know how hard I was crying until I hit my street and a neighbor asked what was wrong. "He's dead," I said. "He's dead."

That was the first time someone I loved died, the first time someone wasn't going to be there the next day or week or year. There would be no more days sitting in the hot white sand next to Grandpa's beach chair as he joked with his golden-brown, raisin-wrinkled friends; no more mornings when I would wake up to find a box of doughnuts waiting for us on the dining table. I would never again hear him laugh or yell or say "For cripe's sake" as only a good parochial schoolboy would.

Sometimes I'll flip through the channels on TV and come upon the show *All in the Family*. My grandpa reminds me of Archie Bunker, that loud person who showed his love in weird ways, but was always there for his family.

As the years pass, I notice my father turning into my grandpa. The way he scratches his head like Grandpa did, the way he clenches his teeth; I have even caught my father saying "for cripe's sake." And sometimes when I look in the mirror and my hazel eyes flash a shade of green, I can see Grandpa in me, too. There are so many wonderful things about my grandpa that my younger cousins will never know. Every time I see a scaly cap or a weathered beige jacket and tinted glasses, or even those funny light blue fishermen caps, I point the person out. "Just like Grandpa," I say. And I can almost see him. Almost. ▣

Generic Flowers on Refrigerators

by Dana Marlowe

i wanna go back
to the days of
lopsided hearts, drawn on
paper with a quarter sun
in the upper right hand corner,
with orange and red rays shooting out at me.
to the when "he loves me"
always occur
and never "he loves me not."
days of generic flowers . . .
a red dot in the center
with too many yellow petals
with symmetrical green leaves on a long stem.

where hopscotch boards appear on
black driveways in heavy
pink
street chalk.
an era when the bell of
an ice cream truck
meant an extra special treat
that humid evening.

the days when white and black and
blue and green and
gray and brown and
purple and orange were
just meaningless colors and not a
judgment
test for skin.
when teddy bears were filled
with love and
comfort, its
right ear hanging by
two thin, brown threads.

i wanna go back
to barbecues and picnics
filled with triangle sandwiches
and hot dogs and
potato chips . . . even the green ones.
when my multiplication tables
received a number-one spot
on the refrigerator.
when inhaling the freshly
cut grass while popping off the
yellow heads of dandelions,
playing with the neighbor's
white bichon frise.
to the days when
i'd construct a building of
blocks and my brother
would knock it down.

i wanna go back
to those days
that are now pictures
in a dusty, maroon photo album
and i want to stay there and
never return.

Basketball and Me

by La Toya Collins

I grew up in a rough neighborhood. The only girl on my block, I always thought I was one of the guys—until my family moved. I had just turned ten when we moved where all the girls were women before their time and the boys were trying to get rich the best way they could, committing any crime they could get away with, stealing from their neighbors and selling drugs to kids.

While we moved in, our new neighbors watched to see what we had—if we were rich or had just a little money. They watched every item coming off the truck to see what it was and where it came from.

I went outside the next day, eager to meet the neighbors. It was in the middle of the summer and I knew the streets would be covered with children laughing and playing. My mom was busy arranging things in the kitchen. Finally at twelve o'clock, kids started to come out. I wanted to go in the house and just peek through the window to see what they were doing, but my dad was sitting under the tree next to me. If I had gone in, he would have known why. So I stayed outside under the tree. We sat for almost an hour before my little brother joined us.

The boys across the street pulled out a basketball goal and I got excited. Basketball was the best thing in the world to me, and I had never played on a real basketball goal. Before we'd used a milk carton or crate nailed to a tree with a five-gallon paint bucket. Here they had a real goal with the thick white net and adjustable backboard. I was dressed in black and red basketball shorts, a black T-shirt, black socks and Michael Jordan basketball shoes, just like always, because I loved the game so much. I was ready to play if they asked. But they didn't. Instead they asked my little brother because they needed a sixth "man."

All the girls in the neighborhood wore sundresses or shorts and tank tops with sandals. They played little games like pitty-pat with their hands and sang songs that went with the rhythm. They also played with jump ropes. I was never into any of that stuff except jump ropes, which I could do really well. My dad leaned over and asked if I wanted to go play with the little girls. My mind was on the boys playing basketball. One of the guys shot the ball and the other, with his shirt off and shorts hanging halfway off, jumped to block his shot. The guy who was shooting the ball fell and got up in a rage yelling, "Foul, man! You fouled me!"

The boy who made him fall yelled back, "You ain't bleeding, so it ain't no foul. Just play and stop crying," and laughed. That made me not want to play anymore.

The next morning I woke up to see if anyone was outside and saw my dad pull into the yard in his truck. He and my oldest brother, who lived in California and played college basketball, got out and pulled a big box off the truck. My brother had just gotten off the plane and was going to spend the summer with us. I was curious to know what was in the box, so curious that I didn't speak to him or give him a hug like I normally did. I was excited because I saw the box had a picture of a basketball goal with a clear backboard and wheels. I was so excited I had to wake my little brother to come see what Daddy had bought. We went in the backyard and put it together.

After we got our goal, people came to play. No one could play unless I played, and that was no problem. I was good, and everyone always wanted me on their team, except my little brother. I think he was jealous. In the neighborhood I was known as Lady Jordan or Little Sheryl Swoopes. The girls in my neighborhood came to our yard to watch and mess with the boys. By then I had made friends with them. We really never hung out together because we were too different. I was always playing basketball.

Because I always played, my skill increased. Playing with boys who were stronger, faster and could jump higher made me even better. It was just my luck that I was playing in the street one day when a guy, a clean-cut white guy (rare in my neighborhood) stopped and watched. When the game was over, he asked my name and, "How would you like to play for a traveling team?" I didn't know what that meant, but I was interested, since I liked to travel and play basketball. He explained to my parents, "She will be traveling all around America and playing with girls her age in various tournaments. She will be seen by college scouts and others. I know she has a long way to go before she starts thinking about college, but this is a great opportunity."

"How much will it cost?" my dad asked.

"I'll pay for her. I will be her sponsor. She has the ability and the talent to go far, and I want to help her get there."

I was shocked that this white man (Coach Mike) was anxious to get me on his team. My parents reluctantly let me play for the Lady Warriors. We had uniforms, and my dad bought me new sneakers. We took airplanes to all our tournaments and stayed in hotels. That was the best summer of my life—I won the MVP trophy at the Women's Basketball Tournament. I will always remember it. Since then I've known basketball is going to be my way out of the "hood," and the only thing that will keep me from becoming a statistic. 回

Photo by Geoff Carr

Still Missing Him

by Michelle LaMarca

I am a seventeen-, almost eighteen-year-old, high-school senior. I appear to the known and unknown as very happy, energetic and strong. In a few months, I will begin a new era of my life—entering the final frontier—but still I look behind. Unanswered questions and dreams hold me back. The door that I repeatedly try to slam continues to reopen, and when I open my eyes, all that I see is his blank face. I can't describe his nose, mouth or eyes. Nor can I see the resemblance I've heard so much about.

The blank face belongs to my father. A man who held me as a screaming baby and quieted my cries. For a short time, I knew him, and my eyes saw his face, but he was killed as a result of an accident. I was still a screaming baby, too young to hold onto memories. So, I can't remember his nose, eyes or touch. I have never seen a photograph, and his life is seldom mentioned, but what I wouldn't give to remember.

I look at many of my friends whose parents are divorced, or their fathers have recently died, but it's different. I can't relate because they have something to hold onto. I have nothing but a seventeen-year-old Raggedy Ann doll I am told he gave me. They can look back and remember the "good times," while I sit and wonder if there ever were good times. In some far-fetched dream, I imagine that somehow or somewhere I will remember something. This is a hopeless dream, I know. But imagine not knowing your father's face.

I have a new father now. He is wonderful, and with my mother, has raised me to be an intelligent and respectful young woman. I feel guilty dreaming and wishing about my birth father, but I can't stop. If I could only remember one thing. One simple memory would satisfy my passion and get me through the nights I cry. But nothing. I only wish that he could hold me one more time and I could feel his touch.

Graduation is coming and soon my new life will begin. What should be one of the happiest days of my life is almost here, and I sit dwelling on sadness. The clear view of my future is fogged with nonexistent memories. When I make my final walk to the podium and turn my tassel to the other side, the only thing missing will be a voice that I can't remember saying, "Michelle, I'm proud of you." 回

I Don't Remember the Car

by Alex W. Hill

I don't remember the day . . . I don't remember the week . . . I don't remember the eight years before. I had to learn everything over again. I had to retrain myself mentally . . . I had to retrain myself physically . . . I had to retrain myself spiritually . . . I had to find out who I wanted to be, since I didn't know who I was.

I was staring up at the fluorescent lights in my hospital room, not knowing who the people around me were. The sterile smell stung at the hairs in my nose. The only other smell was that of chrysanthemums and lilacs, whose sickly sweet odor hung in the air. My mind was full of questions: Who were these people around my bed? How did I get here and why couldn't I move—was I paralyzed? I tried to speak, but all I could manage was a guttural moan—where had my voice gone and why couldn't I speak? Some of my questions were about to be answered, I thought, by that woman who wore worry and concern on her face.

"Thank God you are all right, Alex," she sobbed as she bent to kiss my forehead. I wanted to tell her I wasn't all right. I couldn't move anything and my head felt a pain like that of a log being split by a maul, but my tongue could not remember how to speak. She wanted to know if I remembered her; she wanted to know if I knew she was my mother—I managed a smile. She wanted to know if I remembered Andy and Emily, or my father. Although I didn't, I figured Andy was my brother and Emily was my sister, so I smiled. And who were these old people who spoke in cracking voices? The older gentleman held out his hand—what did he want me to do with it? I certainly did not know. He frowned with disapproval; I was sure that if he frowned any more, his withered face would crack from stress.

"Come on, Alex," he said as he lifted my hand to his. My hand just fell limply back to the bed, "Don't you remember me and your grandmother?" I must say I didn't, but I smiled anyhow—his face told me he did not believe me, though. I didn't remember anyone, or anything, except for some fragmented speech, but without the ability to verbalize, this would not come in useful. Like the blast of an atomic bomb, it hit me—I had been born again. My mind was a tabula rasa. The only ability I hadn't lost was understanding verbal communication. I was confused and saddened—my heart ached as if it had been tied in a knot.

Just then a nurse came in and said, "Time to fix your head," as she gave me a shot of something. I was lifted onto a cart by two orderlies, and the world melted before my eyes as the drugs took effect. I woke up in a different room, with scores of stuffed animals in place of the flowers. I still had my headache, and I guess by the constant screaming I did for the next week, they figured I was in pain. I saw my mother sitting in a chair beside my bed, her eyes glossed over. She sat there looking at me in a curious sort of way for awhile, and then she said, "Alex, if you can understand me, I want to tell you why you are in the hospital." My mother told me that I had been hit by a car when I accidentally went into the street while sledding down our front yard. I had been in a coma for two weeks after the accident, and had a metal plate put in my head.

Over the next week, I was in and out of surgery. I gained strength as a result of five hours of physical therapy a day. Every day, my doctor gave me more solid food, and every day, more of it ended up in the orange pail next to my bed—funny, it didn't taste as good the second time. Toward the end of the week, they took away my wheelchair and gave me a walker. With it, I attended physical therapy from 7 A.M. to 12 noon, went to speech therapy from 1 to 3 P.M., and then across the hall to occupational therapy from 3 to 8 P.M., with a half hour break for dinner. I did this routine every day for two weeks.

The second week out of a coma was much the same. The only difference was I could talk; my speech was slurred, but I could talk! At the end of the fourth week, I was released from the hospital. I had tutoring at home, and the next year, I went into fourth grade. Looking back, I realize that this was quite an accomplishment, since I was hit by the car in the middle of third grade. I started the fourth grade year with a physical age of nine and a mental age of one, although this is not really true because I learned so much in that year.

The image of my body being operated on as I looked on from somewhere in the operating room ceiling still haunts me. ▣

She Said

by Katherine Cincotta

My mother said, Nana
is sick.
I said nothing.
She said Nana
had a stroke last night.
I said nothing.
She said Nana is in
the hospital, dying.
I said nothing.
She said Nana is in a coma.
I said with my eyes stiff, my heart numb,
nothing.
She said, she would want you to come
and see her one last time.
I said
nothing.
She lowered herself to my child
eye level, looked into my shocked face
into my blank mind at my short gasps
for air, said nothing.
I looked right into the white of her eyes.
She began to cry.
I said nothing
I wish I had said something.
There was nothing to say.

My Cinderella Castle

by Maliha Shaikh

When I was little, way back when we had only four people in the family, we used to go to the mall and window-shop. Just past the entrance was a row of jewelry stores. I remember, as clearly as if it were yesterday, pausing to look in the windows, my nose smooshed flat, my breath leaving a moist spot. Sometimes I begged to be picked up to get a better view of the crystal.

The crystal was breathtaking, and though the imitation fruit was tempting, the tiny animals cute, the roses gorgeous and the baby grands commendable, nothing captured my imagination—and my heart—like the crystal palaces. They came in different shapes and sizes, various tints and landscaping. Each Cinderella castle, as my dad and I called them, represented the fairy-tale world of a princess, something every five-year-old girl longs to be.

My dad shared my affection for the Cinderella castles. Once, as he lifted me to see them, he promised, "Maliha, when you turn sixteen, I'll get you your very own Cinderella castle." Only five and full of a child's trust, I believed him.

Over the years, we moved many times, our priorities changed, and we stopped going to the mall as a family. I grew up. Textbooks and novels replaced fairy tales, turning twenty-one eclipsed turning sixteen, finding baggy jeans was more important than designing a hoop skirt, and Diana's life was more interesting than Cinderella's. Often, though, while shopping with friends, I would pause to look in the windows of jewelry stores, always gazing at the crystal palaces. I assumed, however, that my dad had forgotten his promise from a time and place that seemed as distant now as reaching sixteen had seemed then.

We moved to Saudi Arabia, where group excursions to the mall were few and far between. When we did go to a mall, the jewelry stores contained little more than diamonds, gold, more diamonds and more gold. Not even a case of DeBeers could replace the glimpse of a sparkly little Cinderella castle—but there were no more quaint little crystal palaces. The few I did find were so huge, so encrusted with jewels, gilt and other junk that they looked more like the residence of Snow White's evil stepmother than a dainty princess.

Eventually, overwhelmed with culture shock and struggling to adapt to my new school and country, I forgot about my castle. My sixteenth birthday approached, and I was more preoccupied with final exams, plans for the summer, and bemoaning the fates that put me in a country where I couldn't drive than I was occupied looking for my palace.

But just before my family left for summer vacation, my mom brought up the Cinderella castle. She casually mentioned that she hoped my dad would find it in time, but not to count on it, adding that he had been looking for them each and every business trip—which translated to the duty-free shops of just about every international airport. He had never found the right one.

I couldn't believe it. Through moves and mortgages, tuitions and promotions, traveling and working, he had remembered a promise he made to a five-year-old. Not only did he remember, he was determined to honor it. I was touched beyond words, feeling I had had a glimpse of what a parent's love must be.

One hot day that summer, my dad, uncle, sisters and I were in New York City. Our day was filled with museums, interesting technology, amazing streetside sleights of hand and delicious, overpriced food. Somehow, on our way back to Grand Central Station, we found ourselves in an expensive shop in Rockefeller Plaza. My guess would be that my dad had something to do with the navigation.

Our browsing was disrupted by a shriek from my youngest sister. Rushing to see what was the matter, I found them all standing in front of a large glass case where, on the fifth shelf, sat my crystal Cinderella castle.

A tiny, simple castle perched high upon a mountain, textured on the sides, and with a flat, sheer, insurmountable surface in front, it was accessible only by the tiny meandering steps protruding from the facing precipice. It was perfect. It was The One.

As I stared, speechless, my dad asked the saleswoman to take the castle out of the case. When it was placed on the counter before me, the feeling that it was The One only increased—while the sides were frosted, the front was crystal clear and, looking into it, I could see a lake under and inside the mountain, glinting and reflecting into eternity.

I held my breath as my dad asked the price and, in

shock, heard the saleswoman announce the impossible, ridiculously high amount of $600. My heart sank, but she followed this bombshell with a series of discounts. By virtue of being the very last one, my perfect crystal palace was reduced to the bargain price of $160. Still ridiculous. I turned and started walking out the door, barely able to see through my tears. To have come so close, only to lose my childhood dream, was unbearable. I stopped when I realized no one was following me— they were all gathered around my dad, who was pulling out his credit card. Utterly overwhelmed, I just stared.

Packed securely in a box with layers of tissue, the castle didn't leave my dad's hands; he gave it into my over-protective safekeeping only on the train ride home.

At the house, I showed Cinderella's castle to my young cousins who, once they got over its delicate beauty, oohed and aahed and put out tentative fingers to stroke it. Then, rewrapped, it was banished to a shelf to await my sweet sixteen.

On the special day, with little fanfare, I gently removed my Cinderella castle from its tissue and placed it on the family-room table to watch the birthday proceedings. After, when the cake was in the fridge, the candles in the trash and the presents scattered, I brought the castle upstairs and reverently placed it in a spot of honor on my bureau.

It sits there now, tangible evidence of a love so great that my palace, glinting and shimmering with rainbows, dulls in comparison.

And one day I will, with more of that immeasurable love, present it to my sixteen-year-old daughter.

And I will tell her this story. ▣

Miracle on Eighth Street

by Kun Jia

Even in the farthest reaches of my mind, not one disappointing memory of my childhood lingered. My mind's eye never failed to conjure up a blissful scene of me romping in a playground, jumping on a springy mattress or watching a little wooden boy with a long nose on TV. This pleasant nostalgia often made me wonder when I had crossed the point of no return into a world of regrets and worry.

Last Saturday morning, as I was peering at the New Jersey Turnpike, thoughts of visiting the old fairyland coursed through my mind, along with how I wouldn't be able to separate my sticky skin from the seat when we arrived in Hoboken.

"Mom! When are we gonna get a new car?" I asked, scrunching over for the nonexistent cold air from the air conditioner.

"When money starts growing on trees," my mother replied. Dad delved into the technicalities of automobiles and air conditioners. This lecture, combined with the suffocating heat and the fact that my dear mother was perfectly cool despite my feeling like melting rubber, made the ride almost unbearable.

"I hate being poor. What's next—food stamps?" I

ranted, not heeding the annoyance on my mother's face. For a moment, it looked as if she would say something, but she just started cleaning the dashboard with a tissue. *What's the use,* I thought. *Nothing could make this piece of junk look less like trash.* But I didn't make my thoughts known, lest there would be another war between Mrs. Deng and Miss Jia. So, in what felt like an eternity, but was probably only fifteen minutes, we arrived in. . .

"What the—" I blinked my sweat-soaked eyelids and made a feeble attempt to process the scene.

"Look, it's our old house. Remember that nice Indian girl next door? What was her name? . . . Patel. Remember? She used to baby-sit you," my mother asked. I did, but could not remember, or accept, what met my eyes. The sidewalks were cracked, on the verge of crumbling, and Stone Age apartment houses lined the street. Our clunky Isuzu turned onto 8th Street; the street sign looked as if it had barely survived a hurricane.

"This is Hoboken?" I asked in disbelief.

"You don't remember your hometown? Did you know this was Frank Sinatra's hometown?" my not-a-Sinatra-fan mother asked with her subtle yet discernible Chinese accent. So these were the origins of the Jia immigrants.

"1437 8th Street!" my jubilant father announced. It was frightening to look at the decrepit two-story apartment house with a big crack in the front window. It revealed nothing of the innards; yellowing newspaper was taped haphazardly inside. This was no treasure chest full of toys. The only attempt at decoration was a little flower-pot, out of which sprung a dandelion.

As we parked, I wondered if anyone still lived here.

Then the front door was thrust open and a little girl, who couldn't have been much older than I was when I lived there, came pouncing out. She slammed the door behind her, and I wondered how the old portal could survive the impact.

While my parents visited old friends, I focused my attentions on the little girl and tried to find a little angel underneath the filth and baggy hand-me-downs. I found her playing with a naked and arm-free Barbie doll as dirty as its owner.

She squinted at me with curious, dark eyes, and, for a flickering moment, I thought I caught a glimpse of another little girl I once knew.

"Hi, what's your name?" the girl asked, pronouncing every syllable in that drawn-out way kids have. "I'm Princess Emily, and this is Princess Rita." She waved the tattered royal doll in my face.

"Hello, Princess Emily and Rita," I said, stooping down, "I'm just plain old Karen. What are you and Rita playing?" I inquired. I was anticipating some make-believe game, but to my surprise Emily was sincere in her claim to royalty and prestige. Could it be that this poor little girl was incapable of seeing the wretchedness that surrounded her?

"We're going to play at Cinderella's house. You wanna come?" Without waiting for a reply, Her Highness grabbed my wrist and led me into her royal abode.

I was home. Not the home with the stream, garages, Sony entertainment system and Jacuzzi, but the one with the makeshift eating area, the cramped bedrooms rented out to various immigrant families and one tiny bathroom. We went past an old woman with a foul-smelling stew on the rickety stove, the man fixing the light bulb on a dangling wire, the narrow hallway, and knocked on Cinderella's door.

"Hello? Is anybody home? I wanna play with Cinderella," Emily declared. Cinderella, or a fair-voiced Emily, replied, "Come in, Princess Emily." We did, and I couldn't believe it. This wasn't only the room Emily shared with her mother, this was the room I lived in eight years ago! To the right still stood the bunk bed my father had made for me. The white paint was cracked, but I was Princess Karen and this bed was my throne. Suddenly, I didn't see the shabbiness; the bunk bed was a vessel on which I could climb and watch the world below.

Emily pretended to be Cinderella and recited her plight with her evil stepmother and stepsisters as I sat on the floor, not caring about the dirt, and listened. When Her Highness began to fuse Cinderella with the Little Mermaid, I decided it was time to find my parents. "Bye-bye, Princess Emily, I have to go. It was a treat meeting you. I hope to see you again some time. Okay?" I said.

"Okay," Emily replied.

I walked briskly into the hallway to the bathroom. The door was ajar; there wasn't much to see, just an olive green toilet, a grimy bathtub and a sink. While washing my hands, I glanced at the mirror and saw the little girl who used to stand on a stool to reach the sink. The face in the mirror smiled.

On my way out, I passed the old cook with the magic potion, the butler polishing the chandelier and the royal subjects convened in the great hall. I made my royal exit just in time to find my parents walking toward the Isuzu pumpkin coach. I marveled at the beautiful veil that had colored everything with a child's fantasy.

"So, people are still living in the old place?" asked my father.

"Yep. And they're really nice. Kind of reminds me of us back in those days."

"Wow, time sure goes fast, doesn't it?" remarked my father.

"Yep," I replied, and lay back against the cushioned seats to enjoy the breezy trip home. ▣

9 Creativity

Art by Alexander Lukas

A Stained Letter

Fiction by Jarod Rhoades

Over the past few months, I have acquired an obsession with creating things. Whenever I am not accomplishing something, I get a craving to grab a pencil and draw, get a pen and write, get a knife and whittle, or anything of this sort. When I think back, I can almost define the exact point this behavior began, but I cannot discern the reason or why I feel, subconsciously, that it will better me in some way. This was a period of intense happiness, stress and confusion, followed by deep sadness, loneliness—and my present obsession with accomplishment.

My archaeology class was conducting a research project in the mountains of Oregon. We were staying at a cheap hotel on the highway in a small town near the dig site. I had been put in charge of the data arrangement, which was really too much work for one student to handle. I was going to attempt it to make a good impression on my professor. One evening, I walked in the rain to a café in an attempt to find a quiet environment to begin formulating the introduction for this task. I sat with my coffee and tried to put the words together in my notebook. My ideas refused to flow, but still I tried. A half hour into my failed attempt, a young woman walked to my table and asked if she could sit with me. I obliged, and she sat and made conversation. Throughout our talk, I noticed how beautiful she was. I kept looking at her hair; it was excessively shiny. Her eyes were a deep brown and glistened in the artificial light.

"Did I ask your name?" she said.

"No. It's Aaron Martin. You didn't tell me yours, either."

"I am Elaine Robbens. Nice to meet you." She stuck out her hand for me to shake. "What are you doing in town?"

I explained. While I spoke, she looked right into my eyes. Then she told me her story. The day before, she had returned to her apartment and found her boyfriend making love to a woman on their kitchen floor. She had kicked him out, throwing his things out the third-story window. A considerable amount of terrible words immediately followed, until Elaine slammed the window shut, leaving the boyfriend standing in the frigid winter air. Throughout this story, I could feel my hatred growing for her boyfriend. I was trying to discern whether I disliked the man because he was despicable or if there was a deeper reason, as Elaine explained that she was tired and wanted to go home. I left the café that night with her phone number and an empty sheet of notebook paper titled "Introduction."

Back at my hotel room, I found myself invigorated, unable to sleep. I lay down in the overly springy bed with my eyes open, and I realized that all I was thinking about was this girl. I made up a scenario in my head: I would call her the next day, meet her somewhere and sweep her off her feet. As I pondered this, my thoughts dissolved and I floated into sleep.

When I awoke, the sun was shining through the window. The first thing that came into my head was the night before. The whole incident replayed like a videotape, and then I remembered my plan, almost forgotten like a dream on the edge of waking. I took a shower, brushed my teeth, and dressed in relatively attractive clothing (a gray dress shirt and black slacks), all the while acting out the day in my mind. Since it was Saturday, I had no immediate tasks to complete with my research group.

Around noon, I worked up the courage to dial her number. It rang twice, and the unmistakable voice of Elaine Robbens answered—a soothing, soft sound. My heart jumped once and I went into my plan. It worked beautifully. We were to meet at Tony's Italian Restaurant, a small, quiet place. I left the room thinking myself brilliant for what I had accomplished.

As I walked down the road, a profound sense of joy coursed through my body. I felt the best I had ever felt. I arrived at Tony's and sat to wait for Elaine. She soon appeared, and we had a late lunch, picking up our conversation where it had left off. The more I heard about her, the more amazing she seemed. I absorbed every detail I could, and still I needed more.

When we finished lunch, I asked if she would accompany me to my hotel room, and she agreed. We split the bill, which seemed an outrageous amount. Once in my hotel room, I settled into a uncomfortable chair and asked her if she would like a drink. She quickly said yes, so I produced a bottle of wine I had been saving in case I came across a particularly sleepless night. I poured it into two plastic cups and we started talking. My nerves loosened a little, as well as my tongue. Gradually, my inhibitions drifted away and our conversation grew more personal and open. I began to dominate the conversation. I spoke of my project. I spoke about my writing. I spoke about my stress and frustration, all the time gulping wine. I spoke about Elaine's boyfriend, whom I had grown to hate in twenty-four hours. I could not stop rambling. I wanted this girl to know everything about me. I probably talked for more than an hour. We lay on the bed and began to speak quietly with great meaning to our words.

"You mentioned something about writing earlier," Elaine said.

"Yes, writing is the only way I can express myself the way I want to. My words don't mean very much when I speak."

"I'd like to read some of your writing someday," she said.

"Maybe I'll let you," I said. "Elaine, I want to tell you something. Well, I am not very good with words, but I'll try. I met you yesterday and I feel really good about it," I said.

"Yes, I feel really good, too. I needed someone to talk to and you are such a good listener to hear my problems. It's really too bad that you don't live here. I feel a strong friendship growing between us. Maybe you could give me your address and we could write. I don't think my problems are quite over, and I'd like to have someone to listen," Elaine said.

I wrote down my address on a piece of scrap paper, and she did the same.

"That's not really what I was trying to get out, Elaine. It's something a little deeper than that. I have had a desire to see you all day."

"Please, Aaron, don't say it, please."

"What I have been feeling is more than friendship, I hope."

"Aaron, no, I'm not ready for another relationship. Please, don't say it."

"Elaine, I think I am falling in love with you," I said.

"No, no, I don't want to hear this," she was walking toward the door. "I'm sorry, I just can't say the same thing." She opened the door and left me sitting in my hotel room, desperately trying to discern what to do, and what I had done wrong. My day ended exactly as it had begun: wanting her beside me, thinking of when we would see each other again. A sense of loneliness settled over the room.

I left town the next week, having never heard from her again.

I never finished the research paper. When my professor asked what I had accomplished, I presented a single piece of paper with "Introduction" on the top, covered with random scribbles. The assignment was taken out of my hands, leaving me with a simpler task.

A week after I returned to my apartment, I was reading a book when my mail slot opened and a white envelope slid in. I noticed the return address and eagerly tore it open, tearing the letter in the process. Elaine wrote that she was sorry and did not want me to be angry. She hoped I could forgive her because I was one of the best friends she'd ever had. At the time I thought it quite ridiculous that she considered me one of her best friends.

We had known each other for only one day, barely time to establish a deep friendship. Then I realized how hypocritical I was. I told Elaine I loved her that second day, and I still did. I picked up my pen and started to write.

Elaine and I wrote for a long time. In those letters, I found Elaine more amazing than I had thought. She had spent her life in the forests of Oregon. Her father had been a successful writer and thinker, so she had an easy childhood, financially. When she was a teenager, she grew tired of getting everything she wanted and started a business making clothes. She rented an apartment and supported herself. All she wanted from life was simplicity and serenity, a cozy home in the woods with a garden and frilly drapes. It was an ironically possible dream for a girl like Elaine. Almost every one of her letters contained a reference to this life. I wrote of my love for her. I mentioned it, unfettered, at the end of every letter. There was never a reaction from her.

Elaine needed someone to listen to her problems and dreams—and I was that person. She did not love me, and I soon realized I was only the outlet for her subconscious, but still I grew more attached every day. I depended on those letters for happiness. When I woke in the morning, my first thought was whether a letter would slide through my mail slot. It became my life to read Elaine's curvy, schoolgirl penmanship, and to respond by proclaiming my love for her.

After six weeks of this game of tag, I received a letter explaining that Elaine had gotten back together with her boyfriend. I read the letter again, disbelieving. This perplexed and saddened me, so I wrote her some questions.

Her reply came with no explanation, but more about her life history. The next letter I wrote would be my last. I digressed into philosophy. I spoke of love in a poetic way, delving deeper into the mind. The letter ended with a full page of my proclamation of love, the reasons behind it and my deepest feelings. I sealed the envelope, frightened and anxious for the reply.

That night, and the next two, I was restless. Perhaps it was the thunderstorm that put me in a jittery mood, but I believe it was something much more important. I woke on the fourth day after only two hours of sleep. Tired, I lay down on the couch and switched on the television, but my eyes stared straight up, not seeing, and my ears shut off. I stared for an hour. A familiar sound knocked me out of my trance, and I looked with unbelieving hesitation at the television. A picture of Elaine hovered in the corner as the newscaster spoke.

"The identity of the driver killed in the fatal crash on Highway 58 yesterday has been confirmed as that of Elaine Robbens, an Oakridge citizen. The daughter of the esteemed writer, William Robbens, was killed when another car swerved into the oncoming lane, causing a head-on collision. Her family is mourning her death." I stared with my mouth open. Then I was in the bathroom without realizing I had ever gotten up, vomiting into the sink. I splashed water on my face. Leaving the water running, I stumbled into the living room again and fell, face first, injuring my nose on the floor. Then my squeaky mail slot opened and one envelope slithered in. Mechanically, my hand picked it up. Slowly, I ripped it open and started to read.

Aaron, I was wrong. What I was feeling about you was deeper than friendship. Today, I packed some things and left Leonard. By the time you read this, I may already be there. I am coming to see you, Aaron. I need a place to sleep, and I know you are kind enough to find some room for me. I hope you can forgive me for what I have done to you, and I think I'm in love with you. I'll see you soon.

—Elaine

Some blood from my nose dripped onto the white paper and glowed. Disgusted and startled, I dropped the letter to the floor and wept. Something I had never had escaped me. Two dreams had been destroyed, and I cried uncontrollably. What I lost was everything I ever had, and the blood pooled up on the floor as it dripped from my face, a vermilion puddle of thick syrup.

• • •

A week ago, I burned that stained letter. The fire took away the evidence, but left the pain. It has been five months since I sat in the café with her, and I have just begun to focus on one project. My obsession continues, still an enigma. It may be an advance in my mental processes, or a breakdown of my soul. Obsession supports me, drifting from room to room in my apartment, pointless, mindless, endless, forever. 回

Backwards

by Lauren LeRea

i am crouched next to the body
   of my husband—
on a cold dirty floor of the
   main street convenience store.
tears stream back upward
   toward my eyes
as my knees and hands lift me from
   my sprawled position.
i fly backward through the glass door
   into my 1972 silver Buick which speeds
back into the thick fog of that
   winter's night.

words scribbled on a policeman's notepad
   are erased as blue ink refills his pen.
and the pad and pen slowly replaced
   in the empty black pocket of his
     sheriff's overcoat.

blood stains are removed from
   a white plastic covering
as it is rolled to the end of my
   husband's feet

reaching the pale hands
of a young paramedic.

and a swirl of skim milk and blood is undone
as milk flies through the air into
   an awaiting carton
      rising from the ground.
and blood fills the bullet hole in the chest
   of my husband in a gray wool coat.
a short stumpy man in a black mask
   soars backwards into the store
and he replaces his revolver in his
   faded jean jacket.

and lights now appear
   in my husband's hazel eyes
as he sees money
   filling the register
      by the clerk
while the masked man
   reverses out of sight.

and my husband walks back
   through the aisle
replacing the wet carton
   of skim milk
and he makes his way back
   to the parking lot
as his keys go from
   pocket to door . . .

and i want to rewind time
like that
and tell you, tom
to get the
milk
tomorrow.

Photo by Yoo Jean Han

Don't Melt, My Snowflake

Fiction by Megan Morrow

I leaned over my math book, thinking hard—or trying to. I hated math. I just couldn't concentrate when it came to algebra. But I knew the real reason I couldn't think: my brother, David.

I slammed the book shut, and stared at the swirling snowflakes. Christmas would be here in a week . . . but would my older brother, who had run away?

Probably not. He skipped last Christmas, so why should he come this Christmas? We hadn't heard from him since he left. David and I had been close, with less sibling rivalry than in most families, and this time of year just brought out the worst feeling of emptiness without him.

I found myself concentrating on the snowflakes swirling around in the wind as if they had no place to go. *I wonder if David is like one of those snowflakes,* I thought, *getting blown around with no place to go. Or,* I thought, biting my lip, *is he like the snowflake that gets caught on a windowpane and melts?*

I shook that thought from my head. If I had just one wish, I'd want David home for Christmas.

• • •

I sat in algebra class the next day staring down at my unfinished homework. *This really stinks,* I grumbled to myself. *I haven't been turning in finished papers all week. I'm sure to flunk this semester. And I won't get into college, all because I canned algebra freshman year. And it'll be all David's fault for being a great brother, then leaving to go who knows where with me wondering whether he's dead or alive. All because he and Dad had a stupid fight.*

I don't think I listened to a thing in class that day. All I remember is the feeling of dread when I passed in my incomplete assignment. After class, the teacher called me to her desk to "talk."

"I think I know why I'm here, Ms. Rodkin," I said, just to let her know I was aware I had been slacking off.

Ms. Rodkin was tall and pretty. She looked as if she were in her thirties, though I knew she must be in her mid-forties considering the number of years she had been teaching.

She peered at me over her wire rims. "I just wanted to know if I should be concerned about anything. As of now, your algebra grades are going way down."

"I know, it's just. . . . I'll try to do better. I'm sorry."

She looked concerned. "Is something wrong? If you're having trouble . . ."

"No, really, I know I can do better. I just haven't been able to concentrate." My toes were wiggling inside my shoes to get to study hall, and my eyes kept wandering to the door. I guess Ms. Rodkin could sense that I didn't want her help, as she made a shooing motion with her hand.

I gladly hurried toward my destination.

"I miss David, too, you know."

Ms. Rodkin's words stopped me in my tracks. I was puzzled. How had she known what I was thinking? I knew my brother had always done well in math and, since he also was a bit of a class clown, he managed to build friendly relationships with his teachers. It didn't surprise me she remembered him. But how had she . . .

"How—how did you know?" was all I could manage to blurt out. She had caught me. I felt like a criminal who had been tricked into revealing herself.

"I know everything," Ms. Rodkin winked at me. "The seniors call me Miss ESP."

Then her face immediately flooded with guilt. "I'm sorry," she said quickly. "I mean, I know it's a sensitive. . . . It's none of my business."

I didn't want her to feel like an intruder, so I gave her a warm but subtle smile.

"That's okay." I looked down at my feet. "Guess you can't easily forget him, huh?"

"Sometimes I turn around and expect to see him making a funny face at the person sitting in front of him."

I laughed. I knew what she meant. Even now, after more than a year, I would walk into a room and expect to hear his funny laugh that always annoyed me, or to tap me on the shoulder and then run and hide. Or sometimes, I would imagine that I heard him calling me "Sassy," his nickname for me.

I didn't want to remember all those nights hearing Dad and David fighting downstairs when they didn't know I was home. I didn't want to remember that horrible morning we found David, his things and his car gone. I could hear Mom crying and screaming at Dad for being so rough on him. I blanked my mind and tried to push these thoughts out.

"I know exactly what you mean, Ms. Rodkin," I said.

The teacher fingered the bracelet on her wrist. "I miss him in my classes. He was a wonderful student." She paused. "He was good at algebra."

I forced a laugh. "Too bad he isn't here right now. He could be helping me."

"Hmmm. Well, if you're having trouble, let me know."

All of a sudden, her expression changed. She stared out the window, seeming lost.

"You know, I had a sister, Myrah," she said sadly. "When I was twelve and she was fifteen, she got fed up with my parents and decided to try the world out on her own." She shook her head.

I was silent for a minute. "I—I didn't know that."

Ms. Rodkin looked up at me, blinking. "Well, now you're the only one here who does," she said in a voice just above a whisper.

We were both silent. I shifted my backpack on my shoulders.

She winked at me. "Go on, get out of here," she said softly. "Go to study hall."

• • •

The days before Christmas were slow and boring. Normally, David and I would take off and go skiing, except for the days we told each other we had a headache and couldn't go, but we always knew that meant we needed to go Christmas shopping for each other. I could still go skiing with my friends, but what fun was that when they couldn't amuse me by trying to drink hot chocolate through their nose?

Christmas Eve dinner was a sea of tension. We invited the relatives who lived nearby. They arrived with seemingly cheerful faces. Everyone complimented my mother on her wonderful hors d'oeuvres and breathed in the luscious aromas from the kitchen. I could tell from the way my dad kept looking out the window, and the way my mom stared into space every so often, that things were not okay. It certainly didn't help when we sat down to eat and my grandmother laughingly said to my mom, "Oh, that boy never does show up on schedule, now does he?" My mother cleared her throat, but I could see her body tense.

I sat next to my cousin Jason, who let out loud belches after every few bites. I nibbled my biscuit, fighting the urge to stuff it down his windpipe. Across was Uncle Randy, making one dumb joke after another. I concentrated on Aunt Rebecca's stories about teaching first grade.

I helped my mom load the dishes into the sink and offered to wash them. It took me about an hour to finish, and by then all our company had left, stopping in the kitchen to kiss me good-bye and say Merry Christmas.

I decided to go to bed right away. I was exhausted from all our preparations for the company; I knew my mom must be tired, too. I wanted to tell her that she could go to bed, that she didn't have to bother with the Santa job this year, but she probably would have been offended. So I kissed her and Dad good night.

As I lay in the dark, I tried to imagine what my brother was doing right now. Was he picking through garbage cans, trying to find a halfway decent supper, or was he safe and warm at a friend's house? Or was he a melted snowflake?

I chased that thought from my mind. "David," I said softly, "wherever you are, whatever you're doing, I hope you're having an okay Christmas."

• • •

I woke up at 1:00 A.M. with a start. Had I heard something downstairs? I listened carefully, not moving. Nothing. Probably just a dream. I pulled my comforter back over my head.

I heard it again: footsteps, downstairs. My bedroom was over the living room, where the steps seemed to be coming from. They were faint—but clear—through the heating vent.

At first I thought it was just my parents putting presents under the tree, but the footsteps were nowhere near the tree. I knew it was silly to be scared, but just to make sure, I rolled out of bed and tiptoed down the hall to my parents' bedroom. My mom and dad were both sound asleep.

I began to panic. Who was walking around downstairs? A burglar? A murderer? I shuddered. I didn't feel like getting chopped to bits at 1:00 A.M. on Christmas day, even though I would probably make the front page of the newspaper.

I scolded myself for having such a gruesome imagination. It was probably just Uncle Randy or somebody.

Forgot his hat or something. I decided I'd go down and offer him cookies. I couldn't sleep anyway.

I started down the staircase. From the middle of the stairs, you have the view of our entire living room. I looked down into it and saw a man. It was not Uncle Randy.

This person was thin and wore torn jeans. I could only see him from the back, but I could tell that he didn't belong in this house. I was really scared. I wanted to get my parents, but I knew I couldn't get to the top of the stairs without this stranger noticing me.

I spotted the flashlight that we kept at the top of the staircase. If I could reach it, I could throw it at the back of the guy's head to knock him out. It had to work. It worked in the movies, didn't it? I took a deep breath and stepped up one stair, very, very softly.

No creak. So far, so good. I let out my breath quietly, then sucked it in again to prepare myself for the next step.

I grabbed the flashlight, grasping it so hard my knuckles turned white.

I stepped down one stair. No creak. Then the next . . . *Creeeak!* I stopped in horror. I listened. My heart was beating so loud I was sure the man could hear it. He didn't seem to be reacting, so I got myself ready to throw.

I drew my arm back and planted my foot on the stair. My victim was bent over with his back to me, just where I wanted him.

Ready . . . aim . . . *Whapp!*

"Aaaaaggghhhh!"

I'd hit him! But I hadn't knocked him out.

"Sassy, why'd you do that?"

I held my breath.

"David!" I exclaimed, forgetting to keep my voice down. David was the only person on earth who called me Sassy.

I ran toward him. He was hunched over holding his head. I pulled him upright and grabbed his shoulders, not believing it was true, that it was really him.

I stared at him. He had gotten thinner, his cheeks were sunken in, and he needed a shave. He looked more rugged. There was more to him than when he had left. It was in his eyes.

It was pain.

David had gone through a lot of hard times since that September. He looked like he hadn't gotten a good night's sleep in a while. And he had a bump on his head from me. A great way to welcome him home.

I smiled.

"I'm so sorry! I thought you were a burglar or something."

He smiled crookedly. "That's okay. After what I've been through, I'm used to it."

We were interrupted by my mother's shriek.

"David Scott, you're home!"

There were lots of greetings, questions and tears.

David told us he had bunked out with some friends a couple of towns away, and they kicked him out for no good reason.

"Not real good guys," as he described them.

I silently disagreed. I thanked these good guys, whoever they were, for sending David home for Christmas.

Every year for Christmas I had asked for something unimportant, something I really didn't need. Sometimes Santa gave it to me, sometimes he didn't. That year Santa outdid himself. I didn't care if I never got another gift in my entire life, as long as I had my brother to tell me new jokes, help me with my algebra and call me Sassy. ▣

Photo by Kate Rakus

Timmy the Toad— A Fictional-But-Not-So- Fictional Parable

Fiction by Paul Constant

Timmy the Toad was *not* a happy toad. His father, Corporal Punishment, was very mean to him. His mother, I. N. Difference, was a cruel woman who didn't like having a son. She wanted to be a musician. Timmy grew up very sad, but also very mad. He was mad at his parents for not loving him. He was mad at his school for rejecting him. (Timmy was very shy in school.) In fact, he was mad at the whole town of Amrica for just existing.

So one day, Timmy, the not-so-happy toad, went to Shootem Up, a local gun dealer, and bought a gun. Of course, Timmy had to wait five days before Shootem could give him a gun, but that just let him plan even more. Timmy decided to get revenge on his parents and the world by shooting someone. One day, he saw ol' By Stander walking in Amrica's town square and *boom!* With a shot, he got By right in the patoot! They took By to the hospital and removed the bullet from his posterior, and then they took Timmy to court.

When the judge asked Timmy, "What caused you to do this?" Timmy got scared. He decided to try to get out of it by blaming someone else. He said, "Well, sir, I saw Mr. T. V. Violence the other day, and he was pretending to shoot someone and it looked like fun!" The judge, of course, was shocked. He said, "Well, what about the gun? Didn't you get the gun from someone?"

Timmy the Toad thought about it for a minute, and said, "Yessir, I did get the gun from someone. Mr. Up, the gun dealer. He saw how upset I was, he should never have sold it to me!"

Well, the whole town of Amrica heard this, and the mayor of Amrica, Hi Steria, said, "Well, obviously, Timmy here is the victim! I say we round up T. V. and Shootem, and throw them right out of Amrica! Then it'll all be okay."

So, the town threw out Shootem Up, the gun dealer, and T. V. Violence, the play actor, and they thought all was well. One day, however, Timmy the Toad decided he was sick of life again. So, in a fit of fury, he grabbed a butter knife and poked ol' By Stander again, right in the derriere! The people of Amrica again got together in court, and decided that poor Timmy had been victimized a second time. They decided to blame the company in Taiwan that made the knife, and devised a plan to drop immense amounts of bombs on the knife company. The Amrican citizens were tittering amongst themselves about their plan, when, as usual, that old busybody, Vocef Reezon, decided to speak.

Vocef quietly began, "Now, I didn't particularly enjoy watching T. V.'s little plays. I thought they were stupid and senseless. But don't you see? Amrica was built on freedom. I don't think everyone—no matter how stupid or senseless—should have their freedom taken away from them. T. V. didn't commit the crime, so why should his freedoms be taken away?"

He paused for a moment, nervously cleared his throat and began again, "And, though it's not totally wrong for Shootem to have some restrictions placed on him, like it or not, Amrica's laws do say that we can have weapons. Although Shootem is selling weapons, we have to protect his rights. Taking his rights away could have horrifying results. So we take them away. Who's next? Where does the line stop? We can't let this happen. Everyone's rights are important."

Vocef's chest filled with pride as he began again. He was happy with how he was vocalizing his beliefs. Surely they couldn't disagree? "But there are cases when someone's rights have to be infringed upon, and that's when they take away someone else's rights by breaking the law. And if those rights are infringed upon, then we have to punish the person who breaks the laws. It's time to draw the line. People must start taking responsibility for their actions. T. V. didn't shoot By Stander in the patoot, and neither did Shootem Up. Timmy the Toad did. And that's what's important. He's the one who broke the law. T. V. was not hurting anyone by putting on stupid little revenge plays. We're only hurting ourselves by searching desperately for someone to blame for your actions. Thank you."

Vocef stopped speaking, sat down, and watched as the assembled citizens of Amrica stared at each other in blind confusion. Finally, Hi Steria stood up and shouted, "Let's throw Reezon out, too!" All of Amrica agreed that this was a good idea. Then they went on with their plans to bomb Taiwan.

And the citizens of Amrica lived happily ever after, at least until Timmy the Toad decided that he was upset with the whole story and dropped an entire store of pornographic magazines on By Stander's head, but that's a different story altogether.

Names have been changed to disguise (thinly) the guilty. 回

One-Fifth of a Second

Fiction by Timothy Cahill

The beads of sweat that cover his face are not due to the heat, although the temperature is a blistering 102°F. Nor is the slightly nauseous feeling in his stomach the result of the illness he succumbed to several weeks before. And the lump in his throat is in no way related to the sadness that accompanies a personal tragedy, though his share of grief has been great. These are all physical manifestations of overwhelming fear.

There are moments in life that will irrevocably alter one's destiny. The fate of one's hopes, dreams and aspirations hangs in the fragile balance of a single snap judgment. It is the fear that he will not succeed that now wraps its dark claws around his mind and fights desperately to paralyze his will. *But it will not,* an inner voice exclaims within him. *It cannot.*

His hand emerges from his pocket in a motion so fluent that the clerk at the counter is already staring into the face of death by the time his eyes widen in shock. The clerk is not yet afraid because he does not realize what is happening. It is only a matter of seconds before the storekeeper will comprehend, react and escape.

The clerk's life means nothing to the man with the

gun. It cannot. It will not. He can afford no hesitation. The world the clerk inhabits is relevant only because he is here, now. He must be treated as an obstacle and nothing more. Self-preservation demands it.

The man has no name, no face, no life. But he unquestionably has eyes. The eyes are still opening, and—for the first time—they exhibit fear. He sees the eyes, and inescapably, he sees the fear. And he stops. His hand stops. His mind stops. His heart stops.

It requires only one-fifth of a second to pull a trigger. But such a measurement ignores the fact that time is an entity unto itself. In the blink of an eye, he sees the clerk's fear, and sees beyond it. He sees sadness and concern. The man is real. He is flesh and blood. Perhaps he is afraid not for himself, but for a family, his family. A wife he loves, children he has raised, parents he supports.

His grip on the gun tightens and the blood drains from his hand. He thinks thoughts that would require minutes to say. He considers choices that would require hours to ponder. He reaches a decision that would require a lifetime to understand. The eyes are a portal into a world in which he dares not tread. The man cannot be real. Yet it is already too late. He has seen more than he can accept, more than he can ever understand.

It requires only a pound of pressure to pull a trigger. But it is an amount of force that is now impossible to overcome. He can steal this man's money, but he cannot steal his life, only end it. There is no way to comprehend what he sees in the clerk's eyes; he can only envy it, cherish it.

The eyes now possess an inkling of confusion. He peels his gaze away from the eyes and directs it to the gun in his hand, a gun which suddenly bears a weight he can no longer support. The weapon slips from his grip and clatters loudly to the tiled floor as he sinks to his knees and covers his face with his hands. Yet the vision remains ingrained in his mind. The image of a man one-fifth of a second away from death. One-fifth of a second that would become an eternity. ▣

Ophelia and Me

Fiction by Shana Onigman

It happened one October afternoon when I was driving down Route 1 in the pouring rain. She was beside me in the car. She hadn't been around a lot for quite awhile, but then, it never was all that surprising when she showed up, even though her visits were so arbitrary.

"I've been wondering," she said, breaking a long silence, and then she stopped.

When she's wondering something, it's usually nothing good. I waited for her to continue. I should have guessed, though, that she would stop right after saying it, just to mystify me.

"What?" I said, rather predictably.

"I've been wondering . . . ," she repeated, dreamily.

It was easy for her to be dreamy. It's always easy to be dreamy on a rainy October day if you're in the passenger seat. If you're in the driver's seat, you've got to watch the road, and you can't just dream and wonder about anything, unless you've got really good car insurance and not much interest in seeing tomorrow.

"What have you been wondering?" I said disinterestedly, hoping to humor her until she shut up. She glanced at me, irked by that obvious annoyed way that I persisted in being practical by keeping my attention focused on the road. Never mind that her life depended on me keeping my mind focused.

"I was wondering what it'd be like to be insane," she said suddenly.

I rolled my eyes. "Insanity," I told her, "is a very trite subject."

"Oh, but it's so interesting!" she said. "Who wrote, 'Isn't it joyous to be insane'?"

"My ex-boyfriend wrote that in a letter to me," I said, annoyed that she was making me remember that. "I didn't know you read that letter."

"No, no, I mean besides him," she said, ignoring my accusation. "Someone famous?"

"Probably," I shrugged. "He wasn't one for original statements." I smiled to myself over my little dig—he would have called me bitter if he'd heard that.

"You're still bitter?" she asked, turning to me.

"About what?"

"About him."

I switched the windshield wipers to a higher speed in response. They squeaked as they slid back and forth, and I forced my eyes not to follow, not to be hypnotized.

"No—though it wasn't that long ago, you know."

A car, doing about eighty, swooshed past me on my left. A surge of panic jumped into my throat and then settled back into my stomach as disgust. "Jerk," I spit softly at the speed-demon.

"Oh, I don't think he was that bad," she said.

"What?"

"Your ex-boyfriend. He wasn't such a jerk most of the time."

"No," I sighed, "he wasn't."

"But I don't know if he was right."

"Right? Right about what?"

"About being insane."

I could feel myself losing it, between the bittersweet, raw memories she was heaping on me and the stress of driving against that rain with the hypnotic swish and squeak of the windshield wipers. I pulled into a McDonald's parking lot, resting my head against the steering wheel.

"Why are we stopped?" she asked.

"So you can have your say and let me alone," I said bluntly, not caring if I was rude. "Fine. Get it over with. You're thinking about insanity, which is trite, which he thought was joyous, which you think is interesting, which I think I don't want to think about. What about it?"

"It shows up in a lot of books and movies and plays."

"Yeah. That's why it's trite. People have been writing about insanity for a long time, since Greek tragedies. The main character in almost every Greek tragedy was a little crazy, at least by today's standards. We'd call anyone today who kills their kids or their parents insane, and that's what most Greek characters did. And then Shakespeare—he wrote about insane people. And even today, every other bestseller is either a biography or an autobiography of someone who has done time in an asylum. Same with movies. It's all the same. Every writer is obsessed with it."

"Aren't you obsessed with it? You're a writer."

I bared my teeth at her, rather than grinned. "I'm . . . not . . . every . . . writer," I said.

"Granted."

"Thank you."

"Shall we go to McDonald's?"

"I hate that place."

"Get a vanilla shake?"

"If you get one, I'll end up drinking it."

"You like them anyway. We'll both get one."

"No, they're not healthy, and they're too expensive."

"But they're good."

She knew I had won, and lapsed into silence. Thinking she had finished, I thankfully started the engine again.

"What about Ophelia?" she said suddenly.

"What about Ophelia?"

"Well . . . in *Hamlet,* she went insane, right?"

I groaned, realizing she hadn't dropped the subject. "That's the common belief."

"You don't think she really did."

I turned the engine off. This was going to take longer than I thought.

"No. Ophelia wasn't really insane, she just wanted attention. Wandering around singing senseless songs and talking to imaginary friends doesn't make you insane."

"It doesn't? What does?"

"I don't know." I shivered. "I mean, maybe it does, but if it did, it would mean I'm crazy."

"What's wrong with that?"

"Let's go to McDonald's."

Twenty minutes and two vanilla shakes later, she repeated the question. She wasn't one to let go of questions easily.

"What's it like, insanity?"

"How should I know?" I said. "Confusing. There are books about it. You should read them."

"I don't read books," she said.

"Then how do you know about *Hamlet?*"

"You know. I know."

I acknowledged this silently, furious at the fact that she had to bring it up, and sucked hard on my straw, trying to ignore the stares from other McDonald's patrons and shaking my head so my dripping hair fell over my eyes.

"But what's it like to be really insane?" she insisted.

"Why do you ask?" I growled.

"It's important. I think it must be . . . dark. Not knowing. Dark. Cold. You think?"

"I don't know," I admitted, "I'm not insane. Or at least I don't think I am. Yet."

She smiled then, a long, slow, strange smile.

"Aren't you?"

And I was startled to find that I was sitting alone in a McDonald's booth, with one half-finished vanilla shake in front of me and one untouched, with a straw sticking out of it.

And I was talking out loud to myself. 回

Evidence

Fiction by Mark Denoncour

David shut the door and fell into one of the hard plastic chairs, his body cold and stiff. He removed his baseball cap and placed it on his lap. Covered with snow, it blended with his coat. He pulled his coat sleeve back and looked at his watch: 11:53. He had just made it.

Through the glass panel he could see the man who would be executed in a little more than five minutes. The man was short and black. His head was completely shaved. Despite the distance between them, David could see sweat on the man's forehead, glistening in the overhead lights.

Rot in hell, David thought.

He had good reason to think that. David had been the key witness in the trial that put Eddie Grouner in the electric chair. David was the first officer to arrive at the scene, the first to notify the police and the first to speak to the media about the crime.

David again looked at his watch: 11:54. The time was crawling by. Any minute though, the chief warden of the Worthington Penitentiary would step up to the condemned man, say his lines, the switch would be pulled and Eddie Grouner would be dead. So David really didn't care what the time did. It was just that he was very, very tired. He hadn't been sleeping well lately.

Staring at Eddie, David began to think back to that cold September night, and what he had told the police. . . .

• • •

Cold. Swirling, wiggling cold woke David up. He rubbed his eyes and pinched the bridge of his nose. Where was it coming from? David pulled himself from the bed. It was coming from the window, he realized, and lumbered over to it. His hands pushed it shut, but he heard something. It was a horrifying scream from down the street.

Now jolted completely from sleep, David flung open his bedroom door and ran downstairs where he grabbed his coat, shoes and gun.

Four houses down, David found Megan Hooran, Eddie's fiancée, on the floor. The body had at least five bullet holes in the head, and more in the chest, with blood seeping out, dyeing the carpet a dark, heavy red. Beside her ravaged body stood Eddie Grouner in a pair of badly faded gym shorts and no shirt. On the carpet next to his foot lay a sleek, black revolver.

• • •

That had pretty much been the end of Eddie Grouner. For a year he had remained clean, and some of the officers were discouraged that he would have committed such a hideous crime. Many, however, were not surprised. Eddie was a notorious criminal with no respect, and the majority of the officers (including David) hated him. Eddie had a list of robberies that spread for miles, but somehow he had managed to slip through the holes of the justice system unscathed. Even though staying clean for a year was something, it was not nearly enough to earn sympathy from the jury. Plus, the evidence against him was overwhelming. The bullets found in Megan Hooran's body were all perfect matches with the Baretta .380 found at Eddie's feet, which had his fingerprints all over it. That type of gun was also one that Eddie had used several times in small robberies. In addition, Eddie had no alibi, and could only wildly insist that David had committed the crime, not him.

● ● ●

David stared at his watch: 11:58. Footsteps boomed, and David looked up. The warden was on the platform, standing next to Eddie. David slouched back in his chair and thought, *Let the show begin.*

The warden coughed, cleared his throat and spoke, "Edward Smith Grouner, you have been condemned to die. . . ."

David listened intently. *Soon, very soon,* he thought. *You don't look so smug anymore, Eddie. Is the thought of death bothering you? I hope so.*

" . . . God save the . . ."

It was all going well. But, of course, why wouldn't it?

" . . . anything to say before your sentence is carried out?"

Eddie narrowed his glance on David. He spoke in a low, calm voice. "I did not commit this crime. God knows this, and you, David, will never see heaven."

A smile creased David's face. So perfect. If only the police had checked.

A black mask was pulled over Eddie's face. The warden approached the platform. Once again he spoke to Eddie, although Eddie could no longer see him.

"Edward Smith Grouner, electricity shall now be passed through your body until you are dead, in accordance with state law. May God have mercy on your soul."

David's smile widened. If only the police had checked his coat pockets that night. They would have found the pair of gloves David had used to carry the gun to Eddie's home. They would have found the silencer David had attached to the Baretta .380—a weapon confiscated two years earlier, which Eddie had used in a robbery—covered with David's fingerprints. But, of course, they hadn't checked David's pockets. They trusted David's story and accused Eddie of murder.

The next day David had thrown away the silencer in a bag of trash. The gloves he had burned in his fireplace. Now there was only one more piece of evidence that needed to be destroyed.

"Roll on two!"

The overhead lights dimmed and a dull buzzing noise filled the air. David realized at once this was the generators powering up.

A loud thump cracked the silence as Eddie Grouner's body heaved against the metal restraints of the electric chair. After several moments, Eddie's body stopped moving.

The buzzing halted abruptly, and the lights came on, illuminating the small room once more. David put on his cap and walked silently out the door. ▣

The Passion of a Fine Young Man

by Kevin Robert Mulcahy

the cap is off
but the ink is gone
and hope
is a rope
i hung myself on
they'd like me to do
tricks in my cage
'cause passion's in fashion
and i'm full of rage
they'd like me to hit
some sickly sweet note
it's late
and i hate
whatever i wrote
they'd like me to be
what i am not
but happy
and sappy
i must have forgot
they'd like me to try
to seize every day

tomorrow
more sorrow
i feel sick anyway
they want me to think
quite positively
and tonight
i might
just watch more tv
they forced off the cap
and the passion is gone
and hope
is the rope
they'll hang themselves on

Fourteen Days of a Fruit Fly

Fiction by Caitlin Bennett

The man on the corner told me we are to die shortly after we are born. His eyes were worn with the lapse of time and hardship; his lips chapped from harsh days and frigid nights. I dropped a coin in his rusted can. He shook his head in raw acceptance of what he did not want, but needed.

The little girl pressed her face against the mesh metal fence. I studied her. She looked directly at me and smiled. The smile went as easily as it had come. She told me that every day after this one will be exactly the same, and we will wane until we are nothing. She was not aged in years, but in something equally as powerful.

My mother nodded and walked away from the long, straight lines of stone. Her eyes were lined with moisture from tears that drowned something inside. She told me that tomorrow isn't always there, but today is.

The taxi screeched to a halt at my feet. I opened the door cautiously and the man asked where I wanted to go. I told him I wasn't sure. He said I could go anywhere, for a price.

I shoved piles of dirty clothes into the washer. I hardly

ever do my wash. The lady in the laundromat said the colors had to be separated from the whites. But I didn't know why.

The old woman tapped my shoulder with her creased finger. I revolved in my solitary orbit to face her. She interrogated me on what I would be when I grew up. I told her I didn't know. She responded that, for a suspended moment, possibilities are endless. After that moment, all is lost.

My sister kicked me sharply in my left shin. The agony spread through my entire limb and it went numb. She told me that pain is a part of everything, and everything is painful.

My best friend ran away. I tried to catch her, but my unpracticed feet stumbled. I attempted flight without wings to carry me. She told me that life is a test. She raves that distance and time are the ultimate tests of love. Will I pass?

The teacher in the front slammed his pointer against the green blackboard. He screamed for me to pay attention, and then assigned me detention. He told me my world is not my own.

The lady in the detention room directed me to take my seat. She told me to take what is given.

The delinquent next to me cursed in dismay as he cut his finger with the knife he was using to carve his initials in the desk. He told me to leave my mark on the world.

My father sighed, weary from monotonous hours. He told me life is hard and to make a life of what you love. Happiness, said he, is priceless.

My seventh husband filed for divorce. I didn't sign a prenuptial agreement, thinking that today was forever.

He told me to live in the present, but always think for the future.

The judge said I should have been smarter.

My cat settled onto my lap with the utmost of pleasure. She told me not to think too hard or too long about any one thing.

The coach stood silently watching as I ran along the winding path in the cold sleet. Not a word flowed from his solemn mouth. He told me that if I didn't believe in myself, other people wouldn't either.

The doctor told me I was dying. He said I'd be dead in six months, then prescribed an apple a day.

The mortician commented that I look good in purple eye shadow, but that I am rather pale. She told me to try some more blush on the cheeks. Of course, I didn't hear her.

Yet I heard everything at first. Then I told myself it was time to live. By then it was too late.

A fruit fly buzzed around my corpse. I thought it was looking for a meal, but instead it landed on my nose and stared directly into my eyes. It told me I was lucky because I lived so long and had so many chances. It said that every moment of life is precious, and I am fortunate to have had so many moments. A fruit fly lives for fourteen days, and then it is gone. ▣

Watching Mommy and Daddy

Fiction by Jennifer Cohun

I "really can't tell you anything else," the woman in the gray suit said unsympathetically, but my mother still cried. Nothing could stop her. I watched them from above, not making a single noise. My mother had just gotten home and found a disrupting sight in our usually simple house. Nobody could change what had happened today.

All of a sudden the door slammed open, but without a noise I could hear. My father stood there with tears flowing down the cold curves of his face, just like the river we visited so often. His fingers curled and then straightened, curled and then straightened. They stopped, and he quickly crossed the strawberry red carpet of the living room toward the stereo. Everyone in the room stared as though he would start to throw furniture or blow up like a nuclear bomb.

His fingers shook as he sifted through my CDs. He picked out my favorite Tori Amos and slipped it in the player. You could hear the flawless noise of the CD against the player as his hands shook. The volume, which he had altered, now shook the house with an awful roar. Not one of the uninvited houseguests made a move to stop him. The graffiti of the song drifted word by word in everyone's presence.

My father crossed the room once again, but this time to my mother. He pulled her close is if no one was watching. They sat down on the wooden-framed antique sofa my parents had allowed me to choose. It had to be the most beautiful piece of furniture in the room. They clung together, not talking. The teary mist had been forgotten. As though nothing had happened, our little party was now ending and all of the strangers were disappearing. Someone turned off the light near the sofa.

Mother got up and started swaying to the music. My father joined her as if the two of them did this on a regular basis. I had never seen them together like this, or even hold hands. A slow rhythm came on, and the two of them stood close, not dancing, not yet touching. Staring into one another's eyes. Would anything, even this, interrupt their love for each other? No, they imagined without even knowing the other's thoughts. It was not a time for talking. I watched the two of them staring blankly, not knowing when to stop looking, afraid to find something. My mother sat down again. My father stood for another few minutes, then started to lie down in a fetal position in an effort to ward something off or away from him. He stopped the thought and put his head down lightly on her lap.

I watched Mother and Father, Greta and Dorin. They slept until four in the morning and as if it were timed, they both awoke at the same moment. Mother looked around to see if she were still in a dream, but, unfortunately, it was still the night before. I still sat up in the loft covered in a smooth and silky cover. Though my eyes were locked with a door bolt never to open again, I saw Mother sit up, stand, and go to the kitchen. She came back with a knife lying softly on her arm like an infant.

"If you should need an exit from your misery, I will follow gaily." Smiling, Mother set the knife down on the glass coffee table and set herself down once again.

Father stood up slowly, unsure of himself, but all the while staring at the knife. He picked it up as softly as Mother had placed it down. I heard a kitchen drawer open and close, and then Father walked back to the living room, the knife no longer in his arms.

A knock on the front door didn't surprise my parents, as if it were a play. My father got up to answer the door. Two men stood at the front door and entered without being asked. Mother stood, and tears started to fall from her jeweled eyes like a broken pearl necklace. What would Mother and Father say? Lightly, but very sure of himself, one of the men spoke, "Would you like to show us where the body is?" 回

Hitchhiker

Fiction by Randolph Paulsen

Wet chunks of white slush fell from the sky and made a temporary home on our windshield. The light, pretty snowflakes of two hours ago were a fading memory.

"Will they give up our room if we're not there on time?" I asked, my voice wavering slightly.

"I just don't know, Jim. I wish I could tell you," said my mother.

"Do you mind if I turn on the radio?" I inquired rhetorically as I reached from under my blankets to turn the dial, not waiting for an answer. The click of the knob, some fuzzy reports telling us how crazy ski vacationers (like us) were to be driving in such weather, and then static, unintelligible. . . . I switched it off. I sighed, pulled my blankets over my head, put the car seat into a reclining position and closed my eyes.

I woke up half an hour later and looked around. The empty backseat glared at me. The blackness outside the safety of the headlights threatened to swallow me whole. The windshield wipers squeaked with untiring monotony. My mother kept driving—speedometer reading a steady 35 m.p.h., 10:47 in glowing green light . . . still sleepy.

"How much farther do we have to go?" I mumbled through my dreariness. I squirmed under the covers, trying to work out the kinks in my limbs, and sat up.

"Can't be more than an hour now," my mother told me. Our destination always seemed on the horizon.

I shivered. "There's something up ahead," I noted. Peering through the storm from between sticky eyelids, I saw the large shape of an automobile. Brightly burning emergency flares marked its position. Between the flares, standing like a ghost in a parka, was a man with his right hand out of his pocket, a gloved thumb extended toward the shrouded sky.

"Looks like a hitchhiker," said my mother.

"Let's pick him up," I suggested adventurously. The car pulled to a stop in the breakdown lane, next to the man's car. The man ambled to my window. He had an obvious limp. The man stood right outside my window, the steam of his breath pulsing from deep in the blackness of his hood, turning the glass milk-white. He tapped on the window; I rolled it down.

My mother leaned over, one hand on the steering wheel. "You need a ride?" she asked. I sank down in my seat, trying to avoid being noticed.

"How far north are you going?" he said, rather kindly actually.

"We're going as far as Sunday River."

"Ah, yes," he said as he looked at our roof where skis were strapped.

"Thanks, I just need to find the first motel. Triple A will take care of the car once it stops snowing." He stood there for an awkward moment.

My mom broke the silence, "Well, hop in."

"Thanks." He brushed the latest layer of snow from his jacket before he yanked open the sticky back door, and landed with an audible bounce. He pushed the hood of his parka back so that it sat like a pillow behind his head. He rubbed his hands together and breathed deep, reviving breaths into his cupped palms. A rough grunt and a sniffle cleared his nose and throat. It was when he put his hands into his lap that I first saw his face.

He had a thin, weathered complexion. I guessed that he was about forty. He had wide-set dark brown eyes, but that wasn't what caught my attention. Running from the top of his cheekbone all the way down to the lip of his muscled jaw was the biggest scar I had ever seen anywhere. When I say anywhere, I mean anywhere. It was bigger than scars in the movies. It was so deep and long it looked as if you could unzip it and take his face off his skull. I observed that no stubble was growing out of the scar, then I realized I had been staring at his face for quite a while.

He cleared his throat and pulled his coat collar up, as if he were trying to hide something terrible. I suddenly felt ashamed and settled back into my seat, my eyes closed tight trying to blot out the image of the stranger's face.

"So, what's your name?" asked my mother, trying to start a conversation.

"Oh, it's Jeffrey," he said, "Jeffrey Rowes. I'm from Rhode Island. I was on my way to Canada when my car died. My brother and his family live up there. We were planning on spending Christmas together." He sighed and rolled his eyes. "Now with this storm, I don't know if it's worth it. How much longer is this . . . " he pointed out the window, "supposed to last?"

"I read that it should continue well into tomorrow. But then somebody told me it could last three days," she sounded confused.

Nothing was making any sense to me. Everything that came out of their mouths turned to jargon before it reached my ears. The only clear image in my mind was that of the monstrosity behind me. I began to fantasize. Jeffrey was a fugitive who had ditched the car he had stolen after breaking out of an institution for the criminally insane. Then he had hitched a ride with some innocent ski vacationers, and fed them a bunch of lies about who he was before shooting them and burying them in the snow on the side of the road, while he drove off in their car in the middle of the worst snowstorm in eighty years and made his way safely across the Canadian border, never to be heard from again, and all the while the innocent ski vacationers lay in the snow, shot through the head, the blood in their blue corpses turned to ice, their bodies left undiscovered until the spring when it wouldn't matter anymore.

And then I saw Jeffrey's hand reaching between the two front seats. My heart thumped so hard that I felt it press against my throat. I swallowed and with a flurry of motion and sound I slapped that hand and threw my bundle of blankets blindly into the backseat screaming, "He's a murderer, Mom! Don't listen to a word he says, he's lying! He's gonna kill us both and leave us at the side of the road! He's a murderer!" I swung around and looked frantically behind me where I saw Jeffrey.

He was pressed into the seat, his eyes wide open, staring straight at me. His mouth hung slightly open in a look of surprise, disgust and fear. I looked at his hands; his fingers were dug into the cushion of the seat to the point where it would have taken a crowbar to pry them loose. My eyes moved back up to his face. I looked into his wide-set dark brown eyes, and I saw, for the first time, that Jeffrey Rowes was nothing more than a man.

"I wanted to hear the radio," he breathed. He swallowed and tried to stop shaking. "I think I'd better get out here," he said, his voice barely above a whisper. Without speaking, my mother stopped the car. Jeffrey reached for the door handle. Mom started to speak, "Jeffrey, I—," but he silenced her with a wave of his hand.

He slowly opened the door and stepped out, leaving the night's happenings behind him. All the while I sat in my seat, my eyes staring at nothing. I rolled up into a ball of guilt and tried to make myself disappear. I knew I wouldn't sleep for a long time.

My mother drove. Jeffrey became a speck and then he was gone, lost in the curtains of snow and darkness. Neither my mom nor I said another word that night. ▣

Jonathan's World of White

Fiction by Adrienne Scheibel

Jonathan Furst sat completely still. His large brown eyes followed a fly crawling up his arm. He watched it closely. He had no impulse to brush it off, but only to study its movements. Jonathan watched as it stuck its black tongue out to touch his skin.

Then he watched as the fly flew to the window, past the iron bars. It tried to escape, only to be stopped by the same glass barrier that kept him in the asylum. Jonathan knew how it felt.

He may have sat there with the fly for hours. He may have sat there for seconds. He did not know, he did not care. He did not even think about it. Time had no meaning to Jonathan Furst. In fact, many things had no meaning for him.

His life was an eternal world of white walls, white women in white skirts, white doctors in white coats, and screams of confusion and insanity.

The world was broken only by the one person who came to visit him. This was The Brother, the tall intelligent man who claimed responsibility for Jonathan. He came only on the fifth day of every month.

Yes, on the fifth day of every month, Jonathan would

feel the fresh air and bright burning yellow and orange sun on his large face. He lived for the hour or two of blue sky and green grass that was spent outside, away from the towering red brick building that held the world of white he knew so well.

But Jonathan's demented mind forgot easily. Therefore, when he was brought to this bright happy world of color by the only person who loved him, he would forget that he would eventually be returned to the inside of the asylum. There his world was blank.

Jonathan turned to the calendar on the white wall with a slow deliberate movement of his head. His eyes were blank and his mouth barely moved when he spoke, "May. May fifth. May fifth," said Jonathan's smooth voice.

He barely ever spoke to anyone but The Brother. Every year for five years, he had waited all month for the fifth day to arrive and bring with it his brother.

The Brother never missed a day, and Jonathan never missed seeing him come. Jonathan waited by the window, staring blankly through the bars he had come to ignore. He began to watch as people walking down the street crossed over to the sidewalk farthest away from the building as they approached the asylum.

They never looked back, especially if they had seen the many blank minds hidden by the blank faces that stared down on them. If they had ever experienced the shrieks that radiated from that part of the building, they would never return to that section of town.

Jonathan wound his hand around one of the iron bars and was immediately entranced by its image. He studied it as he had studied the fly, then let his eyes fall, unfocused, only to begin studying the pattern of the tiled floor. He did not even notice the state he had left his eyes in. If he had noticed, he wouldn't have cared. He could stare forever at anything, even a black spot on the wall where another patient had spit his dinner in a fit of delirium.

He would sit, stare and wait. Wait for The Brother to come.

Jonathan continued to sit in that white room full of beds with sheets that reeked of uncontrolled bladders. Unlike most smells that often disappeared after you had been exposed to them for a period of time, Jonathan was unable to free himself from the smell of the room, even after five years. It was this smell and the sounds that kept most people away. Most people, but not The Brother. The Brother did not like the smell either, but he loved Jonathan, and so he still came. Everyone else in his outside world had abandoned him, and Jonathan was waiting to see the black car that brought his brother. The Brother's sleek sedan always pulled up to the curb in front of the building. The Brother always parked at the same place, at the same time, and made the same movements.

He'd slowly remove himself from the car, rub his eyes as if he could not keep the sleep from them. Gingerly, he would approach the large steps that projected from the entry way. With slow, smooth movements he climbed, he was always so sure of himself. He would stop, always on the fifth step, as if hesitant to go any further. Jonathan would hold his breath, wondering if this would be the time The Brother turned away, returning to his car and not entering the world encased behind the brick walls. Anyone passing by would think he was unsure of entering the building that held a whole separate planet. But Jonathan knew The Brother always came to see him. The Brother would then continue up the steps to the cold sterile doors. There he would pause again with one hand extended to the door. And Jonathan was always afraid for that one short moment. For that one short moment when his brother would pause at the door, he knew fear. He was afraid that The Brother would not enter, and Jonathan would be left there forever. But he always came, and Jonathan was always assured as The Brother left. He promised to return saying, "Maybe next time I'll take you away from here, Jonathan."

And Jonathan knew The Brother would not lie, that The Brother loved him and that he would have taken him away from the world of white if he could.

Maybe today would be the day The Brother would take him away.

One of the uniformed white women came into the room with a breakfast tray. He ate only a few tiny spoon fuls of the cereal placed before him. Five to be exact. Five because today was the fifth of the month, and it was th day that The Brother came. Five was a special number o that day because The Brother was a special person.

Jonathan ate his cereal slowly. He listened to tl sound of his eating amplified in his ears. He did not tas his meal, for taste was not a priority in Jonathan's life. F life had no priorities except The Brother's visit. Duri the visits Jonathan did not sense the uncomfortable air that always filled the room during The Brother's visits. To Jonathan, "uncomfortable" was a normal feeling because that was all he had ever known from anyone. It was a feeling he had mistaken for security and love. He didn't know any different.

And then the same woman brought Jonathan his lunch. Once again, he ate only five bites, and again eating was not the priority. Lunch merely meant The Brother was near, as he usually appeared as the lunch tray was taken away.

Jonathan readied himself.

Jonathan sat at the window, surrounded by the white walls and white nurses with white shoes in a room full of the shrieks of insane human beings. He began to wait for The Brother.

The Brother who came every fifth day of the month, right after the lunch tray was taken away by the woman in the white skirt.

He sits and waits for The Brother.

The Brother who never really existed except in the white world of Jonathan's blank mind. ▣

How to submit writing, art and photos for the monthly *Teen Ink* magazine and the next *Teen Ink* book:

You must be twelve to nineteen years old to be published.

- Include your name, year of birth, home address/city/ state/zip, telephone number and the name of your school and English teacher on each submission. Most published pieces are fewer than 2,500 words.

- Type all submissions, if possible, or print carefully in ink. We can't return any submissions, so keep a copy.

- Label all work fiction or nonfiction. Be sure to include a title.

- Affix name and address information on the back of each photo or piece of art. Please don't fold.

- Include the following originality statement in your own handwriting after each submission: "This will certify that the above work is completely original," and sign your name to affirm this is your work.

- Request anonymity. If due to the very personal nature of a piece you don't want your name published, we will respect your request, but you still must include name and address information.

Other information:

If published in the magazine or book, you will receive a free copy together with an environmentally sound wooden pen and a special *Teen Ink* Post-it pad.

All works submitted become the property of *Teen Ink* and all copyrights are assigned to *Teen Ink*. We retain the non-exclusive rights to publish all such works in any format. All material in *Teen Ink* is copyrighted to protect us and exclude others from republishing your work. However, all contributors retain the right to submit their work for publication elsewhere and you have our permission to do so.

Writing may be edited and we reserve the right to publish our edited version without your prior approval.

Send all submissions to:

Teen Ink
Box 97
Newton, MA 02461
E-mail: *Book@TeenInk.com*
617-964-6800

To learn more about the magazine and to request a free sample copy, see our Web site at *www.TeenInk.com*.

All the royalties from the sale of this book are being donated to The Young Authors Foundation

Established in 1989, The Young Authors Foundation, Inc. publishes _Teen Ink_ (formerly _The 21st Century_), a monthly magazine written entirely by teens for teens. This magazine has been embraced by schools and teenagers nationwide; more than 3.5 million students read the _Teen Ink_ magazine every year.

The magazine empowers teenagers by publishing their words and works. It is dedicated to improving their reading, writing and critical thinking skills while encouraging creativity and building self-esteem. After reading more than three hundred thousand submissions from students over the last decade, the editors have selected twenty-five thousand for publication. There is no charge to submit work and all published students receive a free copy of the magazine plus other items.

In keeping with its mission, the Foundation distributes thousands of class sets and individual copies free to schools and teachers every month. In addition, more than twenty-four hundred schools support the foundation by paying a subsidized fee for their monthly class sets.

From its beginnings as a small foundation with a regional publication, The Young Authors Foundation has grown steadily and today is a national program funded with donations, sponsorships, private grants and advertising from companies that support its goals. In addition to funding the magazine, the foundation uses grants and donations to underwrite the following programs:

- *Teen Ink Poetry Journal* showcases more than one thousand young poets and is distributed free to subscribing schools three times a year.

- *Teen Ink Educator of the Year Awards Contest* welcomes nominating essays from students to honor outstanding teachers with cash prizes and publication of student essays in the magazine.

- *Teen Ink Book Awards* donate twelve thousand free books and award materials so schools can recognize students who have shown "improvement and individual growth in the field of English."

- *Teen Ink Interview Contest* encourages thousands of teens to interview family and friends with the winners interviewing national celebrities including Hillary Clinton, Colin Powell, John Glenn, Jesse Jackson, Martin Sheen, Maya Angelou and George Lucas.

- *Teen Ink Web site (www.TeenInk.com)* includes the magazine and many other innovative features and services.

The Young Authors Foundation, Inc., is a nonprofit 501(c)3 organization. See next page for details on how you can become a member, support these programs and receive a monthly copy of the magazine.

Join The Young Authors Foundation and get a monthly subscription to **Teen Ink** magazine.

Only $**25** per year!

Foundation Members Receive:

- Ten months of Teen Ink magazine
- Members Newsletter
- Partner in Education Satisfaction – You help thousands of teens succeed.

The magazine includes stories, poems and art plus music, book and movie reviews, college essays, sports and more.

SUPPORT TEEN VOICES!

☐ **Annual Dues $25***
I want to receive ten monthly issues of **Teen Ink** magazine and become a member of The Young Authors Foundation!
(Enclose Check or include Credit Card Info. below)

☐ I want to sponsor a monthly class set *(30 issues)* of the magazine for a school near me for only $130. *Please send me more information.*

☐ I want to support the Foundation with a tax-deductible donation for: $_____
(Do not send copies of the magazine)

NAME_____ PHONE_____

STREET _____

CITY/TOWN _____ STATE _____ ZIP _____

EMAIL _____

M/C OR VISA *(CIRCLE ONE)* #_____ EXP. DATE ____ / ____

Send a gift subscription to:
NAME _____

STREET_____

CITY/TOWN_____ STATE_____ ZIP _____

Mail coupon to: Teen Ink • Box 97 • Newton, MA 02461 – Or join online: www.TeenInk.com

* The Young Authors Foundation, publisher of *Teen Ink*, is a 501(c)3 non-profit organization providing opportunities for the education and enrichment of young people. While all donations support the Foundation's mission, 75% is designated for the magazine subscription, and no portion should be considered as a charitable contribution.

Acknowledgments

We are most grateful to all the wonderful people who have given so much of their time and energy to make the *Teen Ink* book a reality. Without their support, this would never have been possible. In addition, because of their dedication, hard work and thoughtful input, we believe this book represents the best collection of teen writing possible. We will remember all of these people with the fondest affection:

Our children:

Alison Meyer Hong for being there and supporting us when we needed it the most and Rob Meyer for always challenging us to do better.

Our staff:

Julie Chen for her dedication and incredible attention to detail during the entire book process; and always,

Kate Dunlop Seamans, Tony Abeln, Karen Watts, Kelley Wagers and Barbara Field for their invaluable editorial assistance and technical support for the *Teen Ink* magazine, Web site and the book.

Our book project staff:

Thomas D'Evelyn for his editing, wisdom and encouragement; Denise Peck, Andrew Simpson, Zick Rubin, Michael Hong, Miguel Melendez and Tim Foley for their editorial help and expertise.

Our friends at HCI:

Peter Vegso for his vision; Tom Sand, Lisa Drucker, Susan Tobias, Matthew Diener, Kelly Maragni, Randee Feldman, Kim Weiss, Larissa Hise Henoch, Lawna Patterson Oldfield and all those who guided us so smoothly through our first book publishing experience.

Our board, supporters, friends and family:

J. Robert Casey, David Anable, Michael Dukakis, Katherine Fanning, Milton Lieberman, Ron Reynolds, Susan Weld, Tom Winship, Beverly Beckham, Barbara Wand, Richard Freedberg, Larry Reed, Martin Kaplan, Paul Watts, Debra Raisner, David Raisner, Jason Raisner, Amy Weber Raisner, Glenn Koenig, Michael Seamans, Scott Saltus, Robert Kuchnicki, Ian Lebauer, Paul Roberts, Barbara Raisner, Joseph Rice and our friends at the Newtonville (Ma.) Post Office for their help on behalf of The Young Authors Foundation, the *Teen Ink* magazine and this book.

In addition, we want to thank the following teachers and the more than thirty-four hundred of their students for their devotion to this book and their willingness to read sample chapters to help determine the final pieces. Their feedback and ratings were immeasurably helpful and contributed enormously to the final selection process.

Alabama School of Fine Arts, Birmingham, Alabama—Denise Wadsworth Trimm

Ashland High School, Ashland, Oregon—Tim Cate

Ashtabula County Joint Vocational School, Jefferson, Ohio—Debra Cary, Bernadette Connors, Mary Anne Izenour and Suzanne McCune

Auburn High School, Auburn, New York—Preston Wilson

Barbara Roberts High School, Salem, Oregon—Lorelei Gilmore

Bay Port High School, Green Bay, Wisconsin—Michael Roherty

Bellport High School, Brookhaven, New York—Ramona Hadzima

Black River High School, Ludlow, Vermont—Colin McKaig

Blue Valley Northwest High School, Overland Park, Kansas—Kathy Schmiedeler

Bourgade Catholic High School, Phoenix, Arizona—Marianne Moriarty

Brunswick High School, Brunswick, Maine—Jeanne Shields

Clarkstown High School North, New City, New York—Christine Potter and Mary Tavolacci

Cortez High School, Phoenix, Arizona—Tom Helms and Diane Bykowski

Delta High School, Delta Junction, Alaska—Kathy Vander Zwaag

Denton High School, Denton, Texas—Michelle Biffle and Milton Wallace

Destrehan High School, Destrehan, Louisiana—Lynn Thompson

Druid Hills High School, Atlanta, Georgia—Sherrie Crow

Du Bois Area Senior High School, Du Bois, Pennsylvania—Carole Roberts

Dunseith High School, Dunseith, North Dakota—Marlene Haugse

Edmeston Central High School, Edmeston, New York—Maureen Christensen

Elkton High School, Elkton, South Dakota—Jean Kirschenman

Eufaula High School, Eufaula, Oklahoma—Gale Applegate

Exeter High School, Exeter, New Hampshire—John Ferguson

Falls Church High School, Falls Church, Virginia—Mary Marshall

Framingham High School, Framingham, Massachusetts—Kate Greene

Frontier Central High School, Hamburg, New York—Ryan Collins and Tom Roberts

Frontier Junior High School, Vancouver, Washington—Kristie Neshyba

Gallup Central High School, Gallup, New Mexico—Dr. Mike Woal

Glenbard East High School, Lombard, Illinois—Bill Littell

Highland High School, Anderson, Indiana—Sami Branham

John Dickinson High School, Wilmington, Delaware—Tara Dick and Kristin Zerbe

Kamehameha Secondary School, Honolulu, Hawaii—Ruth Canham

La Mirada High School, La Mirada, California—Andrea Wood

Labelle High School, Labelle, Florida—Al Pellerin and Lynne Pellerin

Macon High School, Macon, Missouri—Lila Petre

Mandeville Junior High, Mandeville, Louisiana—Lee Barrios

Martin Luther King Middle School, Beltsville, Maryland—Bruce Eberwein

Memorial High School, Eau Claire, Wisconsin—Debra Peterson, Fred Poss and Annis Williams

Mercy High School, Middletown, Connecticut—Adrienne Lovell

Mid-Coast School of Technology, Rockland, Maine—Jean M. B. Lawrence and Carolee Weglarz

Millburn High School, Millburn, New Jersey—Marilyn Drennan

Momence High School, Momence, Illinois—Irene Kibbons

Mount St. Charles Academy, Woonsocket, Rhode Island—Donald Hogue

Mundelein High School, Mundelein, Illinois—Jennifer Franco

Notre Dame Academy, Park Hills, Kentucky—Dianna Timmerding

Papillion LaVista High School, Papillion, Nebraska—Margaret Shanahan

Pine-Richland Middle School, Gibsonia, Pennsylvania—John Dolphin, Dr. Susan Frantz, Janet Hanlon and Aleta Lardin

Poudre High School, Fort Collins, Colorado—Kathryn Symmes

Rippowam Cisqua School, Bedford, New York—Cathy Greenwood

Royal Palm Beach High School, Royal Palm Beach, Florida—Kim Grinder

Scituate High School, Scituate, Massachusetts—Christine Berman

Shoreham-Wading River High School, Shoreham, New York—Kevin Mann

South Dade Senior High School, Homestead, Florida—Jim Ford

St. Albans High School, St. Albans, West Virginia—Bettijane Burger

St. John High School, Gulfport, Mississippi—Tommy Snell

Stephenville High School, Stephenville, Texas—Jennifer Muncey

Stewartville High School, Stewartville, Minnesota—David Honsey

Stoughton High School, Stoughton, Massachusetts—Judith Hamilton

Strath Haven High School, Wallingford, Pennsylvania—Emily Farrell

Utica Community Schools Adult Education Program, Sterling Heights, Michigan—Gina Kowalski

Ward Melville High School, Setauket, New York—Faith B. Krinsky

Washington High School, Phoenix, Arizona—Jill Green

Watertown High School, Watertown, Tennessee—Lynda Jellison

Wellington Junior High School, Wellington, Kansas—Chris Hutchens

Whitehall High School, Whitehall, Montana—Lee Ann Gallagher

Wichita East High School, Wichita, Kansas—Jennifer Fry

Williamsville North High School, Williamsville, New York—Lisabeth Pieters

Winnisquam Regional High School, Tilton, New Hampshire—Barbara Blinn and Colleen Mulligan

Wyoming Park High School, Grand Rapids, Michigan—Jeremy Schnotala

Contributors

Rosa Rockmore Baier is a college senior majoring in public health. She is the founder of an organ donation awareness organization and hopes to write a novel someday. She loves cats and enjoys skiing, biking and reading. Rosa's essay was in *Teen Ink* magazine when she was a senior in high school. After it was published, the boy she wrote about figured out that she was the author and they subsequently dated for two years.

Amanda Batz is a sophomore who loves college life. Her most memorable recent adventure was sneaking off campus with a friend to have their ears pierced between classes! She is working toward a double major in astronomy and physics, with a minor in German. She is involved with her school's Campus Activities Board and enjoys golfing, running, reading and photography. Amanda wrote her essay as a senior in high school.

Sarah Bay is a freshman in college studying pre-med. She loves fixing up her very old Saab and has raised over $7,000 for her solar-powered race car team. She and her three sisters love taking pictures of each other, and the photo she took while a sophomore in high school was shot when one of her sisters was playing dress up. She dedicates it to another sister, Kristen, who is the "real photographer in the family."

Caitlin Bennett is a junior in high school. She plays the clarinet with the band, is a member of the drama club, and runs on the cross country and indoor- and outdoor-track teams. She also volunteers at a daycare center and local thrift shop. Caitlin believes every day is a fresh experience and is inspired by life and the ways people live it. To her, "life is the most pure form of art, and the end result is our masterpiece."

Erik Bernstein is a freshman in college who is interested in studying special education and psychology, and is considering a career in counseling. He enjoys creative writing, baseball and making home movies with his family and friends. Erik still remembers the horrible events of his family's home invasion, even though it happened five years ago. He continues to appreciate all that he has in life.

Melissa Bizub is in the ninth grade. She enjoys playing soccer and has lived, breathed and loved horses since the age of four. She currently competes in barrel races, and will begin other events soon. Her family even rehabilitated a horse scheduled to be slaughtered. Melissa's essay was first published in *Teen Ink* magazine last year. She dedicates it to her mother and father, who have always meant so much to her.

Christine Brasch is a college junior majoring in music education and studio art, her two passions. She created her piece for a high school assignment. She had gone to a park where she saw the "most beautiful kid who was so tired and just sat." She was able to make a rough sketch and then created her scratchboard. Christine plays trumpet in various bands and loves to listen to jazz. She is thankful for this opportunity to be published again.

T. K. Broderic wrote his essay during his senior year. He is now a college sophomore studying English and business. He enjoys intramural sports and follows professional teams. T. K. works as a volunteer counselor at a summer camp for children whose lives have been touched by AIDS. He keeps a picture of his dad on his dresser at college and looks at it daily. He is still trying to figure out the gift his father gave him.

Kimberly Burton is a junior in college studying electrical engineering. She is a Taurus and a feminist, and her biggest hobby, besides her track team, is her Web page. She believes "the Internet is the greatest place for a creative mind searching for an audience!" Kim likes mountain biking, warm weather, skim milk, the color blue and the *New Yorker*. Being published in *Teen Ink* magazine during her senior year has kept her writing.

Tiffany Burton is a college sophomore studying business administration. She is a certified cosmetologist and she hopes to open her own salon one day. In her free time she enjoys traveling and spending time with her family. The essay she wrote during her senior year in high school is dedicated to her grandmother, who taught her to write, and to Pops, who encouraged her imagination through storytelling.

Timothy Cahill wrote his fiction piece while a junior in high school. A college sophomore majoring in English, he is a member of the marching band and the mock trial team, and enjoys politics and Ping-Pong. Tim's most memorable college experience has been traveling with the band to cheer on their women's basketball team in the NCAA tournament.

Though the team lost, they rallied from twenty points down to tie the game with one minute left.

Geoff Carr is a senior in high school. He plays for his school's baseball and soccer teams, and enjoys both sports in his free time. He is active in a number of clubs and has a part-time job. Geoff hopes to pursue a career in marine biology after college. He shot his photo for an assignment as a sophomore. He perched on his roof and took a photo of his sister who was down below playing basketball. It is not a trick photograph!

Jinny Case wrote her essay as a junior in high school. Her brother, who is now eleven, has officially been adopted by her parents. Jinny graduated from college this spring, where she was vice president of the Student Sociological Association and a volunteer advocate at a rape crisis center. She is currently pursuing her master's in sociology. She dedicates her piece to her high-school English teacher, Leslee Mahon, who always encouraged her.

David Cevoli graduated from college with a degree in literature, and he is pursuing his master's in English literature. His interests include Spanish language and culture, jazz history, international music and cuisine, songwriting, and playing the guitar. While in college, David spent one semester studying in Salamanca, Spain, and another writing and baking bread in Naples, Italy. He wrote his piece as a senior in high school.

Katherine Cincotta is a senior in high school. In addition to writing, she enjoys playing soccer and pitching for her school's varsity softball team. She loves art and takes classes in drawing and painting outside of school. Katherine wrote her poem during her junior year. She hopes to pursue teaching or writing at a liberal arts college and dedicates her poem to the memory of her grandmother.

Jennifer Clarke loves teaching, and is working on publishing a children's book that she wrote and illustrated. She graduated from college this spring with a degree in elementary education and art. Jenn wrote her essay during her senior year in high school. Her mother's death remains the most significant event in her life and it has directed her on the path she follows today. She dedicates her piece to her mother.

Jennifer Cohun wrote her fiction piece as a sophomore in high school, where she was involved with drama, field hockey and student government. She is in her first year of college and enjoys studying English, learning about the environment and cooking—especially baking pastries and desserts. Jenn spends her spare time walking and hiking in the woods, camping, writing and drawing in pen and ink.

Jennifer Coleman is in the U.S. Air Force and has lived in many areas of the United States and abroad. She has discovered in her travels that abusive relationships are more common than she ever imagined. Since she wrote her essay as a senior in high school, her message has remained the same: "You are not alone. Pick up the phone or walk into a clinic and start the first day of the rest of your life. Good luck, my prayers are with every one of you."

La Toya Collins still loves to play basketball. While in high school, she was on the varsity team and traveled across the country with her summer league. She is now a freshman in college studying economics and accounting. She enjoys hanging out with her friends, dancing, shopping and watching movies. Toya wrote her essay while a junior in high school, and thanks her mom and dad for teaching her the game.

Helen Comber is a sophomore in high school. She is a member of the swim team, drama club, chorus, Model U.N., national history day and the superintendent's advisory council. She enjoys playing the piano, writing and singing with her band, Haven. Helen thanks her band members and friends from CSTF for all their love and support. She dedicates her essay to her grandpa, Victor, and the memory of her grandma, Evelyn.

Danielle Compere is a junior in college studying government and political science. She hopes to pursue a law degree specializing in civil rights and constitutional law. She likes reading (her favorite author is Toni Morrison), dancing, writing poetry, playing basketball and listening to R&B and hip-hop. Danielle wrote her essay as a freshman in high school. She thanks her parents and brother for their love and support, and all her friends for always being there.

Seth Compton is a college sophomore majoring in film and theater. In his free time, he enjoys participating in community service projects and studying Spanish. His interest in soccer has continued from high school, where he was co-captain of the soccer team. In high school, Seth was also involved in theater and the newspaper, and was a member of the National Honor Society. He took his photo during his junior year.

Jessica Consilvio is a college sophomore pursuing her interest in theater. She participates in everything from acting to stage management. She finds inspiration for her photography on the coast with its surrounding beauty. Her most memorable experience was the month she spent in Australia, "the most wonderful place on earth," with three of her brothers. Jess created her cartoon as a senior, when she felt overwhelmed—much the way she still feels in college.

Paul Constant was published in *Teen Ink* magazine many times while in high school. Since then, he has studied English and sociology, and self-published four comics and three journals. His most memorable experiences include visiting Graceland where he wept at Elvis's grave, meeting the president of Ireland and Scotty from *Star Trek*, and being shoved aside by Hunter S. Thompson while working as the mall Easter Bunny.

Kristen E. Conway is a college junior studying photojournalism and history. She is an assistant photo editor for an independent student newspaper, and hopes one day to work for the Associated Press or *Sports Illustrated* magazine. Kristen enjoys baby-sitting and watching movies. She continues to write and is working on several longer pieces, including a screenplay. She wrote her fiction piece as a senior in high school.

Abigail Cook is a sophomore in college majoring in English. She is an avid tennis player and hopes to pursue a career in journalism. Her photograph, shot during her junior year in high school, was the result of an accident. When she was developing her photograph, she used water that was too warm, which consequently "burned" the film and created the finished look.

Mary Mattila Cooper has a degree in music and works in state government. While in college, she played the clarinet in several groups and was conductor for a symphonic wind ensemble. She is active in her college alumni admissions program and enjoys Web design, reading, writing and spending time with her Maine Coon cat, Dexter. Mary wrote her poem during her senior year in high school.

Jennifer Corbett is still good friends with the boy she wrote about in her essay, which was first published when she was a junior in high school. Jen will be graduating from college this spring with a degree in advertising and photography. She is a member of the advertising club, and enjoys art, snowboarding and skiing. One of her most memorable experiences was the summer she spent volunteering in a rainforest reserve in Monte Verde, Costa Rica.

Jillian Côté and her three best friends have upheld their pledge and reunited at the same restaurant for the last two summers. Now a freshman in college, she wrote her essay as a junior in high school, where she was a member of the track team, president of the student council and co-editor of the yearbook. Jillian also enjoys music, and was the lead trumpet for her school's award-winning marching and jazz bands.

Christina Courtemarche has since overcome her problems with incredible effort. She is happy to say, "the miserable fifteen-year-old who wrote the piece is unrecognizable to me. It's a wonderful feeling." Christina is a junior in college studying computer science and mathematics on a full scholarship. In her free time, she enjoys playing guitar, reading and writing short stories.

Kristin Cronkhite is a political science major at a small college where she enjoys tennis and running. She likes to write and listen to music, and plans a missionary trip to Latin America. College has been a "life-changing experience," making her realize that life is "how much you love and how hard you try to do good" rather than acquiring money or academic degrees. Kristin took her photo while a junior in high school.

Lindsay Danner wrote her poem during her junior year in high school, where she was involved in track and field, band, forensics and debate. Now a college sophomore, she is studying advertising and public relations. In addition to being published in *Teen Ink,* one of Lindsay's greatest writing accomplishments was completing her novella, *Adia's Lyric,* while a senior in high school.

Mark Denoncour wrote his fiction piece in the eighth grade. A high school senior now, he runs on his school's winter and spring track teams. He also volunteer tutors adults to improve their reading skills. During the summer, Mark spends most of his time outdoors observing nature, where he believes, "the most beautiful things in life are to be found." In his spare time, he enjoys reading and writing.

Alissa Deschnow wrote her essay while she was a sophomore in high school. She currently works and plans to go to college in the near future. Alissa also volunteers for her church. She says, "My life isn't that exciting, but it's mine."

Joseph DiPasquale graduated from college this spring with a degree in psychology and works as an Internet consultant. In college, he competed nationally as a figure skater and helped raise money for cancer research. Joseph wrote his essay during his senior year in high school. While he will always miss his father, he has learned from his experiences and knows he has much to be grateful for and to look forward to in the future.

Kelly Donald is honored to have the best father in the world, still by her side. After graduating from college with a degree in psychology and sociology, she traveled through Europe and now works in development. She loves reading and being outdoors. Kelly uses her (scarce!) free time to collect Dr. Seuss books, catch up on precious sleep and spend time with friends and family. She wrote her piece as a senior in high school.

Jason Dunlap was first published in *Teen Ink* magazine when he was a junior in high school. He was so excited he ran down the school hallway—but he tripped and fell in front of everyone and was forced to use his magazine to stop his nose from bleeding! Jason is a college junior studying journalism and public relations. He is a member of the surf club and ski team and loves to horseback ride on his parents' farm.

Sasha Dwyer will graduate from college this spring with an associate's degree in elementary education. She loves children and enjoys babysitting, hanging out with her friends, reading and writing. Her favorite color is purple and she absolutely loves chocolate! After graduation she hopes to work as an elementary school teacher and part-time writer. Sasha's essay was originally published during her senior year in high school.

Beth Ezell apprenticed with a horticulturist and now works doing research on herbs for a seed company that she has loved since childhood. Beth took her photo as a high school sophomore. As spring melted the winter's ice, it revealed a doll that had been left behind. She continues to love photography and writing.

Chad Fleming was taught to draw by his father, who's an artist, and since before he could write, has been drawing sometimes even on the furniture. Chad has been working for a number of years to save money so he can go to film school. He loves movies and is interested in editing, fashion and costumes. He created his piece "just for fun" while a senior in high school.

Lisa Gauches is a freshman in college studying drama, with a focus on directing musical theater. While in high school, she was captain of the swim team and president of her school's community service organization. She was also involved with the drama club and student council. Lisa enjoys acting, singing, playing the piano and writing. Her essay was originally published during her senior year in high school.

Micaela Golding graduated from a service academy this spring with a degree in political science and is stationed abroad. She plans to pursue a law degree or become an FBI agent. Her essay was first published during her senior year in high school. She still exchanges birthday cards with Nikki, although they now live far apart. Micaela has run into similar prejudices in other situations, but realizes that those who feel that way are not important.

Pamela Gorlin and her father have worked hard to improve their relationship since her poem was first published during her junior year in high school. She is studying to become an English teacher, after having graduated from college with a degree in literature and rhetoric. Pamela works as a youth advisor at her temple, is a certified aerobics instructor, and is happy to report that she is enjoying her first year as a newlywed.

Marcy Griffin is a college freshman. In high school she played on the varsity softball team as catcher and third baseman, and she was on a traveling summer team. She also played varsity basketball, and enjoys four-wheeling and hanging out with her friends. Marcy wrote her essay during her junior year, and has lived with her aunt and uncle since her mother's death. She dedicates her piece to her best friend, Kim Pieters.

Amanda Hager is a college freshman considering a major in psychology. She has been riding horses for over five years, performing in shows and winning ribbons. Riding is one of the most important things in her life—it has taught her about responsibility and helped her self-esteem. Most of Amanda's writing is a result of her experiences with her friends or boyfriend. Without them, she would not be who she is today.

Andrew Hammer is a freshman in college studying mechanical engineering. While in high school, he was stage manager of the drama club for four productions, and nominated "Super Senior" by the school newspaper. He enjoys bicycling, hunting and mechanics. Andy dedicates the essay he wrote during his senior year to the memory of his mother.

Yoo Jean Han is a college sophomore and a photography major. She enjoys documentary photography and is a volunteer, teaching teens photography. Yoo Jean took her window photo looking out William Shakespeare's home in Stratford, England, as a high school sophomore. Her other photo of a girl, taken as a junior, was a fun attempt at studio photography. She enjoys playing the piano, biking and walking. This summer she returned to Korea to visit family and traveled to Japan and Thailand—a great photo op!

Deanna Harris continues to spend time with her son, Keegan, who now has an adopted baby sister. Her story remains the most significant event in her life, and she hopes her decision will help others be aware that adoption is an option. Dee is now a college sophomore majoring in business. She loves to sing, take pictures, ride horses, work in stained glass and spend time with her boyfriend and family.

Brian Harrison wrote his essay during his senior year in high school. He graduated from college with a degree in American literature and minors in music, psychology and creative writing. He now works as a financial advisor. Brian has composed a small book of poems entitled *Prayers from the Sick Bed,* and credits *Teen Ink* with helping him to embrace the creative joys of writing.

Holly Hester graduated from college with a degree in advertising and now works as director of marketing for a realty agency. She enjoys painting, drawing, writing, photography, boating, water skiing and playing tennis. Holly dedicates her essay to her brother, Scotty, who is now in high school: "You will always be my little munch, running toward me with your arms outstretched, bringing such joy and laughter into our lives."

Alex W. Hill has fully recovered from his accident, thanks to the support of family, friends and the grace of God. He graduated from college this spring with a degree in English and is pursuing his first love, the food industry, as an assistant manager of a restaurant. Alex was editor-in-chief of his college newspaper, and loves camping and outdoor activities. He wrote his essay during his senior year in high school.

Emma Hill, a freshman in college, is considering majoring in psychology. In high school, she spun the sabre for her school's competitive color guard team. She likes writing poetry, dancing, camping with her family and spending time with her two cats, Punkin and Olivia. She also enjoys seeing movies with her friends; her all-time favorite is *Dirty Dancing.* Emma wrote her poem during her senior year in high school.

Kun Jia, a junior in high school, is a member of the track team, math and academic leagues, Model U.N. and Amnesty International club. Kun enjoys reading, playing the piano and spending time with her friends—though never at the mall! She loves watching cheesy movies from the 1980s and is fascinated with all things British. She hopes to visit London one day (once she's done with her SATs and college applications).

Andrea Josenhans, a college sophomore, enjoys horseback riding and writing for her college humor magazine. Her most memorable experiences include meeting Tom Hanks, Steve Guttenberg and most of the 1992 New York Yankees when, at the age of ten, she was batgirl for a day. Since writing about Brandy as a sophomore in high school, she and her family have welcomed Sheba, their new dog, into their lives.

Lori Kessler enjoys playing the piano, writing, playing volleyball and traveling whenever she has the chance. She did attend Anthony's prom, where they had the time of their lives. Anthony was voted prom king, and when he brought Lori to the bus stop for her trip home, they shared their first kiss. Although Lori is a freshman in college, they continue to speak regularly and both have the dream of reuniting one day.

Charles Key is a college sophomore majoring in engineering who loves sailing and soccer. He recalls his most memorable high school experience when his soccer team went to the state finals. He enjoys skydiving and snowboarding, and continues to enjoy photography. Always fascinated by boats, he took his photo with a Nikkormat during his senior year at a beach near his home. He was trying to capture his fascination with the reflections of the boat in the water.

Olivia King is a freshman in college studying biology, with plans to pursue medicine. She wrote her essay as a junior in high school, where she was active in volunteer work and a member of the varsity tennis and volleyball teams. Olivia believes "everything happens for a reason, no matter how hard things seem at the time. If you stay true to yourself, you can get through anything and come out a stronger person."

Melissa Kleinman is a college freshman studying communications and journalism. During the summer, she works as a counselor at the camp she has attended since she was seven. She enjoys writing, hanging out with her friends, listening to music and going to the beach. Since Melissa wrote her essay as a junior in high school, Beth has been in the hospital a few more times, but she continues to do well and enjoy life.

Jaime Koniak graduated from college summa cum laude with a degree in English, and currently is in her second year of law school. In high school, she participated in all three publications: the yearbook, literary magazine and newspaper. She was also staff writer for her college paper and a member of Delta Phi Epsilon sorority. Jaime's essay was originally published in her junior year of high school.

Michiko Kurisu, after graduating from an Ivy League university, is pursuing her love of photography by documenting her father's Japanese garden. She has lived and traveled in sixteen countries, where she has continued to "choose fast camels and avoid puff adders, to kneel and kiss the ground, as Rumi says, in a million ways." She remembers her photo was shot for the first photography course she took with her Nikon 6006. It "was a continuous discovery of seeing detail in new ways."

Michelle LaMarca fondly remembers being published in *Teen Ink* magazine as a senior in high school. The experience was both a great honor and confidence booster. She is now a junior in college studying communications and English, and loves college life. Michelle is extremely active in theater, and still enjoys writing poetry, essays and short stories.

Lisandra Lamboy wrote her essay while a senior in high school. She is now a college sophomore, majoring in psychology. One of the most significant events of her life was receiving her college acceptance letter. Little did she know her life would be transformed! The people she's met and experiences she's had have totally transfigured her world view. She is truly satisfied with her life and looks forward to all that lies ahead.

Alison Lemon graduated from college magna cum laude with a degree in public relations and psychology. While in college, she was a staff writer for the newspaper, and she spent a semester studying in London. Alison is working on her master's in health science, and hopes to pursue a career in women's health and disease prevention. Her fiction piece was originally published when she was a senior in high school.

Lauren LeRea graduated from college this spring with a degree in English/rhetoric and a minor in business. She spent the summer traveling in Europe with friends, and hopes to pursue a career in film or television production. She is an accomplished pianist and recently took up the guitar. She loves music (she has a huge CD collection) and continues to write poetry. Lauren wrote her poem as a senior in high school.

Kendra Levin graduated this spring from a creative arts high school, where she took her photo as a sophomore. Deciding to "just kind of mess around with double exposure," she took a whole roll of backgrounds and then shot the roll again with a girl from her class. Having won a number of awards, Kendra plans to continue her interest in the arts, especially writing, in college.

Alexa Lin wrote both her personal essays during her senior year in high school. She has since graduated from college and is working full-time.

Anamaria Lugo graduated from art school and currently works for a department store as a visual merchandising manager. She took her photograph in high school during her senior year for class assignments.

Anamaria enjoys photography as a hobby although she doesn't have much free time now!

Alexander Lukas is a sophomore at an art institute majoring in illustration. He drew his cartoon as a sophomore in high school, just for himself. While in high school, Alex was involved in art and theater, primarily behind-the-scenes work, including lighting, sound and set design. One of his favorite artists is illustrator Chris Van Allsburg.

Doug Mahegan is a senior in high school. He enjoys sports, and is active in football, wrestling and lacrosse. Doug took his photo using an automatic camera as a sophomore. He and his two friends were at a local beach. Having forgotten what the photography assignment was, they were just having fun when Doug snapped his amazing shot.

Dana Marlowe wrote her poem while a senior in high school. She graduated from college with a degree in communications, and a minor in sign language interpreting. While in college, she had a story published in a regional magazine and a column published in the *Chicago Tribune*. She is pursuing a graduate degree in communication studies, and continues to enjoy writing and public speaking.

Jessica Mazonson is a college freshman. While in high school, she played field hockey and was very active in community service, including educating peers on racial issues, being trained to combat domestic violence, and volunteering at a woman's shelter. Jessica took her photo as a junior for a photography assignment to "show emotion." The photograph of her best friend was shot at the beach.

Robert McKee is a junior in high school and is considering a career in journalism. He spends much of his free time working at a local restaurant while maintaining honor roll standing. Like most teens, he tries to enjoy his summers. Bob thanks *Teen Ink* magazine for first publishing his essay last year, and he thanks his ninth-grade English teacher, Carole Roberts, for encouraging him to submit his work for publication.

Kathleen McMillan wrote her essay as a senior in high school. She has studied theater art and film, and worked in restaurant management. She recently decided to pursue her degree to teach English, after remembering her high school English teacher, Jean Eckblad, who cried while reading Kathleen's essay aloud to the class. Kathleen dedicates her poignant piece to this teacher who meant so much to her.

Elizabeth Ames Miller is studying to be a physician's assistant. She graduated from college with a double major in mathematics and theater. Recently married, she and her husband love to spend time on the water, fishing, sailing and exploring. Her brother now owns his own business, and is happily married with seven-year-old twin sons. Lyz's essay was originally published when she was a senior in high school.

Tiffani Morehead is a freshman in college studying elementary education. She is a member of Future Educators of America, and was an All-American cheerleader and homecoming queen in high school. During the summer, she works as a lifeguard. She participates in the annual Multiple Sclerosis Walk and enjoys swimming, shopping and four-wheeling. Tiffani's mother has fully recovered since her accident and is happily remarried.

Megan Morrow wrote her fiction piece in the eighth grade. She is now a high school senior who loves dance, movement, music and a variety of arts-related activities. She has been singing and playing the flute since she was very young, and she enjoys figure skating and being in musicals. Megan is active in her school's leadership program and continues to write.

Pamela Jourdain Moul will never forget having her work published in *Teen Ink* magazine while a senior in high school. She credits her teacher, Phil MacSweeney, who had a special gift for making English enjoyable. Pamela received an associate's degree this spring, and plans to pursue her bachelor's in communications. Recently married, she enjoys reading, cooking, gardening and writing in her spare time.

Kevin Robert Mulcahy graduated from college with a degree in philosophy and psychology, and now works as content developer for a dot-com. He hopes to pursue a Ph.D. in developmental neuropsychology. He enjoys playing guitar and (sporadically) studying Irish (Gaeilge) and is slowly writing a book of "philosophical fiction," just for fun. Kevin's poem was published during his senior year in high school.

Brendan Murphy, a sophomore, receives a full academic scholarship at his parochial high school. He is an honor student involved with both student government and the speech team. In addition to playing hockey, he runs track and is a member of his school's volleyball team. Brendan has worked as a lifeguard and landscaper, and also volunteers at a local Irish cultural center and as a youth hockey referee.

Kelly Murphy is a junior at an Ivy League college studying government and religion. She coaches a local swim team and is a member of a Division I women's track and field team. This fall she will be studying Spanish language, culture and history in Barcelona. Kelly wrote her essay during her senior year in high school. Although A. J. was not one of her best friends, his death remains one of the most significant incidents of her life.

Miranda Noonan graduated from college with a degree in journalism and music. She spent a year in Dublin, Ireland, and now works for an investment manager. She likes singing, theater and spending time with her nephew. Mandi wrote her essay as a senior and she dedicates it to her mother, who has been her driving force, and to her high-school English teacher, Billy Marshall, who always gave her that extra push.

Amanda O'Loughlin wrote her essay as a sophomore in high school. She graduated from college this spring with a degree in drama and anthropology. She enjoys theater and singing, and has been studying tap, ballet and jazz since she was four. Amanda is a devoted activist for HIV/AIDS education and awareneness, and has participated in the AIDS Walk since 1989. She dedicates her piece to the memory of Uncle Jay.

Shana Onigman graduated from college this spring with a degree in theater and music. She enjoys road biking, swimming, hiking, playing the violin and participating in all aspects of theater. Shana was published many times in *Teen Ink* magazine while in high school, and she describes the first time with a line from a James Taylor song: "The sky opened and the earth shook."

Travis Ostrom is a freshman in college. He enjoys studying physics and dreams of being an astronaut. In high school, he founded a roller hockey team and volunteered as a hockey coach at the YMCA. Travis loves swimming, scuba diving and being near the ocean. His most memorable experience was when he caught a 350-pound marlin while deep-sea fishing with his dad. He thanks his English teacher, Nina Johnston.

Michael Pagano is a freshman in college studying biology. As photography editor of his high-school newspaper and yearbook, Michael pursued his interest in photography. He also was a varsity soccer player for three years. His photographs were frequently published in *Teen Ink* magazine. The one featured in this book was taken during his sophomore year in high school.

Randolph Paulsen wrote his fiction piece as a freshman in high school, where he organized the first-ever public high-school team for the local AIDS ride and was a member of a professional break-dance troupe. He is now a freshman in college studying sociology and English. He still enjoys writing short stories and poetry. Dolph thanks his mom, dad and Jesse, and all those who gave him some slack or a helping hand over the years.

Jennifer Perry graduated from college with a degree in hotel/restaurant managment and works as an assistant general manager for a family-run hotel. Having created her drawing as a sophomore in high school, she was inspired by the recent passing of her uncle, who was also her godfather. Jennifer continues to take time to paint, draw and write. She feels it's important to remember how art and creativity have helped make her the person she is today.

Mark Phelan works for majority leader, Congressman Dick Armey. He graduated this spring with a degree in history and is a member of Phi Beta Kappa and Pi Kappa Alpha fraternity. He enjoys baseball, tennis and running. He wrote his essay as a junior in high school. Although the loss of his mother was a traumatic time, it has inspired and driven him to succeed in college and beyond.

Elizabeth Pile is a college sophomore pursuing a master's in occupational therapy with a minor in psychology. She loves to run, write and spend time with her family and friends. Elizabeth is involved in many activities both in and out of school, including soccer, working as a residence hall assistant and volunteering with the Special Olympics. Her essay was originally published during her senior year in high school.

Gregory Platt is a computer animation major at an art institute. His interest in art began in second grade, and he won many competitions in high school. He loved working with the drama club, where he progressed from stage crew to designing the previously rented sets. Greg created his piece in his high-school art class. It is a variation of *trompe l'oeil* (or deceive the eye) theme, which makes it realistic while giving the illusion of 3-D.

Allison Poole recently graduated from college with a degree in English and psychology. She is pursuing a master's in international service and plans a career with a nonprofit children's service organization. She enjoys hiking, going out to eat and spending time with her friends. Allison's poem was originally published when she was a freshman in high school. She dedicates it to her grandma, Barbara, who gave her a love for reading.

Heather Quinn graduated from college with a degree in psychology and a minor in education. She is pursuing her master's in education and teaching preschool part-time. She loves her students and the ways their little minds work! Heather enjoys reading, hiking and gardening, and continues to write short fiction and poetry. Her essay was originally published during her junior year in high school.

Melanie Race wrote her essay as a senior in high school. She graduated from college this spring with a degree in anthropology and minor in women's studies. She is a gay-rights activist, and while in college served on the board of an agency that serves gay, lesbian, bi, trans and questioning youth. Mel also worked in her college events office, and was an officer of the Gay/Straight Alliance and Catholic Students Union.

Kate Rakus recently graduated from college with a degree in environmental studies. She took her photo as a sophomore in high school.

Andrew Raymond is a senior in college majoring in business management.

He enjoys everything about cars and hopes to make the automotive industry his future. He relaxes by playing golf and skiing. Drew took his photo as a senior in high school. It was just a "random shot"—when he walked into a room in his house, he noticed the way the sun was coming through a window and knew he should grab his camera.

Andy Redden is a senior in high school. He works as a manager at a local grocery store, and enjoys playing video games, watching movies and eating Chinese food with his girlfriend. He likes biking and reading, including every issue of his favorite comic book, *Strangers in Paradise*. Andy dedicates his poem to the memory of his brother Mike, and in gratitude for his strengthened relationship with his brother, Chaz.

Alison Reemer is a college senior studying marketing and journalism. She was a writer and editor for her college newspaper and secretary of her sophomore class, and is a member of Alpha Chi Omega sorority. She is an avid runner and enjoys playing volleyball. Alison wrote her essay during her senior year in high school. She dedicates it with love and respect to Grandma Bella and Grandpa Meyer in honor of their bravery.

Benjamin Rhatigan is now closer to his other grandfather, his "zayde," since writing his piece as a junior in high school. Benjamin is a college sophomore studying English and international relations. He enjoys reading and writing short stories. He dedicates his essay to his former English teacher, Faith B. Krinsky, who was his guiding light through high school and who helped him further find himself.

Jarod Rhoades wrote his fiction piece as a senior in high school, where he acted and directed many drama productions. He also compiled and edited a collection of short stories, poems and essays by young writers. Jarod's greatest influences include Faulkner, Joyce, Steinbeck and Nabokov. He is a college sophomore majoring in geological sciences. In addition to his short story work, he is writing a novel.

Caroline Richards graduated from college with a degree in economics and women's studies. She works as a researcher at a consulting company, and is considering a future career in publishing, editing or economic policy research. She enjoys running, Rollerblading, waterskiing and reading. Caroline's poem was originally published in *Teen Ink* magazine during her junior year in high school.

Jacqueline Savage recently received her master's in social work and now works with a domestic violence intervention program. Her desire to help children developed after spending summers at her parents' camp. Writing poetry and fiction remains her passion. She thanks her dad, mom and brother, Rob, who nurtured her confidence, enabling her to submit her piece as a high school freshman. She also thanks Ben, whose love and wisdom are a constant support.

Adrienne Scheibel wrote her fiction piece as a junior in high school. She graduated from college with a degree in psychology and education, and she is a second-grade teacher. She enjoys traveling, making scrapbooks and reading. After college graduation, Adrienne and her roommate drove across country in three days. For the next year, they spent their free time learning country dancing and preparing to become teachers.

Lisa Schottenfeld is a senior in high school. She has performed in many of her school theater productions and volunteers as assistant director for her temple's drama club. She is editor-in-chief of the newspaper and literary magazine, sings in the school chorus, and participates in a student-run debate group. Her passion is Shakespeare. Lisa dedicates her poem to "students everywhere who refuse to fit themselves into the mold."

Christopher Scinta wrote his poignant piece as a senior in high school. The character of Kayla is a conglomeration of every close friend he has had, and the story was inspired by a friendship he had many years ago. Christopher is a college sophomore studying ethics, society and law. He enjoys photography, music and sports, and is a soloist for his church choir. He and a friend recently completed a screenplay.

Jessica Seifried is a college sophomore studying international affairs, political science and English. She is active in community service and enjoys writing, biking, Rollerblading and swimming. She wrote her essay as a junior in high school. She dedicates it to her dad, and thanks her mom, brother Michael, Nana, Aunt Kathy, Uncle Bob and best friend Sally. She also thanks her teachers who have helped her along the way.

Charlie Semine is a college sophomore majoring in theater with minors in English and Italian. He recently participated in the Royal Academy of Dramatic Arts for the summer. Charlie took the photo of his younger sister during his sophomore year in high school for a photography class assignment entitled "shadows." He is a member of his college's only improv comedy troupe, and plays the sax and sings.

Maliha Shaikh is a freshman in college. She is an avid reader and enjoys horseback riding and kung fu. She has lived in Pakistan, Indonesia, Saudi Arabia and the United States. She is passionate about travel, recently indulging her love of history with trips to Italy and Egypt. Her most memorable experience was the Muslim pilgrimage, Haj, which she performed earlier this year. Maliha wrote her essay as a senior.

Aaron Shield, having received his degree in Italian studies, works as project manager in Romance languages at a translation company. During college, Aaron studied French, Spanish, Portuguese, Hebrew and Italian. He plans to pursue a Ph.D. in linguistics, and hopes to teach and do field research. Aaron's introspective piece was originally published when he was a high school sophomore.

Stephen Siperstein is a junior in high school and a musician "to the core." He has been playing the guitar and piano for years, and has even taught children how to play. Photography is a fairly new avocation for Stephen, although he has already had an exhibition in his hometown.

Amy Spota is a student at a fashion institute majoring in illustration. She created her ballerina during her junior year in high school as part of an assignment in scratchboard. She has studied dance, including ballet, and likes the lights and darks of her piece. Amy hopes to design children's books someday.

Kate Staples is a junior in college studying physical therapy. She loves helping people, and worked at a nursing home for three years during high school. Her interest in physical therapy was also inspired by her mother, who is a nurse. Kate enjoys writing, skiing, and playing lacrosse and tennis. She dedicates her essay, first published when she was a senior in high school, to the memory of her grandparents.

Gina Nicole Statuto wrote her piece when she was a high school junior. As a college sophomore studying political science and criminal justice, she hopes to pursue a law degree. She is an avid reader, loves the theater and opera, and enjoys training exotic birds. She has been competing in horse shows for five years, and even owns her own horse. Her fictionalized piece is dedicated to her loving father, who will always be there on her course through life.

Kaidi Stroud is a college sophomore studying English and creative writing. She wants to pursue a master's in secondary education. In high school, she was captain of the track and cross-country teams, and was involved with the newspaper and yearbook. She is now a member of her college club lacrosse and track teams. Kaidi's poem was first published during her senior year in high school. She still writes poetry.

Cassandra Stuart wrote her essay while a high school senior. As a sophomore in college studying government, film/television and journalism, she enjoys running, writing, traveling, public speaking, cooking and participating in a variety of outdoor and community service activities. Cassie is a varsity rower and ice cream scooper extraordinaire, and has traveled to England, Spain and Japan.

Cassandra Summerill is in the ninth grade. She wrote her reminiscence of her hero while in the seventh grade. She is a member of her school's basketball team and yearbook committee. She volunteers for a local no-kill animal shelter, helping to collect funds and supplies. A local newspaper even featured a story about her and her work there. Cassie and her family love animals. They have three dogs, a cat, six birds, a rabbit, a hamster and some ducks!

Jessika Teegarden works as a licensed massage therapist and chiropractor's assistant. She enjoys spending time at the beach, Rollerblading, playing the piano and guitar, drawing and writing. Jessika has been married to her husband, Aaron, for five years. Her poem was originally published during her senior year in high school.

Andrea Trask is a college sophomore. She works as a resident assistant and enjoys theater, writing, playing softball and singing. She is a member of the drama club, and is a charter member of both the Yo-Yo club and medieval history club. Andrea has spent her summers working at the YMCA and as an ITS consultant for her college. Her piece about Sheldon's death, which impacted her whole community, was first published when she was a high school sophomore.

Anna Tudor was a sophomore in high school when her poem, which was inspired by an experience she had when she was eleven, was published in *Teen Ink* magazine. As a senior, she is active in student government and drama, and plays the French horn in the school band. Anna spent this summer taking college courses in philosophy, film and international relations, and traveling in Spain with her family.

Lauren Vose is a college sophomore active in drama production. She has even founded a tap group, capitalizing on her lifelong love of dance. A public policy major, she taught a course on date rape at her college and spent a summer volunteering in Honduras working for a social service organization. She wrote her piece as a junior in high school when the whole school was devastated by the death of a classmate.

Heather M. Walker wrote her poem as a high school sophomore. She combined details of her own past into Mystery's character, leaving the rest to fiction. Being published many times in *Teen Ink* magazine remains one of her favorite accomplishments. Besides writing poetry, Heather enjoys painting, playing the pan flute and free-form dancing. She also adores nature walks, swimming in rivers and lakes, and all creative endeavors.

Greg Walters and his girlfriend are still happily together, having celebrated their second anniversary last spring. Greg is a freshman in college majoring in business. He enjoys all sports, especially water sports, and is active with his church. In high school, he was president of the National Honor Society, vice-president of the Honor Choir, and the announcer for his school's football games. He wrote his essay as a senior.

Kathleen Waters, a high school junior, is a member of the archery team, which has taught her patience, and the art club, which has taught her to appreciate beauty. She enjoys photography and volunteers her time with special education students. Katie thanks her English teacher, John Dillon, for encouraging and believing in her. She dedicates her piece to her mom, who has sacrificed her life to help others.

April Weber wrote her essay as a junior in high school. She is now a college junior studying studio art and education, and dreams of becoming an interior designer in the future. During vacations, she works as a teacher at her high school and spends summers in the Adirondacks. Although she and her friend attend schools in different states, they remain close. April will always care about her, and she knows her friend feels the same way.

Margaret Wetherell wrote her personal piece as a sophomore in high school. She studied computer science in college and works as a hardware engineer. In her free time, she enjoys reading and Rollerblading. She dedicates her essay to her mother, Ruth, who has since greatly improved and is now doing well. Margaret appreciates the changes her mother has made that have enabled their family to become closer.

Whitney Wiggin decided to spread her wings and attend college in a completely different part of the country, which has been an interesting experience. She loves traveling and the outdoors, and enjoys boating, skiing, running and flying. A junior, she is majoring in communications and public affairs. Whit took her photo for fun as a senior in high school, where she also volunteered at a Spanish-speaking elementary school.

Laura Yilmaz is a freshman in college considering a major in East Asian studies. She is extremely active in the theater and has worked as the costume designer, set designer and makeup chief for her high school drama club. She loves art, and especially enjoys drawing in pencil. Laura's essay was originally published in *Teen Ink* magazine during her junior year in high school. She dedicates it to her sister.

Permissions *(continued from page vi)*

"The Girl with the Red-Violet Hair." Reprinted by permission of April Weber. ©1997 April Weber.

"Checkered Feet." Reprinted by permission of Kristin Cronkhite. ©1998 Kristin Cronkhite.

"Kayla." Reprinted by permission of Christopher Scinta. ©1999 Christopher Scinta.

"Open Rose." Reprinted by permission of Michiko Kurisu. ©1993 Michiko Kurisu.

"Raindrops and Tears." Reprinted by permission of David Cevoli. ©1993 David Cevoli.

"Mystery Thawing." Reprinted by permission of Heather M. Walker. ©1993 Heather M. Walker.

"The Trees That Cried." Reprinted by permission of Jacqueline Savage. ©1991 Jacqueline Savage.

"Old Doorknob." Reprinted by permission of Seth Compton. ©1996 Seth Compton.

"Can You Stand the Rain?" Reprinted by permission of Jillian Côté. ©1999 Jillian Côté.

"Sam and His Tomatoes." Reprinted by permission of Kate Staples. ©1997 Kate Staples.

"Matt Keegan (Sitting Next to Me)." Reprinted by permission of Kristen E. Conway. ©1997 Kristen E. Conway.

"Girl Screaming." Reprinted by permission of Jessica Mazonson. ©1999 Jessica Mazonson.

"It Hurt Not to Cry." Reprinted by permission of Deanna Harris. ©1999 Deanna Harris.

"Baby's Face." Reprinted by permission of Christine Brasch. ©1998 Christine Brasch.

"Crimson Tears." Reprinted by permission of Laura Yilmaz. ©1998 Laura Yilmaz.

"Just Like a Movie." Reprinted by permission of Erik Bernstein. ©2000 Erik Bernstein.

"Dear A. J." Reprinted by permission of Kelly Murphy. ©1997 Kelly Murphy.

"Safe for the Night." Reprinted by permission of Amanda Hager. ©2000 Amanda Hager.

"Wendy and the Monkey Bringer." Reprinted by permission of Elizabeth Ames Miller. ©1992 Elizabeth Ames Miller.

"Leaving Dad." Reprinted by permission of Kimberly Burton. ©1998 Kimberly Burton.

"Don't Be Afraid to Ask." Reprinted by permission of Greg Walters. ©2000 Greg Walters.

"Student Under Books." Reprinted by permission of Jessica Consilvio. ©1998 Jessica Consilvio.

"Would You?" Reprinted by permission of Amanda Batz. ©1999 Amanda Batz.

"Coming Back to Life." Reprinted by permission of Melanie Race. ©1996 Melanie Race.

"Saving My Brother." Reprinted by permission of Holly Hester. ©1991 Holly Hester.

"Weight of the Matter." Reprinted by permission of Christina Courtemarche. ©1995 Christina Courtemarche.

"From the Other Side of a Locked Door." Reprinted by permission of Caroline Richards. ©1993 Caroline Richards.

"The Tattoo." Reprinted by permission of Alissa Deschnow. ©1993 Alissa Deschnow.

"Rowboat." Reprinted by permission of Charles Key. ©1998 Charles Key.

"The Rain." Reprinted by permission of Allison Poole. ©1994 Allison Poole.

"Good Night and Good-Bye." Reprinted by permission of Robert McKee. ©1999 Robert McKee.

"The Things We Take for Granted . . ." Reprinted by permission of Cassandra Stuart. ©1998 Cassandra Stuart.

"Passing the Guardrail." Reprinted by permission of Elizabeth Pile. ©1998 Elizabeth Pile.

"Sheldon the Fisherman." Reprinted by permission of Andrea Trask. ©1997 Andrea Trask.

"Tree Trunk." Reprinted by permission of Anamaria Magda Lugo. ©1992 Anamaria Magda.

"Reliving the Nightmare." Reprinted by permission of Alison Reemer. ©1997 Alison Reemer.

"Holding On." Reprinted by permission of Kaidi Stroud. ©1998 Kaidi Stroud.

"Skating Paradise Lost." Reprinted by permission of Joseph DiPasquale. ©1996 Joseph DiPasquale.

"Wood Stakes on Beach." Reprinted by permission of Whitney Wiggin. ©1998 Whitney Wiggin.

"Bargaining with God." Reprinted by permission of Kelly Donald. ©1996 Kelly Donald.

"Christmas Cookies." Reprinted by permission of Helen Comber. ©2000 Helen Comber.

"No Visitors at This Time." Reprinted by permission of Andy Redden. ©2000 Andy Redden.

"Grainy Hand." Reprinted by permission of Abigail Cook. ©1996 Abigail Cook.

"Perfection." Reprinted by permission of Alexa Lin. ©1994 Alexa Lin.

"My Worst Day." Reprinted by permission of Margaret Wetherell. ©1994 Margaret Wetherell.

"Constant Fear." Reprinted by permission of Heather Quinn. ©1989 Heather Quinn.

"Feast Fit for a King." Reprinted by permission of Emma Hill. ©1999 Emma Hill.

"'What Did You Say?'" Reprinted by permission of Mark Phelan. ©1995 Mark Phelan.

"Four Melting Heads." Reprinted by permission of Chad Fleming. ©1996 Chad Fleming.

"Father Figure." Reprinted by permission of Pamela Gorlin. ©1993 Pamela Gorlin.

"The Greatest Gift." Reprinted by permission of Jinny Case. ©1993 Jinny Case.

"Ballerina." Reprinted by permission of Amy Spota. ©1996 Amy Spota.

"My Friend, Beth." Reprinted by permission of Melissa Kleinman. ©1999 Melissa Kleinman.

"Danny Lee." Reprinted by permission of Tiffani Morehead. ©2000 Tiffani Morehead.

"Exit: My Hero." Reprinted by permission of Amanda O'Loughlin. ©1994 Amanda O'Loughlin.

"My Cinderella Castle." Reprinted by permission of Maliha Shaikh. ©2000 Maliha Shaikh.

"Miracle on Eighth Street." Reprinted by permission of Kun Jia. ©1999 Kun Jia.

"Cartoon Boy." Reprinted by permission of Alexander Lukas. ©1997 Alexander Lukas.

"A Stained Letter." Reprinted by permission of Jarod Rhoades. ©1998 Jarod Rhoades.

"Backwards." Reprinted by permission of Lauren LeRea. ©1996 Lauren LeRea.

"Metal Window." Reprinted by permission of Yoo Jean Han. ©1997 Yoo Jean Han.

"Don't Melt, My Snowflake." Reprinted by permission of Megan Morrow. ©1996 Megan Morrow.

"Curved Stones in Snow." Reprinted by permission of Kate Rakus. ©1995 Kate Rakus.

"Timmy the Toad—A Fictional-But-Not-So-Fictional Parable." Reprinted by permission of Paul Constant. ©1994 Paul Constant.

"One-Fifth of a Second." Reprinted by permission of Timothy Cahill. ©1997 Timothy Cahill.

"Ophelia and Me." Reprinted by permission of Shana Onigman. ©1996 Shana Onigman.

"Evidence." Reprinted by permission of Mark Denoncour. ©1997 Mark Denoncour.

"The Passion of a Fine Young Man." Reprinted by permission of Kevin Robert Mulcahy. ©1993 Kevin Robert Mulcahy.

"Fourteen Days of a Fruit Fly." Reprinted by permission of Caitlin Bennett. ©1999 Caitlin Bennett.

"Watching Mommy and Daddy." Reprinted by permission of Jennifer Cohun. ©1995 Jennifer Cohun.

"Hitchhiker." Reprinted by permission of Randolph Paulsen. ©1997 Randolph Paulsen.

"Jonathan's World of White." Reprinted by permission of Adrienne Scheibel. ©1993 Adrienne Scheibel.

Books for Living
Books for Life